K9 PROFESSIONAL TRACKING

K9 Professional Training Series

K9 **Scent** Training
A Manual for Training Your Identification, Tracking and Detection Dog
Resi Gerritsen · Ruud Haak
K9 PROFESSIONAL TRAINING SERIES

K9 **Behavior Basics**
A Manual for Proven Success in Operational Service Dog Training
second edition
Resi Gerritsen · Ruud Haak · Simon Prins
K9 PROFESSIONAL TRAINING SERIES

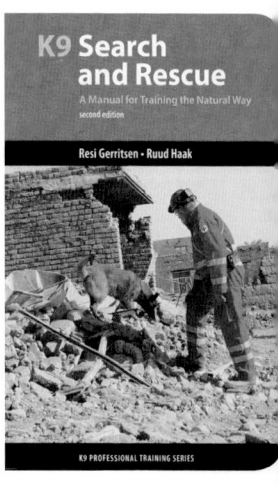

K9 **Search and Rescue**
A Manual for Training the Natural Way
second edition
Resi Gerritsen · Ruud Haak
K9 PROFESSIONAL TRAINING SERIES

K9 **Drug Detection**
A Manual for Training and Operations
Resi Gerritsen · Ruud Haak
K9 PROFESSIONAL TRAINING SERIES

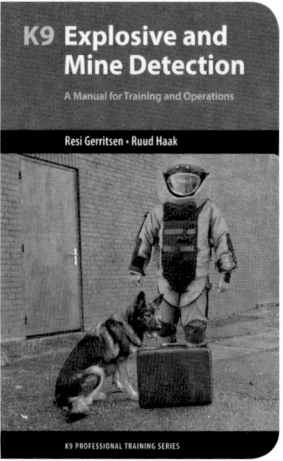

K9 **Explosive and Mine Detection**
A Manual for Training and Operations
Resi Gerritsen · Ruud Haak
K9 PROFESSIONAL TRAINING SERIES

K9 **Schutzhund Training**
A Manual for IPO Training through Positive Reinforcement
second edition
Resi Gerritsen · Ruud Haak
K9 PROFESSIONAL TRAINING SERIES

See the complete list at
dogtrainingpress.com

K9 PROFESSIONAL TRACKING

A Complete Manual for Theory and Training in Clean-Scent Tracking

Second edition

K9 Professional Training Series

Dr. Resi Gerritsen
Ruud Haak

An imprint of
Brush Education Inc.

Brush Education Inc.
www.brusheducation.ca
contact@brusheducation.ca

Cover design: John Luckhurst; Cover image: Swedish police officer Fanny with her police tracking dog, the German Shepherd Dog Torneryds Arko. Photo by Micke Månsson.

Interior design: Carol Dragich, Dragich Design

All photos are from the collection of Ruud Haak, except where noted on page 283. Illustrations by Chao Yu, Vancouver, based on original drawings by Ruud Haak.

Printed and manufactured in Canada

Library and Archives Canada Cataloguing in Publication

Title: K9 professional tracking : a complete manual for theory and training in clean-scent tracking / Dr. Resi Gerritsen, Ruud Haak.
Names: Gerritsen, Resi, author. | Haak, Ruud, 1947- author.
Description: Second edition. | Includes bibliographical references.
Identifiers: Canadiana (print) 20210378646 | Canadiana (ebook) 20210378689 | ISBN 9781550599121 (softcover) | ISBN 9781550599145 (EPUB) | ISBN 9781550599138 (PDF)
Subjects: LCSH: Tracking dogs—Training.
Classification: LCC SF428.75 .G47 2022 | DDC 636.7/0886—dc23

Contents

Preface

Our young dog Tessa sits a few yards before the starting point of the track I have laid, eager to begin. She has to wait until I attach the tracking harness and the 33-foot- (10-m)-long tracker leash. Then it's time to be on our way...

On the Track

Standing beside the tracking stake that marks the start, I give Tessa the command "Smell" and make sniffing sounds. Tessa sniffs intensively on the ground, and when I think that she has picked up enough scent, I allow her to begin to work out the track with a quiet and drawn-out "Seeeek." I see how she picks up the odor of the track, and I follow her only when I feel the knot in the leash, which indicates that the end of the line is coming up.

We first walk straight ahead over a field with short grass, and after about 330 feet (100 m), we cross an asphalt road over which a car has just driven. Then we enter a wooded area. "Good girl," I tell her. She is tracking through the woods with concentration and isn't distracted by some people walking on a nearby path with their barking dogs. She doesn't even notice a rabbit that jumps away in the distance.

Full of diligence, she arrives at the first turn. She overshoots the turn for about 3 feet (1 m), loses the odor, and then searches back,

Figure 0.1 Tessa waits impatiently to work out the track.

first in the wrong direction and then, with tail-wagging, she shows that she is again on the right track. "Well done!" I praise her.

After about 660 feet (200 m), the track changes from woodland covered with leaves to a dry, sandy surface. Tessa has to work a bit harder now: I note that she tracks more slowly. But I also notice her relief as she, after about 165 feet (50 m), finds the first article with my scent behind a little hill. She radiates joy when she retrieves the leather keyholder for me. I don't immediately put the article in my pocket, but first smell it as if I am checking her work, and after that I reward her exuberantly.

Then I encourage her with "Good girl, seek further" to follow the track over the sand. We don't go much farther, because again we enter the woods and track in a straight line for about another 330 feet (100 m). When we reach the cross-track, she hesitates a bit, but then follows my track again. I encourage her with a "Good work." About 16 feet (5 m) before a stone, there is a turn, and after first having smelled to the right, she takes the correct direction to the left. "Good girl," I say when she takes the acute-angle turn correctly.

She finds the second article with my scent, although she first overshoots it by a couple feet (0.5 m) before she locates the article under some leaves. Out of the woods, the track makes a curve over a concrete road, and she tracks that change correctly after a brief orientation. The track carries on for about 660 feet (200 m) and then, about 66 feet (20 m) after a right-angle turn, it ends, where she finds her last article: a tennis ball in a large sock.

She jumps on "her" article; she knows she may walk around with it and play. This play time allows her to let the excitement built up in her by the intensive tracking flow away.

I am very satisfied with Tessa's achievements and let her know that clearly. For sure there is still some work to be done, but she has already mastered the technique of tracking, even though she is still a young dog. Her passion and tenacity in following the track hold a lot of promise for her future as a tracking dog.

With tracks like these, a dog with the right characteristics can train to become a tracking dog that can work out tracks that are miles long and hours old, tracks of unknown persons, and tracks over different sorts of surfaces. The training must build slowly, step by step, and the dog must learn to solve the problems it encounters. Only then will you have a reliable tracking dog you can count on.

Introduction

Tracking uses the dog's sense organs to access a world that is normally closed to us: the world of odors. For a dog, tracking is the most normal and simple thing in the world. But for a lot of handlers (and instructors), tracking and training for tracking can be frustrating. First, handlers must give up their sense of control and learn to put their confidence in the dog's expertise. Second, handlers and trainers can't smell what the dog smells, so they can find it difficult to troubleshoot or understand what is going wrong. In the face of trouble when tracking, handlers may lose heart and confidence, leading to failure.

With no other part of dog training is the bond between handler and dog so important. You can't achieve anything by violence or pressure. Only a good understanding between handler and dog will lead to success. With tracking, handlers must decide to follow the dog in his world and to recognize his superiority in this area. For some handlers, this is a big hurdle.

However, although the dog's ability to smell is much better than ours, he doesn't instinctively know how we want him to use it. That's what we have to teach him. Once we do, we can have confidence in the dog's superior olfactory system.

In this book, you will discover the many possibilities of the dog's nose. For successful training, it is very important that the handler knows what the dog is doing and what is happening with the track. Handlers often make it difficult for their dogs because of faulty insights or the wrong approach to training.

Even experienced handlers are sometimes frustrated by their dog's mistakes when learning to track. At the root of their frustration is usually the assumption that the dog understands without any doubt what is desired of him. A dog has an excellent sense of smell, but we have to teach him to follow a human track. We have to make the dog understand what we want and ensure he enjoys the process.

But before we can teach the dog, we need a clear understanding of how the dog perceives scent and how he uses those perceptions to track. That's why this book covers so much of the scientific background to scent perception and tracking. This theoretical background will help you understand what the dog is doing when tracking and why. It will also make you better able to modify training if your dog encounters problems.

In This Book

We begin in Chapter 1 with a look at some of the early research on tracking dogs from the late 19th and early 20th centuries, when the field of police and tracking dogs was in its infancy. Although recent research has added to these early studies, the historical research has many valuable, practical insights into tracking dogs. Chapters 2, 3, and 4 are devoted to the physical process of smelling: how the anatomy of the dog's nose leads to the perception of odor. Chapters 5, 6, and 7 delve into the odors of the track — what the dog is smelling — and conditions that affect the track, such as temperature and humidity. Chapters 8 and 9 explore the equipment and preparations for tracking training and tips to set you and your dog up for success. The rest of the book details how to train a dog for tracking, from preliminary exercises when a puppy is just 8 weeks old, to advanced training for cross-tracks and older tracks. We also talk about common mistakes — and how to avoid them.

Odor and Scent

To maintain clarity about the various concepts used in training, we use the terminology recommended by the Organization for Scientific Area Committees for Forensic Science (OSAC), Dogs and Sensors Subcommittee. OSAC replaced the Scientific Working Group for Dogs and Orthogonal Detector Guidelines (SWGDOG) and makes standards and guidelines for the canine detection community.

According to OSAC, the term *odor* refers to the "volatile chemicals emitted from a substance that are able to be perceived by olfaction," while *scent* refers specifically to the "volatile chemicals emitted from a live human."[1]

Clean-Scent Tracking versus Mantrailing

There is no doubt that tracking dogs can help solve crimes, especially when looking for evidence that may have been hidden or discarded. If a dog arrives at a crime scene quickly, it may even be able to lead investigators to a fleeing perpetrator. Tracking dogs can also help in the search for missing persons by search and rescue teams.

However, to be useful to search and rescue operations, tracking dogs must be able to work *clean-scent* trails, which means they can follow a particular smell in the footprint of a person, independent of the type of ground it is on and any other tracks or tempting smells that interfere with the person's track.

Here we are not talking about so-called mantrailers, dogs that follow the smell of a person from fallen skin flakes or volatile organic compounds (VOCs). This form of searching has not yet been scientifically proven and is not therefore seen as a reliable search method in the professional dog world.

Dog handlers in the world of mantrailing, especially well-meaning amateurs, tell exciting stories about the larger-than-life performances of their dogs. However, many of these canine performances have, in fact, resulted in a miscarriage of justice, usually because handlers influenced their dog's work. Our book *K9 Investigation Errors: A Manual for Avoiding Mistakes* discusses these types of cases.

Because we have too many doubts about the effectiveness of mantrailing, this book does not discuss how to train dogs in this method. Mantrailing as a field requires a longer development time and more research to prove its credibility. Instead, we will help you train your dog professionally to become a clean-scent tracking dog that is capable of performing at a high level on both paved and unpaved surfaces. These methods are based on years of experience with police forces and search and rescue teams from around the world.

DR. RESI GERRITSEN AND RUUD HAAK

DISCLAIMER

While the contents of this book are based on substantial experience and expertise, working with dogs involves inherent risks, especially in dangerous settings and situations. Anyone using approaches described in this book does so entirely at their own risk and both the author and publisher disclaim any liability for any injuries or other damage that may be sustained.

Early Research on Tracking Dogs

Throughout our careers, we have closely followed research about how a dog's nose functions, as well as research into searching and tracking. In addition to new research in these areas, we have read many old studies and have even tried some of the experiments ourselves. Early research in tracking dogs provides many valuable discoveries, yet few trainers today know about it. To prevent the loss of the scientific results of such research, this chapter includes summaries of some of the most important data from this wealth of information.

We begin with a brief history of the use of dogs for tracking and police investigation. Although people have used dogs for tracking since ancient times, scientists and researchers became interested in studying dogs more closely during the 19th century, when enthusiasm for police dogs experienced a surge around the world.

The Earliest Tracking Dogs

There is evidence of tracking dogs in the service of forensic investigation as far back as the ancient Greeks. A papyrus found in Egypt contained a satire by Sophocles (496–406 BCE) called *Ichneutai* (The Trackers).[1] This somewhat risqué burlesque describes the theft, well known in mythology, of Apollo's herds by Hermes. Sophocles describes how satyrs, masquerading as herding dogs, pursued the track of the stolen herd and thief.

In the time of the Roman empire, Plinius (also known as Pliny the Elder, 23–79 CE) described six categories of dogs in his *Naturalis Historia*: *villatici* (home- or guard dogs), *pastorales pecuarii* (shepherd dogs), *venatici* (hunting dogs), *pugnaces* and *bellicosi* (fight- or war dogs), *pedibus celeres* (sighthounds) and *nares sagaces* (tracker dogs).[2]

Much later, in the late Middle Ages (1493), Heinrich Mynsinger wrote and published *Puoch von den valken, habichten, sperbern, pfaeriden, und hunden* (*Book of hawks, goshawks, sparrowhawks, horses, and dogs*).[3] The author based his book on much older sources and describes regular police-dog training that involved training dogs to stand up against a man clothed "in a stout coat of skins lest the dog should bite him during his education." The dogs were also trained to track the trail of a thief, much in the same way that bird dogs (retrievers) were taught to search for partridge and quail.

Figure 1.1 Historical records are clear that humans have long employed dogs' tracking abilities. Tracking scene, a miniature from *Livre de chasse*, a medieval book about hunting by Gaston Phébus, written in 1387–89.

Figure 1.2 Woodcut from Mynsinger's 1473 book that describes how dogs are trained to trail thieves.

Police Dogs in Belgium

Around 1890, dog enthusiasts near Malines, Belgium, started to systematically train their Malinois, the short-haired Belgian shepherd dog, for protection and tracking work. Louis Huyghebaert, in particular, encouraged the training of the dogs in nose work. In an article from that time we read the following:

> While we walked together along the canal, Mr. Huyghebaert gave me his wallet, and during a moment when his dog Tom was not watching, I threw the wallet in the brushwood about 3 meters from the road. After walking on for a longer distance, Tom's master began to search his pockets and gesticulate as if he had lost something. Immediately the dog went back to the place where we had briefly paused and came back without having found anything. Seeing his master still inspecting his pockets, he ran back again, first tracking and then searching with his nose in the air. Soon he came back with a triumphant look in his eyes and the wallet in his mouth.[4]

In March 1899, police commissioner Ernest Van Wesemael of Gent, Belgium, introduced three police dogs to his force. By the end of the year, the town had 10 police dogs, and by 1910, more than 30. All were Belgian shepherd dogs, mostly Groenendaels and Malinois trained for both protection and nose work.

Figure 1.3 At the end of 1899, Gent, Belgium, had 10 police dogs. The far right of this photo shows the kennel concierge, Police-Lieutenant De Meyer, and in the middle of the group, De Meyer's wife, who fed and cared for the dogs.

The use of these police dogs was such a success that soon many other Belgian towns, and towns from other countries, followed their example. Numerous newspaper articles full of praise caused such a demand for shepherds that even all the look-alikes of Groenendaels, the black long-haired Belgian shepherd dog, and Malinois were exported to England, France, Germany, Russia, Argentina, and the United States. In most of these countries, police-dog-training societies were founded.

Police Dogs in Germany

Austrian lawyer and cynologist Hans Gustav Adolf Gross, often called the founding father of criminal profiling, broached the idea of using dogs as police assistants in Germany near the end of the 19th century. Gross taught as a professor at the Franz-Josephs-Universität Czernowitz in Western Ukraine, Prague University, and the University of Graz. He also established the Institute of Criminology in Graz. The release of his book *Handbook for Examining Magistrates, Police Officials, Military Policemen, etc.* in 1893 is marked as the birth of the field of criminology, applying science to the fields of crime investigation and law.[5] He also adapted various fields of study to the needs of criminal investigation, such as crime-scene photography, footprints, handwriting analysis, and the use of police dogs. In 1896, he published an article, "A Police Assistant," praising police dogs:

> Above all, the dog should be a faithful, always alert, always
> attentive companion, who is equipped with far sharper
> senses than man, perceives much more than man, and
> so can warn him about the dangers of objects, as well as
> about many other circumstances that man would have oth-
> erwise overlooked.[6]

In 1896 in Hildesheim, Germany, a few police-dog enthusiasts were inspired by Gross's article and began training dogs for surveillance and tracking. Police dogs and their use also captured the interest of journalists and the general public. This interest increased significantly when the dogs began to work as "detectives" investigating criminal cases. The dogs became even more popular once they helped solve a few homicides, with keen interest from all over the world. The police dog movement, at that time still in its infancy, grew quickly.

Dog Detectives

Police dog literature in these early years ascribed heroic, almost unbelievable feats to the animals. Dog enthusiasts such as Friedo Schmidt, who wrote books about the work of police dogs, cautioned that a successful track by a police dog must be seen only as an indication and not as evidence. But police and judges at the time accepted the results as conclusive. This wholehearted faith undoubtedly led to many excesses. An event described by veterinarian J. Hansmann about the work of a tracking dog illustrates how far wrong an investigation could go with a too-enthusiastic acceptance of a dog's indication:

After a burglary, indistinct footprints were found in
the vicinity of the house at two different places about
100 meters distance from each other. A police dog handler
from Berlin started with his dog at one of these spots. The
dog picked up a track leading to the railway station. There
investigators learned that an unknown, suspiciously behav-
ing man with a backpack, who could be described exactly,
travelled from this small station with the first morning train
to Berlin...

But the dog handler went back to the crime scene
and brought his dog to the second place where indistinct
footprints were found. The dog now followed a track
3 kilometers in another direction to a secluded garden
house. In the garden, the dog stopped at a spot that had
been recently dug up. Here the greater part of the spoil was
found.[7]

This example demonstrates the value of having a good police
dog working in crime investigation, but it also shows how easily
we can make mistakes in the interpretation of the dog's work. If
the dog handler had stopped after the track leading to the railway,
the conclusion would have been that the man with the backpack
had carried the stolen material away. This would not have led to a
proper resolution of the case at all.

Veterinarian Friedrich Clater wrote in 1914 that "the police
dog has become extremely important in recent years, and the
performance of some police dogs is almost miraculous."[8] The
word *miraculous* indicates the widespread attitude towards police
dogs at the time. Some dogs were believed to have properties that
bordered on a kind of psychic perception.

In the face of such claims, and with the use of police dogs growing more common, scientists wanted to test dogs' abilities and better understand them. The work of some of the most important
pioneers in this research are described in this chapter. Although
we have certainly learned more about how dogs smell and perceive

odors since these studies, they still hold value for handlers in better understanding the myths and realities of dog tracking work.

George John Romanes

In 1885, the Canadian-Scots evolutionary biologist and physiologist G. J. Romanes performed experiments on the ability of dogs to follow human footsteps. He used his own dog for the research and published his work in the scientific magazine *Nature* in 1887.[9]

While his dog was held by a helper, Romanes walked through a shooting ground. After about a mile, he disappeared out of sight, and the helper let the Setter go. The dog hurled itself with full enthusiasm and speed on the track of its handler and quickly caught up with him. Even when Romanes rubbed his shoes with aniseed oil, giving the track a strong aniseed odor, the Setter followed his track after only brief hesitation.

In another test, Romanes lined up 11 people, one behind the other. He stood in front and led the group forward, each person stepping in the footsteps of the individual who walked in front of them. After about 590 feet (180 m), Romanes turned right with five helpers behind him, while the six others went to the left. His Setter was brought to the shooting ground and began to track. At the branch, the dog at first walked on, then it searched more intensively and located the correct track to the right. With that action, it was accepted that the dog was able to find and work out the track of his handler out of a mix of 12 human scents, and later on out of six tracks. However, Romanes's dog did not succeed in working out the track of a stranger. He didn't even want to work out the track of a gamekeeper he knew well.

Next, Romanes decided to exchange his boots with those of a person his dog didn't know and both laid tracks. The dog worked out the track laid by the stranger wearing his handler's boots, but he didn't pick up the track of his handler with the strange man's boots, even when he was encouraged to do so.

Romanes continued his tests and laid a track in socks he had worn for a while. The dog didn't pick up this track either, but when Romanes laid a track in bare feet, his dog worked it out, although slowly and with some hesitation. When his handler was wearing new boots, the dog didn't localize the track.

Romanes then glued brown paper onto the soles and sides of his old boots and laid a track. In the beginning, the Setter didn't pay much attention to the track, but that changed when he came to a place where a piece of paper was loosened from the heel of the boot. The dog recognized the track of his handler and followed this cheerfully, even though the gap in the paper was only a fraction of an inch in size.

Romanes surmised that the dog was working out not just his handler's track, but also those of his hunting boots. The track was therefore a composite odor consisting of the leather of the boots and the scent of his feet. The dog could, however, very clearly distinguish the scent of his handler from that of the boots, as proved by another experiment.

Romanes walked about 164 feet (50 m) in his boots, then almost 984 feet (300 m) in his socks, and after that another 984 feet (300 m) in his bare feet. His dog worked out the track until the end. Romanes concluded that the dog, after first following the mix of scents, could recognize a single part of it and could also follow this single part. This all was worked out correctly by the dog as long as it was his handler's track, but the Setter didn't succeed on other people's tracks.

Romanes's work was impressive, but all his tests were done with his own dog, which had an especially excellent nose and a strong bond to Romanes. He was not able to duplicate his efforts with other dogs.

Friedo Schmidt

The first person to systematically research the tracking skills of dogs, and publish on the subject, was Friedo Schmidt from

Stralsund, Germany, in 1910.[10] He suggested that human "scent substances" penetrate shoes and fall to the ground to form a track dogs can smell. In similar fashion, human scent substances penetrate gloves and are deposited on touched articles. He observed that a dog's physical condition can impact its ability to track and that poor food or a long journey has a negative effect on a dog's abilities. He also proved that trying to hide an individual human scent, or to lay an "odorless track" with new shoes, made tracking more difficult for the dog, but not impossible.

In his book *Criminal Trails and Police Dogs*, Schmidt also described how articles found at a crime scene should be saved and stored:

> By no means should the article be left at the scene or be taken in hand by the criminal investigator. This must be common knowledge to every man working at the crime scene. The article may also not be wrapped in paper or packed in a wooden or cardboard box because before long it will take the odor of the strange material.
>
> I suggest glass containers as the best means of storage. Glass is an inert material. Substances like sweat, blood, etc. incur no changes in contact with glass. Every separate

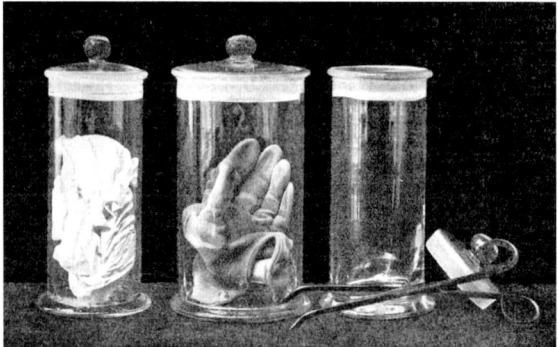

Figure 1.4 Friedo Schmidt had a clear understanding of how evidence should be preserved for later investigation.

article, as well as size allows, must be put in an appropriately sized, wide-necked, sealable glass-receptacle equipped with a glass-stopper. Such containers have the advantage of transparency, so that the article, for instance a handkerchief, can easily pass from hand to hand and important details, such as a monogram, can also be observed whilst in the receptacle.

Inspector Bussenius

A summary of the first milestones in tracking and suspect identification by dogs cannot ignore the contributions of Inspector Bussenius from Braunschweig, Germany. A skilled police-dog trainer, Bussenius and his dogs provided many early successes to support the police dog movement. In particular, the successful use of his German Shepherd Dog Harras von der Polizei in the Duwe murder case at Hagenhof near Braunschweig in June 1903 gave the world the first proof of the value of a dog in the investigation of homicide cases. The Duwe case is often seen as a turning point in the history of the police dog. Friedo Schmidt summarized the case in 1911:

> An eleven-year-old girl was killed at the Hagenhof farm in the German village of Königslutter near Braunschweig on June 3rd, 1903. The forensic research team did not come up with results, although one of the farmhands was suspected. After days of continuous but fruitless investigation, the public prosecutor asked Inspector Bussenius to try to find the murderer with his German Shepherd Dog Harras von der Polizei. After their arrival at the Hagenhof farm — four days after the homicide — all 12 employees of the farm were placed in a line in the yard. Harras was brought to the crime scene, where Inspector Bussenius commanded him to sniff the bloodstains and the surrounding area. The dog immediately picked up the track. First he briefly scanned one of the forensic investigators who had visited the crime scene earlier. Before long, the dog left him and continued

tracking. The dog then sniffed each person standing in the line, the one after the other. Suddenly, when he reached the eighth position in line, Harras hurled himself at the man, who cried out loudly in protest. The accused man was the suspected farmhand Duwe. The test was repeated two times. Each time, the people in the line changed positions, but the result was always the same: Harras hurling himself furiously at Duwe and not paying attention to the other persons. After that, Duwe was arrested. In the beginning, Duwe tried to deny the murder, but soon he made a full confession…. For Harras's work, a dog enthusiast sent one Reichsmark to the Braunschweig police department one week later to buy a reward of beef steak for Harras.[11]

Figure 1.5 A German police officer with his tracking dog at the beginning of the 20th century.

Konrad Most

Around 1913, people began to look at police dogs' nose work with a more critical eye. An outspoken critic was Berlin police dog trainer Konrad Most, who supported the use of dogs on patrol, but wasn't convinced dogs should be used in detective work. As head of police dog training at the German breeding and training facility for police dogs at Grünheide, near Berlin, Most had several police tracking dogs available for his research on tracking. Initial results from his tests were poor: the dogs he tested were distracted by cross-tracks and lost the track altogether when it changed direction.

Figure 1.6 The police dog training school at Grünheide, Germany, was the source of many important studies on tracking dogs.

After proving that a dog could easily move over from one track to another, Most then investigated why. His research concerned two primary questions:

1. What odors form a track for a dog?
2. How old can a track be for a dog still to be able to follow it?

At this time, there were two main theories about how dogs follow a track, each with its own supporters.

According to one theory, a dog follows the individual scent a person has left on the ground. Experiments conducted by Romanes in 1887,[12] Zell in 1909,[13] and Blunk in 1926[14] supported this theory.

According to the other theory, the dog follows the odor caused by the disturbance of the ground where a person has placed their foot. This theory also had widespread support. For example, in 1905, Brough concluded that dogs were not able to follow a track once it had been crossed by another.[15] In this view, dogs cannot distinguish between the disturbance caused by the original track and the cross-track because they are the same odor.

MOST'S TRACKING CROSS

Konrad Most developed a test for tracking dogs that became known as Most's tracking cross. In this test, shown in Figure 1.7, one track-layer walking from A to C and another track-layer walking from D to E meet each other at point B. The dog starts at A and is supposed to track to C, with DBE offering a tempting cross-track.

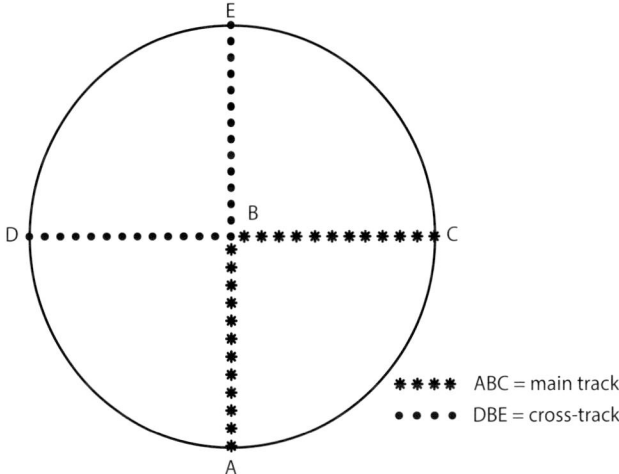

Figure 1.7 Most's tracking cross. One of the most difficult tracking exercises for a dog is to follow track ABC. In many of Most's tests using the tracking cross, dogs tracked correctly from A to B, but at the cross-track went over to E.

Because all the dogs arriving at B followed the track to E or made other mistakes, in 1914 Most concluded the following:

- Dogs are not able to follow the individual human scent in a track; they are not "track-sure."
- Dogs following a track do not recognize the scent of the track-layer when it is on an article.
- Dogs can only follow tracks that are no more than 5 hours old.

During World War I, Most had to stop his research, but in 1920, he repeated his earlier tests with the best tracking dogs of that time. Results were, as they had been before, disappointing and proved that the dogs were not track-sure. With cross-tracks combined with a change in terrain, the dogs always went astray.

In another test, 13 trained dogs were used, one of them a gun dog. The owners were convinced that their dogs could recognize and follow the track of their handler among other tracks. The 52 tests showed 10 correct and 42 wrong results; no single dog did everything correctly. With the presence of a cross-track in the field, the dogs often followed the wrong track and didn't find their handler. The cross-tracks in each of these tests presented serious difficulties for the dogs.

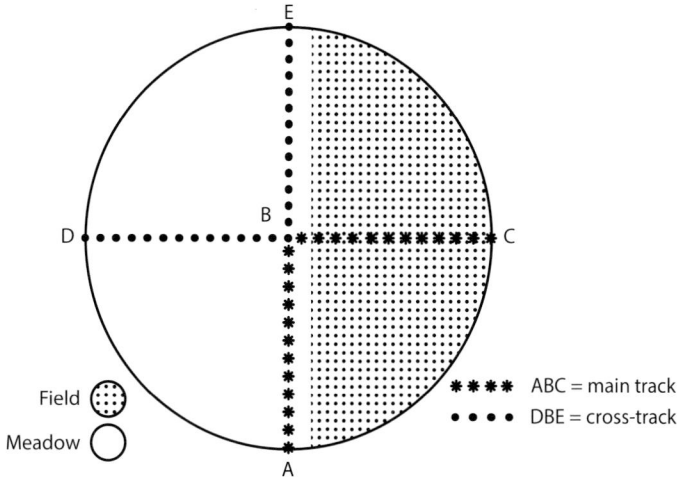

Figure 1.8 Most's tracking cross with a change in terrain, one of the most difficult exercises for a tracking dog.

CONTROVERSY

Publication of Most's research led to much controversy, because supporters of the use of police tracking dogs, such as criminologist

Paul Böttger and veterinarian J. Hansmann, felt the work of these dogs to be threatened.[16] In practice, they were able to prove much better results than Most's tests showed, although many of their results were somewhat tainted by handler interference.

Given the training techniques of that time, Most believed police tracking dogs only followed physical changes to the ground surface, namely the odor of evaporating sap from damaged plants and rotting bacteria. In his view, dogs were not track-sure.

On the other side, German researchers J. Hansmann,[17] P. Böttger,[18] and R. Blunk,[19] along with Rudolf and Rudolfina Menzel from Austria,[20] believed that human scent substances transferred to the ground were leading the tracking dog.

Extensive tests followed: Konrad Most and G. H. Brückner, between 1927 and 1930, performed as many as 1,268 tracking tests.[21] Major R. Belleville conducted a total of 1,458 tracks, with 4,404 cross-tracks, between 1930 and 1935.[22] J. Hansmann and Paul Böttger declared that, between 1925 and 1932, they tested dogs at the Grünheide training institute with "many thousands" of tracks.

Over the course of his experiments, Most modified his point of view and came to believe dogs were able to discriminate between people on the basis of scent. However, neither he nor Hansmann, a later director of the Grünheide training facility, were convinced that this individual scent was what guided dogs when following a track.[23]

THE FLOAT TEST

Konrad Most did many experiments using ingenious contraptions to scientifically determine what dogs follow on a track. One invention used a cable to float a person above the ground surface without touching and damaging the ground surface.

The first tests with the cable-lift were conducted with four well-trained tracking dogs. All dogs were first put to a control test:

Figure 1.9 Konrad Most's float appliance, by which the track-layer was pulled forward just above the ground.

A test person walked from A to B and from there back to A. The dog started to track at A. All dogs tracked from A to B and circled the end point without walking past the end of the track, as a lot of poorly trained dogs do. Without being called, the dogs tracked back to A on their own.[24]

SKIN RAFTS

Tests were then done to answer the question of whether scent substances from a "floating" person fall down to the ground so that the dog can follow them. This was and is still a theory with many supporters. In Most's time, it was thought that some kind of scent substances fall down from someone walking on stilts or riding a bicycle. These substances then float in the air or lie on the ground.

In 1958, R. J. Clifford,[25] and in 1972, W. G. Syrotuck,[26] put forth the theory that flakes of skin called *rafts* fall from the human body and form the scent track. According to Syrotuck, there are about 2 billion cells on the human skin, of which about 1/30 are released daily. This means that more than 40 thousand dead cells fall from our body each minute. On this information, Syrotuck based his theory that tracking dogs follow a trail formed by released rafts.

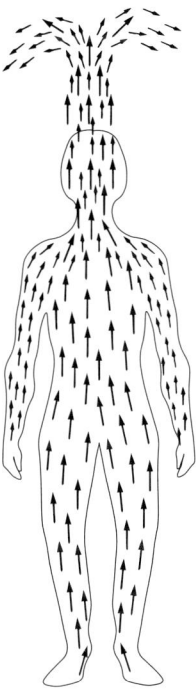

Figure 1.10 Air moves in currents around the human body because of its temperature. According to Syrotuck, this current has a speed of 1.5 miles per hour (2.3 km/h) and carries skin flakes up to 15 inches (40 cm) above the head before they fall to the ground.

Most tested this theory as follows: A test person walks the distance from A to B, where he sits on the plank on the float appliance and is then moved with his feet about 12 inches (30 cm) above the ground. Immediately after that, the dog was placed at A on the track. In all tests, the dogs tracked only as far as B (as they did in the control test) and returned from there after searching. All attempts to teach the dog to track along the path where the person was moved above ground didn't succeed. Konrad Most concluded that human scent substances falling from above do not produce enough of a track for the dog to follow.

However, F. J. J. Buytendijk qualified Most's conclusion as follows:

> If the track of a human, besides footprints, also contains scent substances that fall down from the human to the ground, then it is possible that this total odor complex is what leads the dog, not the scents falling down alone. Most's test does not totally exclude the possibility that, in the normal human track, scents falling from above have a meaning in the whole smell impression. However, the test indicates very well that, under these circumstances, and within the confines of the test, such scents don't produce by themselves a track that a dog can work out.[27]

Even waving arms and legs as a way to shed more skin cells while riding on Most's float appliance didn't bring better results for the dogs. Time could be a factor in these tests, because the dogs were put on the track almost immediately. Dust particles and flakes of skin float in the air and need a certain amount of time to reach the ground. Wind could also cause them to fall up to a few yards or meters beside the track.

But even in our own experiments, on (much) older tracks, we didn't succeed in getting dogs to work out the part of the track that continued under a float appliance, not even when the person on the float appliance was dragged very slowly and only a few inches above the ground.

DRIPPING CANS

In another test, Konrad Most hung dripping cans on the

Figure 1.11 Most's dripping cans.

cable-lift and the human foot track was continued with an odor track of a completely different substance (e.g., drips of juice from meat), while the track-layer was taken in another direction with the float appliance. Even then the police tracking dogs didn't follow the correct track and instead followed the track made by the cans. This test suggested that for a dog to follow a track on his own, without special training, the track must have a biological meaning for him (e.g., odor of meat, game, or a female dog in heat).

PORCELAIN SHOES

In another set of trials, Most used a wooden tracking wheel with wooden (and later porcelain) shoes attached to the outside edge. When the human track was continued by this wheel (the track-layer, again on the float appliance, was transported in another direction), then even the best police dog followed the track of the wheel. For Most, it was clear that the damage to the ground surface and the odors of the plants played an important role in

Figure 1.12 Most made artificial tracks using a tracking wheel with wooden or porcelain shoes attached.

the track odor. The human scents contributed, according to Most, only a small part of the total odor complex.

Most declared that a dog can find his way to his handler based on knowledge of his habits or by following the freshest track. However, Most's point is not valid for every case. If there is only one track in a given terrain, the dog may follow it without perceiving the specific human scent. In such a case, the dog can very easily go over to the track of another person, especially if the track is — as in Most's test — artificially laid in line with the first track.

THE IMPORTANCE OF THE START
Around 1930, after a lot of training, Most successfully taught a group of dogs to stay on the track of their handler, even when this track was approached closely and even crossed over by cross-tracks.

Figure 1.13 A dog working out the track of a stranger.

But it proved very difficult to make a dog track-sure on the track of a stranger.

However, it's important to note that Most didn't initially use a start point (a place at the beginning of the track with a high concentration of scent). After he began making such starts, his results quickly improved. Because of the strong odor at the start, the dog gave more attention to the track he had to follow. As well, the other cross-tracks, younger or older, became less interesting to the dog. However, as Most correctly pointed out, such circumstances never show up in the real-world practice of police work.

In 1938, R. Belleville confirmed the importance of the start: at the beginning of the track, the track-layer should walk around an area of about 1.5 square feet (0.5 m²) for several minutes.[28] If the dog could pick up enough odor at the start, then it could be proven with 86 to 97 percent certainty (with normal ground and weather conditions) that the dog follows an individual human scent on the track. The certainty that the dog would not go over to a cross-track was 100 percent when there was at least

Figure 1.14 The secret to tracking success is giving a strong scent at the start of the track.

10 minutes between tracks. But even after 3 minutes, there was still a reasonable certainty that the dog would stay on the track.

MOST'S CONCLUSIONS

Most's tests indicated that dogs will follow the track laid by the porcelain shoes as if it was a human track, and that using the float appliance meant there was no human scent the dog could follow. Most concluded that tracking dogs follow the mix of odors from damage to the ground surface, odors of plants, and odors of shoes.

With Most's research at Grünheide, members of the police slowly moved away from unrealistic expectations of the police dog. But there was enough scientific evidence of what police dogs *can* achieve that the police administration at Grünheide abandoned its suspicions about the usefulness of dogs in service.

Rudolfina and Rudolf Menzel

In 1930, the philosopher Rudolfina Menzel and her husband, the physician Rudolf Menzel, published a book about the scientific aspects of tracking dogs in police investigations.[29] In that book, they discussed in detail some basic concepts of tracking and gave advice on training tracking dogs. From this important, but not easily available research, we want to discuss some important themes.

PRICKLE THRESHOLD AND THRESHOLD VALUE

The Menzels described two useful concepts for understanding odor perception: prickle threshold and threshold value. A *prickle threshold* is a concept based on the image of a house where awareness lives. Any sense impression approaching awareness, like a visitor to the house, first has to step over the threshold of the house. The higher awareness lives in the house, the higher the threshold to step over to reach awareness and the stronger the prickle has to be.

The *threshold value*, in any given case, is the prickle strength needed to cross the threshold and penetrate the awareness. We can imagine crossing the threshold in two ways: one, that the prickle is just strong enough for us to get the message that it exists (it "prickles" the attention); two, that the prickle is so strong that we can observe certain qualities about it (e.g., that it is strong or weak). Because humans are most familiar with sight impressions, this important difference will be explained using the example of the human eye.

A weak beam of light can be just strong enough for the human eye to observe the clarity of the light without noticing anything else about it. We then would say that this beam of light has passed the *absolute prickle threshold*. As the light slowly becomes brighter, at a given moment the eye begins to observe the properties of the light, such as its color. We then speak of the light passing the *specific prickle threshold*.

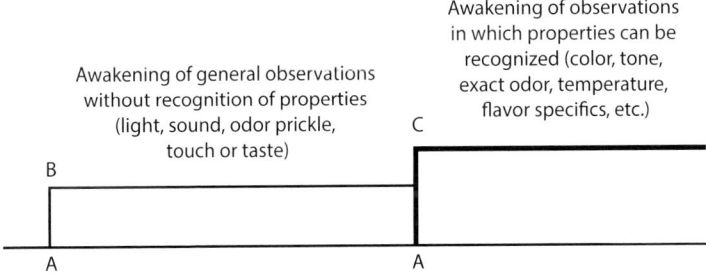

Figure 1.15 Schematic representation of the absolute (A–B) and specific (A–C) prickle threshold.

The same, of course, is true of the olfactory sense. An odor (for instance on a very old human track) can be just strong enough to be smelled by a tracking dog. But the odor may no longer be strong enough to give the dog particular information about it, such as the specific scent of the track-layer. The strength of the scent of this track is above the absolute, but under the specific prickle threshold.

The prickle threshold is not a uniform value. Different creatures have different threshold levels. For instance, some dogs will bark at any approaching stranger, while other dogs will let a stranger into the house without any fuss at all. Between these two are various levels, and even the same creature doesn't always have the same level of prickle threshold. Factors that can influence the strength of a prickle threshold are health, experience, observation, acquaintance, interest, hunger, training, tiredness, and many others.

People are the same. At different times the same person will react differently to prickles coming to them from the outside. Depending on circumstances, we say of ourselves that we are in a good or bad mood, irritated or nervous, and so on. That means our prickle threshold, under the influence of these factors, can change substantially.

Dogs can also be in a good or bad mood, which can alter their prickle threshold in a positive or negative way. The nose of the dog, its finest instrument, is particularly sensitive, especially when we demand its high performance. Here many factors can affect whether the absolute or specific prickle threshold for different odors is high or low. At times, the threshold may be so high that a perception fails to cross the threshold altogether.

Using a dog's nose for our detector and tracking work is not merely a physiological task. In other words, a dog's success or failure with tracking is not merely a question of the capabilities of its nasal organ. It is also a psychological problem, depending on the dog's intelligence and ability to learn, the attention of the dog, and its current prickle threshold.

PERCEPTION AND TIREDNESS

About sensory perception, the Menzels wrote:

> This is not an easy process, but a combination of different factors. In the first place, in order for the dog to make a sensory perception, he must have a fully functioning and well-built registration system (eye, ear, nose, etc.). From each organ there must be a good working nerve connection to the related brain center. Again, these have to function very well. Each part of the system must be functioning

properly in order for an accurate perception to be made. Then there has to be, for each sense, a specific and sufficiently strong prickle and, at last, the dog's attention must be directed to this prickle. Only when all these factors are operating can the dog perceive.

To this view must be added something on the effects of tiredness. Tiredness can play a very important, sometimes deciding, role in perception. It can strike at each of the factors of perception: prickle, sense, and attention. In the nose, for instance, the time it takes to breathe out has to be long enough for the mucous membrane to recover and be ready to carry new information from the next inhalation to the brain.

On the other hand, mental tiredness, fatigue of the brain, plays an important role in how well a dog perceives a track. When we're absentminded or distracted, we sometimes walk or drive down the wrong street without noticing. It may be some time before we discover the mistake. How often have you gone all the way home without thinking about it? To suppose that a dog naturally focuses his attention on the track all the time is illogical. The question is, how far will a dog overshoot a track before it will retrace its path to pick up the trail again? Of course, it is possible to teach a dog to focus his attention on the track for a certain time. Such training requires a strong bond with the dog and correct training technique.[30]

Mental tiredness and a loss of focus during the track can sometimes be seen in very long and difficult tracks, especially when the odor is close to the prickle threshold, or sometimes even under it, so that the dog has to help himself over parts of the track where there is no odor, and hence no prickle. Mental tiredness can also occur when the dog has to work a long time, especially when it is very warm or if the dog is under pressure (from the handler, change of surroundings, unusual travel, etc.). The dog will then, in spite of a normal effort, deliver poor results. Tiredness can also be expressed by reduced attention: the dog slows down, is not inter-ested in the track, is diverted by any little thing, is catching flies, is relieving himself, and so on. You can overcome this tiredness by getting the dog's attention back on tracking with, for example, short pauses and a restart, showing the track with your hands, and encouragement with a "Good boy."

Figure 1.16 Tiredness can play a very important, sometimes a deciding, role in perception.

Physical tiredness can also show up in tracking, particularly on longer tracks. For that reason, it is not advisable to do any tiring work with the dog just before tracking. For better results in track-ing, as in every form of search work, it is best to start with a men-tally and physically well-rested dog.

ODOR SUMMATION

The Menzels also described the concept of *odor summation*. A prickle that is too weak by itself to be perceived (and is thus under the absolute threshold value) can become more noticeable if it is continuously picked up over time. Though separate, the weak prickles following each other will summarize (accumulate and thereby overcome the prickle threshold). These prickles can become so strong by summarizing that they can cross the absolute and even the specific prickle threshold. Eventually a prickle over-comes the threshold of awareness. It hasn't become stronger than the earlier prickles, but through accumulation the weak prickles form a sort of ladder, eventually allowing them to cross the threshold.

It's like having a small pain, such as a headache. We normally don't discover a pain suddenly. Instead, the pain prickles accumulate and summarize, and slowly come to our awareness.

Another way to picture this is to think of being asleep when the alarm goes off. You're so deeply asleep that, at first, you don't notice the alarm. In sleep, our prickle threshold may be so high that even a loud, piercing tone cannot cross the threshold. The alarm continues to ring, so at last the noise summarizes into prickles that can cross the absolute prickle threshold, so we hear the noise in our sleep but don't necessarily recognize it. It's not unusual to dream of fire alarms and sirens until the prickle manages to cross the specific prickle threshold, when we recognize the well-known tone of the alarm and awaken. It is important to understand this summarizing effect and how it impacts dog training.

For instance, in older tracks, the amount of human scent in one footstep can be under the specific prickle threshold, not enough to be perceived by the dog. Only through the summation of the scent prickles, so on a longer track, is it slowly possible for the tracking dog to perceive anything about the scent quality of the track-layer.

However, the summation of prickles doesn't have to take place without interruption. Frequent repetition, even with breaks between prickles, can strengthen too-weak prickles enormously. This is the secret of advertising: a one-time ad can go unnoticed because it doesn't grab our attention, but the same ad confronting us daily will work its way into our distracted brain. In the same way, a certain human scent can, by repetition, work its way into the dog's notice so he can clearly work out in clean-scent tracking very short, old tracks during every training exercise. The easiest way to train, of course, is by working on the track of the handler or a regular track-layer because the dog is so familiar with these scents that the threshold is very low for them.

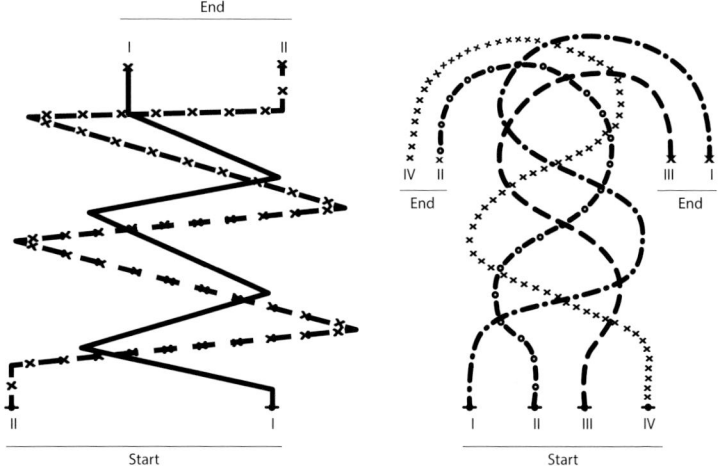

Figure 1.17 Based on his research with these types of tracks, Konrad Most believed that tracking on individual human scent was impossible.

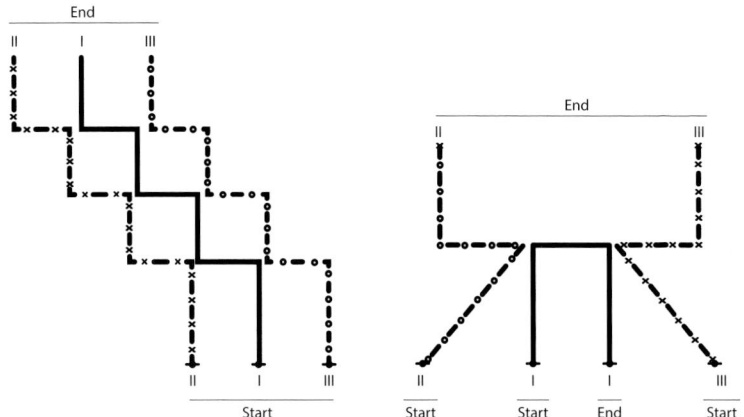

Figure 1.18 With these tracks and cross-tracks, other researchers showed that tracking on individual human scent was indeed possible.

Adapted from P. Böttger, *Hunde im Dienste der Kriminalpolizei.*

ODOR PHYSIOGNOMY

The Menzels also developed the concept of odor physiognomy. It is a well-known fact that certain states of mind or emotions will often produce a particular expression on the face of a human being, the physiognomy of the human. Thanks in part to the Menzels' observations, we now know that the emotional life of a human being can also be reflected in their scent. The Menzels called this the "odor physiognomy." But the difference between the face of a human and a scent is that humans cannot consciously influence or read scent. We can always check our facial expression in the mirror, and because of that, with practice, we can learn to control our facial expressions. Scent cannot be controlled in this fashion.

Because a person's inner life is reflected in their scent, it is easy to understand why animals have problems with some people from the first time they meet, and yet are good friends with other people from the beginning. According to the Menzels, that is also why a police dog will search on the track of a criminal with more diligence and cheer than on a training track, laid by a well-known person. Criminals fleeing a crime are in a hurry and under great tension, which gives them a different, likely interesting scent.

Experiments conducted by the Menzels, and by Friedo Schmidt,[31] eventually led to the important conclusion that how dogs work is determined by the way they are trained. The training method should be closely adapted to the exact purpose of the training, and sufficient controls should be built in to test what the dog has learned.

2

Senses and Perception

The knowledge of historical tracking research, as described in the previous chapter, added to an understanding of the physiology involved in smelling, described in this and the following two chapters, will give dog handlers a greater insight into what is involved in the smelling process of tracking dogs. A handler armed with this important theoretical knowledge has a great advantage over the handler who exclusively practices tracking. This theoretical knowledge can often explain the problems encountered during tracking and, more importantly, can prevent mistakes during training and operations.

Senses

A sense is an organ that can pick up information or signals (prickles) from the outside world (e.g., sight of prey or an enemy) or prickles from the body itself (e.g., hunger). These prickles then are changed into signals the brain can understand (perception), which then provides an appropriate response for the animal.

The primary organs for perceiving the external world are the eyes, ears, nose, skin, and mouth, with the corresponding five sensory systems: visual system (sense of vision), auditory system (sense of hearing), olfactory system (sense of smell), somatosensory system (sense of touch), and gustatory system (sense of taste). For our work with dogs, three of these classic five senses are of special interest: audition, vision, and olfaction.

Figure 2.1 Three of the dog's external senses are of special interest: audition, vision, and olfaction.

It's important to realize that the senses do not operate in isolation from each other. We know that children, for example, learn the spoken word by looking at the face of the speaker. Visual impressions support the recognition of sounds.

Dogs' perceptions are likely also connected. It is illogical to suppose that tracking dogs only use their nose and don't search with their eyes for soil damage or changes in the terrain. Therefore, although our focus in this book is the dog's ability to smell, it's worthwhile understanding a bit about how the other senses operate. It is possible that a dog has a lower prickle threshold for sensory perceptions that naturally cooperate. For example, if the dog sees disturbed ground, it might sniff a little closer, expecting to find a buried object, even if he hasn't smelled any hint of the object.

Figure 2.2 Tracking dogs not only use their noses, but also search with their eyes for soil damage or changes to the terrain.

Audition

Hearing responds to sound waves, which are routed from the outer and middle ear to the inner ear. The inner ear consists of the cochlea for hearing and the vestibular system for balance. The vestibular system sends signals to the vestibular nerve, which joins the cochlear nerve and leads electrical signals to the brain. The cochlea is filled with liquid and has a special membrane covered with small hair-like cells called cilia. Movement of the cilia in response to sound waves provides a signal to the brain, resulting in what we understand as "hearing."

A dog's hearing is a lot better than a human's, who is relatively primitively equipped. Studies show that dogs are able to hear sounds that are four times farther away than humans can.[1] For example, a human can hear a particular sound from 295 feet (90 m) away, whereas a dog can hear it from about 1,300 (400 m) away. Dogs can perceive tones of 30.000 Hertz, which cannot be heard by humans (who hear a maximum of 20.000 Hertz). The dog whistle is based on this principle — it is soundless to humans. As a result of this great discrimination for sound, a dog can recognize the footsteps of its owner or even the engine murmur of its owner's car.

In their 2020 study, Braber et al. quite rightly note that

> little research has been done in investigating the auditory capabilities of the dog. There may be significant mismatches between what we expect dogs (and perhaps specific types of dog, given historic functional breed selection) can hear versus what they can actually hear. This has significant implications for what should be considered if we wish to select specific dogs for work associated with particular hearing abilities and to protect and maintain their hearing throughout life.[2]

For both dogs and humans, auditory structures grow with the individual, which may cause changes in the sensitivity to various sounds. This point is worth keeping in mind when beginning the early training of working dogs, which can start before some breeds (especially large dogs) reach their adult size (18 months for some large breeds). The dog's perception of auditory cues, including its response to verbal cues from a handler, may change as it ages.

Vision

The retina of the eye has two types of photoreceptors. The rods allow perception of light, and the cones allow perception of color. These receptors convert light into impulses that are sent through the optic nerve to the visual cortex in the brain. The brain processes and interprets that information, and "seeing" occurs.

We know that humans normally see better than dogs do, especially at a great distance, although dogs see sudden movements more quickly than humans. The dog's lesser ability to see can be attributed to domestication (being a house pet). This idea was initially suggested in 1954 in a study by Stephan, who investigated the brains of wild animals and house pets and discovered that the areas of the brain where hearing and sight impressions are processed in house pets were 40 percent smaller than in the equal weight brains of wild animals.[3] In 1960, a further study by the Menzels supported Stephan's finding, concluding that canines living in the wild have excellent vision.[4]

In their 2018 study, Byosiere et al. found that

> While dogs appear to be visual generalists, with functional vision during both the day and night, they appear to be more scotopic than humans, meaning that they are highly adapted to function in dim light. In fact, they appear to have developed several ways of improving visual functioning across a variety of ambient light levels. The retina of the dog is largely composed of rod photoreceptor cells, which are extremely helpful in dim light as they can function in less intense light conditions. Only 3% of retinal cells in dogs are cone photoreceptor cells, which are primarily responsible for color vision. This compares with roughly 5% in humans.[5]

Although dogs' visual acuity is difficult to measure, Miller and Murphy estimate that a dog can perceive an object from 20 feet (6.1 m) away that a person with normal vision could differentiate from 75 feet (22.9 m) away.[6]

A dog's ability to distinguish different colors remains controversial. Humans have three types of cone photoreceptor cells — long-wave (red), medium-wave (green), and short-wave (blue), at spectral peaks of 558 nanometers, 531 nanometers, and 419 nanometers, respectively. Dogs have only two types of cones, which almost identically correspond to short-wave and long-wave sensitivities (blue at a spectral peak of 555 nanometers and yellow at 429 nanometers). Because of this, many people suggest that dogs may be unable to perceive differences between green, yellow, and red color cues.

The better sight of humans partly has to do with our height. If you think about how low to the ground the dog is in relation to the human, then it makes sense that the dog's hearing and sense of smell are its primary senses, rather than sight, which benefits from a higher vantage point.

Olfaction

What we know about the nose, and of odor in general, is far from complete. In comparison, we know far more about the other sensory organs. In contrast to audition and vision, there is no physical unit of measurement for smell. Odor is measured simply by whether it is smelled or not, with general, subjective measurements such as "strong" or "faint." Gazit et al. describe odor as "volatile molecules that via olfactory receptors cause a reaction in the olfactory brain."[7] Or, more simply put: odor is perceived (smelled) when molecules from a substance or object travel through the air to reach the olfactory receptors in the nose.

There are many different olfactory receptors in the nose. These receptors are very sensitive and selective, and each receptor is stimulated by a specific type of molecule. These impulses then pass through the olfactory nerve into the cerebral cortex, where the actual "smelling" takes place.

Kokocińska-Kusiak et al. wrote about the significance of olfaction for canines in 2021:

> Although dogs interact with their world via all of their
> senses, olfaction seems to be one of the most important
> because it provides information not only about the current
> status of the environment, but can also allow detection of
> signals from the past (presence of prey, enemies, or some
> new, unknown traces in the surrounding environment).

This complex network of mixtures of smells creates a three-dimensional image of the surrounding world across time, playing a key role in maintaining such basic life activities as finding food, recognizing threats, or finding a reproductive partner.[8]

For our purposes of understanding a dog's sense of smell, Stephan's conclusion is valuable: that the allocortex, much of which is used to process odor, is only slightly smaller in house pets than in wild animals.[9] He concludes that the sense of smell was less affected by domestication than the other senses. Possibly this is because the olfactory organ is an ancient and primitive characteristic, as was confirmed by Salazar et al. in 2019.[10] These researchers found that the olfactory organ also exists in less-developed animals, and further, that it is developed and works even in aquatic animals. There also is some evidence that in dogs olfaction is one of the first senses to be active, even allowing prenatal olfactory learning.[11]

Other information also indicates that the nose is a special sense organ. We are able to recall or describe countless forms of things, but of the hundreds of thousands of odors that we can differentiate, we have only a few words to describe them. In 2013, Olofsson et al. wrote:

> It is notoriously difficult to name odors. Without the benefit of non-olfactory information, even common household smells elude our ability to name them. The neuroscientific basis for this olfactory language "deficit" is poorly understood, and even basic models to explain how odor inputs gain access to trans-modal representations required for naming have not been put forward.[12]

Indeed, odors have a limited number of names. These often have something to do with naming the origin of the odor (it stinks like petrol; this smells like a rose). In many cases, we must make do with describing an odor as pleasant or unpleasant, or with hazy analogies (this odor reminds me of...).

One aspect of odor we are aware of is its intensity. When you see red or green light, it doesn't matter how intense it is. The perception *thresholds* of light of different frequencies don't make a big difference. With odors it is different: the intensity of some odors, and the sensitivity we have to them, can be a thousand times greater than for others. It is not known why this is, although in general, an odor will be observed faster according to how dangerous it is (e.g., smoke). An exception is carbon monoxide, which is odorless to us. This connection between threshold intensity and danger shows us that our sense of smell, for both humans and dogs, is directly related to survival.

What It Means to Be a Smelling Animal

The dog is primarily a smelling animal, meaning that his olfactory system gives him more information about his world than any other sense, and he will perceive through this sense before any other. Hearing is his second most important sense, followed by sight. In most humans, sight is the dominant sense.* This difference is of great importance in making comparisons between humans and dogs, not only for orienting in a room, but also in recognizing articles.

Our room, the room in which we live, is optically built. We distinguish front, behind, above, and under with our eyes. We arrange the articles in a room, or the flowers in a garden, in such a way that our eyes see them, and because of our sight perceptions, we can find our way in it.

Now think how differently the dog experiences the human environment. The dog lives primarily in a world of odor. For most people, a visible item has meaning and therefore determines how we think about our environment. In contrast, a dog orients itself according to clouds of odor.

---

* It should be noted that people with visual disabilities may develop heightened senses of hearing or smell in compensation.

Furthermore, a dog walks on four legs and has its head close to the ground. We cannot really imagine a dog's spatial view, even if we walk on our hands and knees. We have a different physique and, because of that, a different spatial sense of our environment.

Yet having a clear understanding of the dog's perceptions is vital for everyone working with tracking or detector dogs. This understanding is key to assessing the behavior of the dog and working with it as a team.

Figure 2.3 We can't really imagine a dog's spatial view of the world, even by walking on all fours and keeping our head close to the ground.

Differences in Interest

Ordinarily a dog pays attention to completely different items in the environment than humans do. Many things that we ignore, or even turn up our nose to (sometimes literally, because it stinks so much!) are of great importance for the dog, enough to prompt him to study them more closely. Knowing these differences in observation between human and dog can help us better understand the behavior of dogs during tracking.

Because of a difference in interest, our world and that of dogs looks different. This was described clearly by Von Uexküll and Kriszat:

A human and his dog walk together in a town. The handler passes a clothes shop and is very interested in the clothes displayed there; then he goes by a jewelers, where rings and watches lie in the shop window, which he pays attention to; and at last he stops at a bookstore, where he looks at books and magazines. He pays less attention to the butcher shop and walks around a corner into a park and climbs a staircase to a terrace, where he sits on a chair and looks at the nice flowerbeds around him.

The dog experiences the world totally differently when he goes out for this walk with his owner. He passes the clothes shop; the things displayed there don't interest him. These only become of interest when the owner or another housemate has worn them and they have absorbed body scent. Our watches and books also don't interest him. The display is for him nothing more than an unimportant mess of lines and surfaces with uninteresting odors.

But the butcher shop says more to him. The odor of meat and sausages sparks his appetite, and the odor of waste makes him want to roll in it. Also very important for

Figure 2.4 How can the handler just pass by the garbage bin at the corner of the street? Every male dog that passes there plants a fascinating odor "flag."

him (how can the handler go by?) is the garbage bin at the corner of the street. Every male dog that passes there plants a more or less strong odor "flag." The dog studies these very seriously, and only after adding his own flag can he continue his walk.

The staircase of the terrace is like walking up a hill, and he may not even notice that the slope is interrupted by stairs. The rail of the staircase is unimportant, but the cushions of the chairs interest him. They are so very soft. Of the beauty of the flowerbed he probably sees nothing; the park only gets his attention when he sees a mouse emerge.[13]

Figure 2.5 The statue *Zinneke-Pis*, in Brussels, Belgium, was created in 1998 by Brussels sculptor Tom Frantzen. The Flemish word *Zinneke* means "bastard dog."

Because of different interests, humans effectively live in a totally different world from dogs. The dog's interest is much more circumscribed than ours and is, as with every animal, limited to what is of direct importance. We don't know whether the dog really observes the table, cupboards, and mirror on the wall of the living room, or whether he just walks around them mechanically. Of the things on a table, the plates will get his attention only if they are filled with food.

Does a dog ever notice the sky or the tops of the trees as anything other than background to a couple of flying ducks, or to a cat escaping into the trees? Does he note the singing of the birds, even though he can certainly hear them? Does he distinguish between the odor of flowers? Certainly, if he is trained for it, he can distinguish these things, but ordinarily, all such things lie outside his sphere of interest.

Figure 2.6 Only what is shown in gray in this drawing play a role in the world of the dog. The chair and the sofa are interesting because they are comfortable places to lie down. The dining chairs make the food on the table more accessible. All other things from the human world, such as the bookcase and paintings, hold no interest, except, of course, the crumbs that fell on the floor.

Figure 2.7 Human and dog noses: worlds of difference.

An Active Process

An important idea about picking up odors is that it is a more active process than you might initially think. Buytendijk makes the following assertion:

> Mostly one imagines that perception with the sense organs is a passive process.... Sight perception should be the reception of light prickles on the retina; hearing decided by the vibrations on the eardrum; smelling because of particles of odor coming into the olfactory mucous membrane ... This opinion is not right![14]

In fact, what the dog perceives depends largely on his attention or interest. This interest makes the dog actively seek out a sense impression. His interest occurs automatically when the sense impression has a biological meaning; that is, something plays an obvious role in the dog's life. The odor of other dogs is an example of this, as is the movement of a cat or the sound of another dog barking.

However, the attention given to a certain perception can also be decided by experience (including training). The reaction of the dog on noticing the approach of a person or animal he recognizes by odor or sound are examples of perceptions heightened through experience. Humans also have perceptions originating from interest and experience: when a painter, a biologist, and an engineer walk through a landscape, they notice and experience different things because of their different interests and knowledge.

Figure 2.8 Different animals experience their world differently depending on their interests. For example, while a dog walking in a meadow may not distinguish the different sorts of plants, a cow may not see the little mouse trying to find its way through the grass. Their interests relate to the vital needs of each animal.

Training Perceptions

Through training, the dog can be become interested in perceptions that, for an untrained dog, lie far below the perception level. This happens, for instance, with tracking dogs, with detector dogs trained to locate drugs or explosives, or with search and rescue dogs, which search for people beneath debris piles that may contain odors (such as food) that are more naturally interesting to the animal.

Figure 2.9 Through training, a dog can be focused on perceptions that lie far below the perception level of an untrained dog. For example, explosive detector dogs can be trained to find substances that normally hold no interest to them.

Many people have wrongly supposed an intellectual assessment, sometimes even a clairvoyance in the dog. For example, you might hear people telling stories about extraordinary dogs who know what time it is, or that it is Sunday. Yet such knowledge on the part of the dog can be attributed to the dog's ability to learn from experience. For instance, on Sunday, most people wake up later than on working days. Or a dog might sulk when suitcases come out because he's learned suitcases mean his owner will be leaving. A dog's outstanding ability to search for and find the things we train them to find is a result of training, or a fine ability to observe and form connections, not an empathic understanding of our wishes.

THE INDISPENSABLE SENSE

Humans often underrate the importance of their own sense of smell. In 1989, Vroon wrote about this:

> When people were asked which sense they would miss the most, sight was at the top of the list. The sense of smell takes a humble place. But that decision was taken a bit too quickly. The sense of smell was, in evolution, an old and important sense. We simply don't realize how much we are influenced by it. The senses are connected with the brain via nerves. Eyes and ears send, via a long way, their information to different parts of the brain. With smell, it is not that way. A piece of the brain is placed high in the nose. The olfactory organ is in direct connection with the brain.[15]

When the ability to smell is lost, which can happen after a brain injury or as a result of certain viral infections, the people in question not only taste less, but they also expose themselves to dangers because they don't smell the odor of bad meat or discover a little late that the kitchen is ablaze. In addition, the limbic system (which controls behavior and emotions) of these people misses key inputs, which often leads to depression and loss of sexual interest. Depression is more than unpleasant feelings; it also threatens overall health. Long-term depression inhibits the immune system, leading to an increased chance of illnesses.

In his 1985 book *The Man Who Mistook His Wife for a Hat, and Other Clinical Tales,* neurologist Oliver Sacks describes a talented man who lost his ability to smell when he received a blow to his head. This was a serious shock for him:

> "My sense of smell?" he said. "I never thought about it. But when I lost it, it was as if I suddenly became blind. Life has lost a big part of its savor; you don't realize how much taste comes out of odor. You smell people, smell books, you smell the city and smell the spring…a pattern of unconscious background for all the other stuff. My world was suddenly much, much poorer…"[16]

His neurologists did not think he would recover. But suddenly, some months later, his beloved morning coffee, which had become tasteless, began to taste again. Hesitating, he tried his pipe, which he hadn't touched for months, and there also he picked up a trace of the rich aroma he loved so much. He went back to his doctor. But after the doctor tested him carefully, using a double-blind technique, he said, "No, I am sorry, there is absolutely no way. You still have a total disability to smell. But it's crazy that you can 'smell' your pipe and your coffee again…"

What possibly happened is that only the olfactory system (not the brain stem) was damaged, and thus the man's recovered experiences of smell were the result of a powerful smell memory. In drinking his coffee and lighting his pipe, actions associated with odor, he was able to unconsciously call the odors back, and with such an intensity that he thought he had recovered.

HUMAN SENSE ABILITIES

Although weak compared to the dog, human olfactory function is better than people think.[17] In truth, humans have an extraordinary, if underappreciated, sense of smell. For example, humans can detect the scent of fear in human sweat, and they may select mates whose body scent suggests a favorable genetic makeup. Such behaviors must depend on keen olfaction. According to Yeshurun and Sobel, the odorant ethyl mercaptan, which is often added to propane as a warning agent, can be detected at concentrations ranging between 0.2 ppb (parts per billion) and 0.009 ppb.[18] This is equivalent to approximately three drops of the odorant added to an Olympic-sized swimming pool. Given two pools, a person can detect by smell which pool contains the odorant.

Other impressive cases of human olfactory discrimination involve odorants that are ecologically meaningful. For example, human participants in a 1989 study by Lord and Kasperzak could use their sense of smell to differentiate between their own T-shirt from 100 other, identical T-shirts worn by other people for 24 hours.[19] According to Porter et al., a human mother can discriminate between the smell of her baby and that of other babies,[20] and Schaal et al. found that babies can pick out the smell of their breastfeeding mothers from other mothers as early as six days after birth.[21] As Kenneth Hovis, of Carnegie Mellon University at Pittsburgh, stated in 2012, "Early olfactory experience, possibly even before birth, may produce long-lasting effects in both olfactory mucous membrane in the nose and the vomeronasal organ."[22]

However, human odor detection thresholds are very high, so only unusually high odor concentrations spontaneously shift our attention to olfaction.

HUMAN TRACKERS

As with dogs, humans can improve their ability to detect odors with practice. For example, Jess Porter and his colleagues from the University of California, Berkeley, in 2007 found that humans can learn to track an odor trail in a field, and they significantly improve their performance at this task after only four practice sessions.[23] The researchers laid 33-foot (10-m) odor trails, including one of chocolate essential oil, in a grassy field and asked 32 people to find a trail and track it to the end. Those who took part were blindfolded and wore thick gloves and earplugs to force them to rely exclusively on their sense of smell. Two-thirds of the participants were able to follow the odor. And while they were much slower than dogs in tracking an odor, their performance improved over time.

Figure 2.10 A dog's outstanding ability to search for and find the things we train them to find is a result of training, or a fine ability to observe and form connections, not an empathic understanding of our wishes. And although weak compared to the dog, human olfactory function is better than most people think.

In a test by Sela and Sobel in 2010, it was found that humans require two working nostrils to be able to track odors.[24] Such research has proved that the human sense of smell is more powerful than was previously believed and that, with training, humans might be capable of tasks that were once thought to be the exclusive domain of non-human animals.

Practical Tips

Keeping up to date with scientific studies on odor and perception has valuable applications for dog handlers and trainers. Two examples follow of practical ways to put scientific studies to work.

PUPPY SELECTION

In newborn puppies, the olfactory organ is already well developed. Although their eyes are still closed and their ears folded back, closing the hearing canal, they are able to find, by warmth and mainly by smell, their mother's nipples. Bodingbauer posited in 1977 that the speed with which a pup could find that food source was equal to the sensitivity of his sense of smell.[25] That observation could be of practical importance with the selection of puppies if you're planning to train the dog in an area in which the sense of smell is very important, like detector dogs or tracking dogs.

Figure 2.11 Observing which puppies find the mother fastest may be a clue to help breeders and trainers help select puppies for training as detector dogs or tracking dogs.

ODOR AND MEMORY

The sense of smell is connected to learning and memory. Home-sickness occurs in children partly because of unfamiliar odors. A way to prevent homesickness is to allow the child to take along a cuddle toy with an odor of home. In the same way, when you pick up a new puppy, you should request a toy or piece of cloth with the odor of the litter; it will put the puppy at ease when he smells the well-known odor among all the strange, new odors of your home.

All senses can bring back memories, but smells are especially deep. There are cases of people who couldn't remember anything about nursery school until they sniffed a typical "school odor." Probably this recognition of odor also shows why a dog recognizes, even after many years, its previous owner.

FAILURE ODORS

Another example of the relationship between smell and memory is from the following study: people were given a difficult task, which they couldn't do well, and at the same time they were exposed to an unusual odor. Subsequently, when they were asked to complete an easy, ordinary task with the same odor present, they had difficulty completing the task. With conditioning, the odor had become associated with failure. Dogs can make the same connections to "failure odors," such as the smell of certain types of soil or the scent of certain tracklayers.

3

Anatomy and Odor Perception

This chapter covers current theories about how the act of smelling occurs in the body of both humans and dogs. New research is emerging all the time that helps us better understand this important sense. We have tried to present the information as simply as possible and to focus on aspects that are important when working with tracking, scent identification, and detector dogs. We hope that this background knowledge will help you troubleshoot when problems arise during training or operations.

How Sense Organs Function

Thanks to its ancestor, the wolf, the dog has a highly developed olfactory system. Indeed, most predators find their prey by smell. They also recognize family and enemies by odors from tracks and droppings, so their olfactory system gives them information with a high survival value.

As we discussed in the last chapter, a sense is an organ that picks up prickles from the outside world (e.g., odor of prey) or the body itself (e.g., thirst). The prickles become a signal to the brain and the brain chooses an appropriate response.

In general, all sensory organs work the same way. First we'll discuss the general operation of the senses. Then we will revisit each part of the process with more detail on odor perception.

GENERAL OPERATION

Each sense organ has *receptors*. These receptors are located in or on *sensory neurons*. The receptors react to a *signal* in the environment. This signal stimulates the sensory neuron, which results in an *impulse*. This impulse can be thought of as an electric current, running from the sensory neuron through the *nerves*. The impulse is transmitted from one nerve to another, until it reaches the *brain* and the information is processed.[1]

Because we are most familiar with sight impressions, let's use the example of the human eye: the eye contains two kinds of receptors, rods and cones. The *rods* react to the strength of light. As soon as there is light, the rods react: the light breaks down a certain kind of protein, and this reaction is the beginning of an impulse to the brain. After this, new protein is synthesized. When this protein breaking down / rebuilding system does not work well, people cannot see well in the dark.

There are three different kinds of *cones* that each react to certain light colors. When confronted with green light (e.g., from grass), one group of cones react. A chemical reaction in the cones sends an impulse to the brain. In the brain, the information received from the cones is combined with the information from cones that react to red and blue, and all of this information is processed. With certain kinds of color-blindness, something is wrong with one of the cone types; with other kinds, something is wrong with how the information is processed in the brain.

Signal⇒ Receptor⇒ Chemical reaction in sensory neuron⇒ Impulse through nerve⇒ Brain

Problems in perception can occur at any of these stages. Examples of problems include the following:

- The signal cannot reach the receptor.
- There is no receptor available for a certain kind of signal.
- The sensory neuron does not react.
- The nerve does not react.
- The brain interprets the information incorrectly.

These problems in perception apply to all sensory organs, and therefore also to the olfactory system. However, it is not always easy to determine what disturbance is involved when dogs have problems with odor perception. In Chapter 4 we look in more detail at other potential causes of odor perception problems in search and tracking dogs.

External Nose

The skull of dogs, like all mammals, consists of a frontal and a nasal bone. The nasal bone contains the olfactory system, the nose, which includes an external and an internal part.

The external nose picks up air and conducts odor substances to the internal nose. This picking up is stimulated by the cartilage and strong muscles of the external nose, which is the lightly moist, bald part of the dog's upper lip, usually black, although it can be brown, gray, or rose depending on, for instance, the color of the dog's coat. The surface of the external nose is unique for every dog. In fact, a print of it can be used for identification, just like fingerprints are used for humans. According to Bodingbauer, dogs with a large external nose are capable of greater odor achievements than those with a smaller one.[2]

The external nose includes two nostrils, which are the entrance to the internal nasal cavities. With sniffing or more intensive smelling, the nostrils can be widened or narrowed, controlling the amount of air allowed in the nasal cavity. The muscles in the external nose of adult dogs are strongly developed and can be moved

Figure 3.1 The surface of the external nose is unique for every dog and can be used to identify individual animals, just as we use fingerprints to identify specific humans.

to control the volume of air, velocity, and direction when inhaling and exhaling.

FUNCTIONS OF THE NOSE

According to Pearsall and Verbruggen, the nose has several functions:[3]

- As an airway, a connection from the outside world to the lungs
- As an air conditioner, by warming up or cooling down and moisturizing inhaled air. Lungs cannot exchange oxygen or carbon dioxide in dry surroundings as well as they do in more humid conditions.
- As a filter to dispose of dirt, dust, and irritants from the inhaled air
- As a source of reflex functions, like sneezing. Here the nose helps to protect fragile lung tissue from contaminants by expelling them from inhaled air.
- As a sound box for barking or crying. The sinuses provide this.
- As an organ to perceive odors
- As a direction-finder. Both sides of the nasal cavity have an equal capacity to perceive odors. The smallest differences in intensity between these allows the odor source to be determined exactly.

Internal Nose

The internal nose has left and right nasal cavities separated by the nasal septum. Inside the nose are two kinds of epithelium: the respiratory epithelium and the olfactory epithelium. The *respiratory epithelium* has small, hair-like cilia and is coated with mucus. Its function is to clean and moisten incoming air and to warm it to body temperature. The *olfactory epithelium* is located deeper inside the nose. It covers a number of bony plates called ethmoid bones and has many folds, giving it a large surface area.

The structure of the internal nose is different in microsmatics (animals with a poor odor perception, such as humans, monkeys, and birds) than in the macrosmatics (animals with excellent odor perception, such as dogs). In a microsmatic, only a small part of the nasal cavity is given to the olfactory epithelium, while the biggest part is used for normal respiration.

The nasal cavity of a macrosmatic, like the dog, is a labyrinth of folds called nasal conchae or turbinates, which are covered with a mucus membrane. This labyrinth of conchae greatly increase the surface area of the internal nose. The conchae are situated from the "wings" of the nose (nostrils) to the septum. Like the rest of the internal surface of the nose, the conchae are covered with mucous membrane.

In front of the nasal cavity is the conchae maxillaris, where the mucous membrane has comparatively few olfactory cells. The most important function of the conchae maxillaris is to warm and moisten incoming air. The mucous membrane of the conchae maxillaris contains many supporting cells with vibrating hairs on them. This keeps dirt out of the nasal cavity. Dirt that settles onto these vibrating hairs is moved to the throat and esophagus for expulsion from the body.

Behind the conchae maxillaris is the conchae ethmoidalis, which fills the rest of the nasal cavity. The mucous membrane of this conchae ethmoidalis contains large numbers of olfactory cells, which give the dog the ability to scan odors.

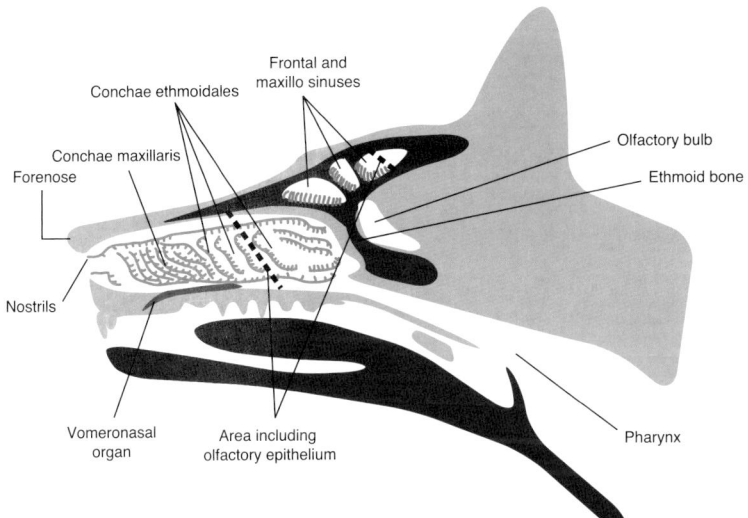

Figure 3.2 Anatomy of a dog's nose. With each inhalation and exhalation, the odor will be led along the conchae and the olfactory epithelium.

Sinuses

In the dog, parts of the sinuses also have olfactory epithelium. In puppies, the sinuses are very small, but they grow as the dog gets older. "The sinuses are larger when the skull is bigger," Wagner notes, adding that "it looks as if this characteristic especially is bound to the searching senses."[4] In other words, a dog's ability to search will get better as it grows.

The maxillary sinus is in the nasal bone, directly above the mouth cavity near the roots of the teeth. Infections in the upper jaw can cause infections in the sinus, affecting the ability to smell. The frontal sinuses are in the frontal bone. Both sinuses have olfactory epithelium.

The Vomeronasal Organ

An important contribution to the dog's odor capacity is made by the vomeronasal organ (also called Jacobson's organ), which is present in the right and left nasal cavities. It is a small, somewhat tubular organ that begins a bit behind the upper canines and goes to the back of the nasal cavity.

The vomeronasal organ perceives different odors than the main olfactory epithelium, and this information is worked out in another part of the brain. The organ has its own nerve connection with the odor center in the brain. It is open to the nasal cavity and connected by little canals with the mouth. The vomeronasal organ helps the dog perceive odors that come into the mouth. Some dogs lick articles to perceive them better and lead the odor to the vomeronasal organ.

FLEHMEN BEHAVIOR

Flehmen behavior — also called the Flehmen response or Flehmening — as seen in horses and cats, is a particular curling of the upper lip that closes the nostrils. This curling facilitates the transfer of pheromones and other odors into the vomeronasal organ.

Figure 3.3 Flehmen behavior in an Andalusian stallion.

According to Nelissen, dogs do not exhibit Flehmen behavior, although some dogs display Flehmen-like behavior.[5] Dogs don't curl their upper lip, but they are frequently seen licking the urine deposits of other dogs, especially females in heat. Some dogs chatter their teeth as they lick or shake their head to bring odors to the vomeronasal organ.

While dogs have more than 1,000 genes for olfactory receptors in the olfactory epithelium, they have, according to Jezierski et al., only nine vomeronasal receptor type 1 (V1R) genes for the vomeronasal organ receptors, which is surprisingly low, as in humans, who have only four V1R genes.[6] In comparison, cats have 21 V1R genes, cows have 40, horses have 42, and rats have 102. That low number in dogs is not a result of domestication, because wolves have only one more.

The Flehmen-like response, which dogs adopt when examining odors left by other animals either of the same species or of prey, helps draw odor back to the vomeronasal organ. This allows dogs to determine the presence or absence of estrus, the physiologic state of the animal they are smelling, and how long ago that animal passed by.

PHEROMONES

The probable function of the vomeronasal organ is sexual: detecting pheromones, which are odors related to sexual behavior. Pheromones contain information about sex, reproductive state (e.g., a female dog in estrus), and dominance. The odors lead to specific behavior by the receiver. A good example is the reaction of a female pig to the odor of a boar (male pig). When she is ready to mate, she will stand in a fixed "mating-stance" when she smells a boar. Boar odor (specifically pheromones) can be purchased. By spraying a little of this odor, a farmer can determine when a pig is ready to mate by her response to the odor. This allows artificial insemination to take place at the correct moment. Odor (pheromones) is also how salmon navigate their way inland during their reproductive period and how butterflies find each other over large distances.

Olfactory Epithelium

There is a variation in the size of the olfactory epithelium of different dog breeds, but there is no direct link between the size of the dog and the size of its olfactory epithelium. In addition, there is no simple relationship between the size of the olfactory epithelium and sensitivity to odors. An animal with a large olfactory epithelium is not automatically more sensitive to odors than an animal with a smaller olfactory epithelium. A German Shepherd Dog has an olfactory epithelium that is 150–170 cm²; humans have an olfactory epithelium of approximately 5 cm². Some odors can be smelled equally well by humans and dogs, but for other odors, dogs are 10,000 times more sensitive than humans.

An important and unique characteristic of the olfactory epithelium is its continuous regeneration: neurons in the epithelium

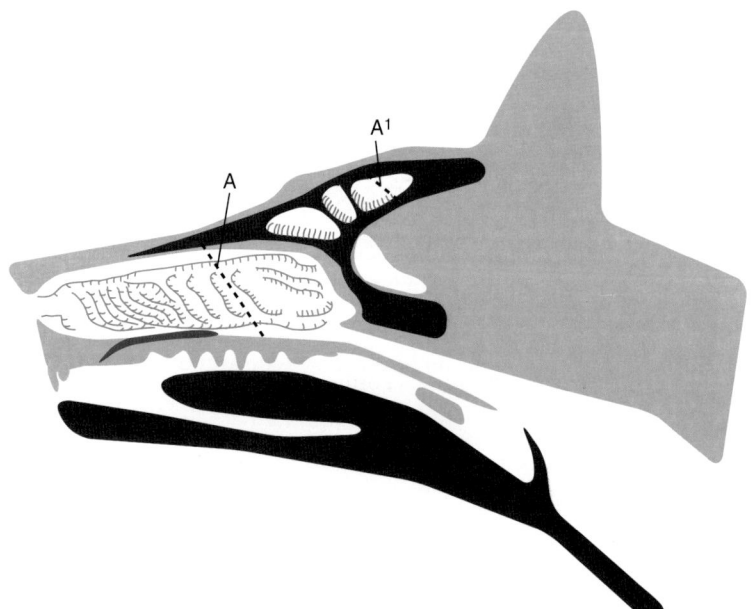

Figure 3.4 Size of the olfactory epithelium of the dog. A = front border and A¹ = rear border of the parts of the nasal cavity and sinuses covered with olfactory epithelium.

live 30–60 days and then die and are replaced with new neurons. This means that if the olfactory epithelium is damaged, it can completely recover in one or two months. Other sensory organs do not regenerate this quickly, suggesting how important the olfactory epithelium is to survival.

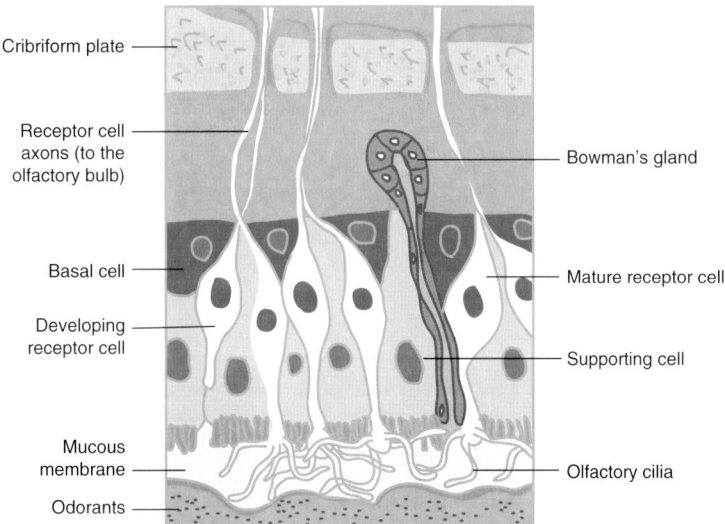

Figure 3.5 A schematic representation of the olfactory epithelium.

The olfactory epithelium is composed of supporting cells, basal cells, and the olfactory cells. The supporting cells, like the name indicates, give general solidity to the surrounding tissue, which includes the olfactory cells. Basal cells grow to become supporting cells or olfactory cells, if the others are destroyed.

OLFACTORY CELLS

The olfactory cells, also called receptor cells, are sensory neurons that give the dog information about the air. The life of an olfactory cell is about one month, after which it is replaced by a new cell formed out of a basal cell. This continuous regeneration of olfactory cells means that a reduced ability to smell caused by damaged olfactory cells is only temporary.

The olfactory cell has odor hairs (cilia) in the mucous membrane lining. Receptors are located on the surface membrane of these cilia, which form an odor-scan system. The cilia are actually extensions from the olfactory sensory neurons.

The density of these olfactory cells differs between species and also changes during the lifetime of an animal. When a young animal grows up, the density of the sensory neurons (and the animal's sensitivity to odors) increases; when an animal becomes old, the density (and sensitivity) decreases.

As seen in Table 3.1, the number of cilia per cell varies among species and appears correlated with olfactory sensitivity.

Table 3.1. Comparison of Human and Animal Cilia*

ANIMAL	CILIA PER OLFACTORY CELL
Minnow	4–6
Frog	6–12
Rabbit	9–16
Rat	15–20
Cat	40
Human	6–8
Dog	100–150

* From M. D. Pearsall and H. Verbruggen in *Scent.*

ETHMOID BONE

The olfactory cells extend from the cilia through holes in the cribriform plate (a part of the ethmoid bone) to the bulbus olfactorius, the spherical expansion of the olfactory nerve in the cerebrum. Due to the enormous number of olfactory nerves, the ethmoid bone of macrosmatics (such as the dog) is much larger than that of microsmatics.

Bowman's glands

The mucous membrane lining of the olfactory and respiratory epithelia are kept moistened by the Bowman's glands. Some of

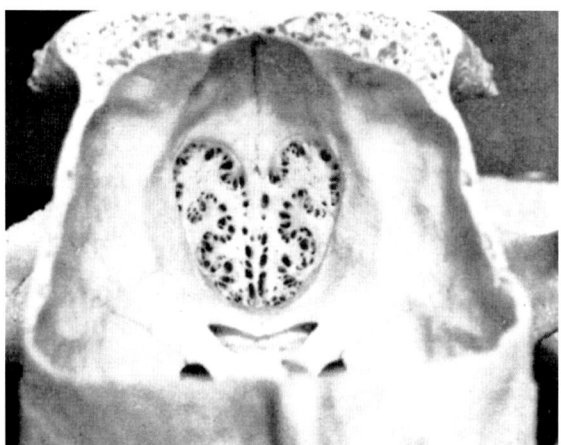

Figure 3.6 The cribriform plate of the ethmoid bone as seen from inside a dog's skull. Olfactory nerves enter the brain through openings in this plate. The cribriform plate of the dog is very large, accommodating an enormous number of olfactory nerves.

these glands produce a watery secretion, while others produce a thick mucous. Scenting materials (odorants) have to penetrate this mucous to gain access to the cilia. The mucous contains odorant binding proteins (OBPs), which play an important role in the contact of the odors with the receptors on the cilia. The OBPs, which are thought to be responsible for transporting and splitting odorant molecules for specific cilia, have been found in the airway secretions lining the olfactory epithelium, but not in the respiratory region.[7]

The nose is the only part of the body where nerve tissue is directly exposed to the outside world. While searching under extreme circumstances (high temperatures and/or dry surroundings) the mucous membrane will be kept moist by the lateral nose glands, which begin to secrete more moisture when the inhaled air has a temperature between 68°F and 86°F (20°C and 30°C). At 50°F (10°C) there is relatively little secretion, but at 122°F (50°C), each gland will secrete about (9 g) of fluid per hour![8]

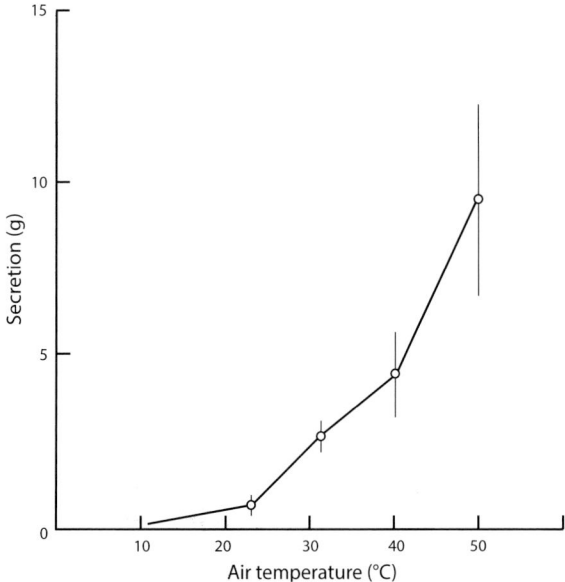

Figure 3.7 This graph shows the weight of the fluid that, depending on the air temperature, is secreted by a lateral nose gland of the dog. The weight given is in grams per gland per hour

Adapted from Blatt et al., in "Thermal Panting in Dogs."

COMPARISONS

Thicker mucous membranes have more room for more cilia than thinner mucus membranes, leading to better smell function. Table 3.2 compares the size of the olfactory area in humans and dogs.

If these values were compared in organisms of the same total weight, then, according to Bodingbauer, the dog is at least 260 times better equipped than humans in odor capabilities.[9] In other words: a human's olfactory area has a surface area that amounts to 1/4,000 of an average adult human's total skin surface. The dog's olfactory surface area is equal to almost the total skin surface of the dog.

Add to that the fact that the average number of olfactory cells in humans amounts about 5 million, while a Dachshund can have

Table 3.2. Human vs. Dog Capacity for Odor Detection

	HUMAN	DOG	DIFFERENCE
SIZE OF OLFACTORY AREA	4–5 cm^2	92–170 cm^2	30x
THICKNESS OF OLFACTORY AREA	0.006 mm	0.12 mm	20x
VOLUME OF OLFACTORY AREA	2.4–3 mm^3	1104–2040 mm^3	600x
PART OF THE TOTAL SKIN	1/4,000	Almost total	
NUMBER OF OLFACTORY CELLS	5 million	125–300 million	50x
CILIA PER RECEPTOR CELL	6–8	100–150	20x
OLFACTORY BULB AS PERCENTAGE OF TOTAL BRAIN	5%	35%	7x

Table 3.3. Comparison of Olfactory Area in Various Dog Breeds*

BREED AND AGE	SIZE OF OLFACTORY AREA IN CM^2
Pekingese, adult	26.89
German Shepherd, adult	152.24
Fox Terrier-mongrel, puppy	10.74
Doberman, puppy	14.39
Dachshund-mongrel, 2 days	11.31
Dachshund-mongrel, 10 days	14.50
Rough Collie, puppy	13.00
Irish Setter, adult	50.00
Gun dog, adult	53.00
Bulldog, adult	41.75
Shepherd, adult	31.50
Airedale Terrier, adult	83.53
Keeshond, adult	86.09
Cocker Spaniel, adult	67.49
German Shepherd I, adult	169.46
German Shepherd II, adult	95.69
German Shepherd III, adult	152.24
Boxer I, adult	121.22
Boxer II, adult	124.97
Pekinese I, adult	26.89
Pekinese II, adult	30.67

* From J. Bodingbauer in *Das Wunder der Hundenase.*

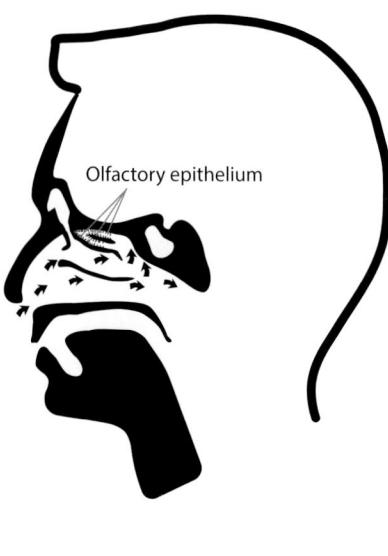

Figure 3.8 Anatomy of the human nose. During normal respiration most of the air flows through the lower and middle conchae. By diffusion or sniffing, odor comes through the upper conchae and reaches the olfactory epithelium.

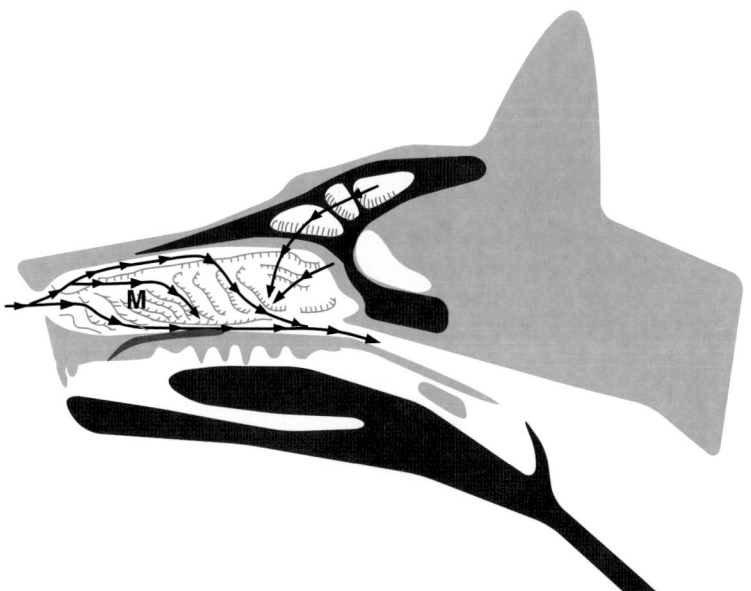

Figure 3.9 An air current moving through the dog's nose, represented by the arrowed lines beginning at the nostrils. Negative pressure comes into play behind the conchae maxillaris (M). Air flow from the sinuses and the conchae ethmoidalis (represented by the arrowed lines coming down from the top right) eliminates the differences in pressure.

125 million olfactory cells, the Fox Terrier 150 million, and the German Shepherd about 220 million. Although there is no known direct relation between the size of the olfactory epithelium and the sensitivity for odors, these numbers are very impressive for the way a dog is equipped for the perception of odors.

In addition, the olfactory bulb of the dog is 35 percent of its total brain, while in humans it amounts to only 5 percent of the brain.

Olfactory Detection Threshold

Relatively little research has focused on the measurement of the dog's olfactory sensitivity. The *olfactory detection threshold* is the minimum concentration of an odor that an individual is able to reliably detect and differentiate from a blank sample. The dog's olfactory threshold has been estimated as being within the parts-per-billion (ppb) to parts-per-trillion (ppt) range for a variety of chemical odors.

Alexandra Horowitz wrote about this in her book:

Scientific measures of the sensitivity of the dog's nose are limited more by the capacity of measuring devices — and dogs' interest in submitting to them — than by their noses. Both pet dogs and tracking dogs have been put through their paces in a variety of threshold detection tasks that ask how diluted an odorant can be before a dog stops noticing it's there.

Pick out a canister with the smell of banana, amyl acetate, from a series of non-banana-smelling canisters, for instance. Dogs keep finding the banana until it is diluted to 1–2 parts per trillion: a couple drops of amyl acetate, one trillion drops of water. Early research with one very cooperative Fox Terrier concluded that she could essentially detect one milligram of butyric acid — think smelly socks — among 100 million cubic meters of air. ... Explosives-detection dogs smell as little as a picogram — a trillionth of a gram — of TNT or other explosive. What might it be

like to notice a picogram of an odor? Since explosives dogs
come to have very fond associations with their search odors,
let's think of an aroma pleasing to our noses: cinnamon rolls
cooking in a home kitchen. The average cinnamon roll has
about a gram of cinnamon in it. Sure, the human nose is on
it, from the moment we open the door of the house. Now
imagine the smell of one trillion cinnamon rolls. That's
what the dog coming in with us smells when we enter.[10]

And according to Jan Kaldenbach:

[Dogs can] recognize the odor of table salt and quinine in a
dilution of 1:10,000,000, compounds which for most people
are totally without odor. It was also discovered that laboratory tests had weaker results than those held outdoors, from
which we can conclude that dogs use their senses more in
the open air.[11]

Based on many laboratory tests, the German researcher Wal-
ter Neuhaus drew several noteworthy conclusions about dogs and
their ability to track:

Dogs can recognize the same odor conditions in a person and an object the person touched, even if that object
has many other odors. This means that a dog on a track that
transitions to different types of surfaces will still recognize
the human scent component of the track, even though the
surface odors of the track might be a thousand times stronger than the human skin scent of the tracklayer. From this,
one cannot deny a dog's physiological ability to clean-scent
track.

This innate ability to discriminate odors does not, however, prove dogs will follow a human scent on a track without careful training. Dogs most likely follow the dominant
smells on a track, which may often be the smells of plants
and soil. However, daily observation of dogs indicate that
human scents are of more interest to dogs than things such
as soil and plants. Because a dog's reliable performance as a
tracker can only be expected where dogs have interest and

passion, it is likely that even an untrained dog will notice and use the human scent component of a track while tracking. From this inherent interest in human scents, it should be relatively easy to train a dog to discriminate an individual scent component.[12]

In order to clean-scent track, a dog must be able to

1. Distinguish a human scent from the other odor components of a track.
2. Further distinguish an individual's human scent from any other human scents on the track or on cross tracks.

Both these conditions have been proven in many tests, establishing the dog's ability to clean-scent track without a doubt. More on this will be discussed in Chapter 6.

Determining Odor Source

By sniffing in combination with turns of the head and body, the dog can locate an odor source. This orientation is helped by moistened membranes of the olfactory and respiratory epithelia. We do the same when we use a wet finger to determine wind direction.

A study of the dog's ability to determine track direction was published in 1993 by Aud Thesen et al., from the University of Oslo, Norway.[13] This ability to detect the direction of a track is of vital importance to predators and is retained in many modern dog breeds. To study this ability, four trained German Shepherd tracking dogs were equipped with head microphones to transmit sniffing activity.

In all tests, the dogs were handled by their trainers. The tests took place between noon and 3 p.m. from May to October 1990 on an airfield near Oslo. The tests were carried out on a dry ground surface, on dry, calm days with fair temperatures (15°C–20°C / 59°F–68°F). One week before the testing started, a grid of 10 × 4 squares, each measuring 6.5 feet × 6.5 feet (2 m × 2 m), was painted on the ground. All the dogs were brought at right angles to the track, where the position of each footprint was known.

The trial began with the dog standing at heel about 16 feet (5 m) from, and perpendicular to, the middle of the track. When given the order to track, the dog went straight forward, as it had been trained to do, while sniffing close to the ground. When it found the track, the dog turned either to the right or to the left.

In the dog's behavior, three phases were observed: (1) an initial searching phase, during which the dog tried to find the track, (2) a deciding phase, during which it tried to determine the direction of the track and (3) a tracking phase, in which it followed the track.

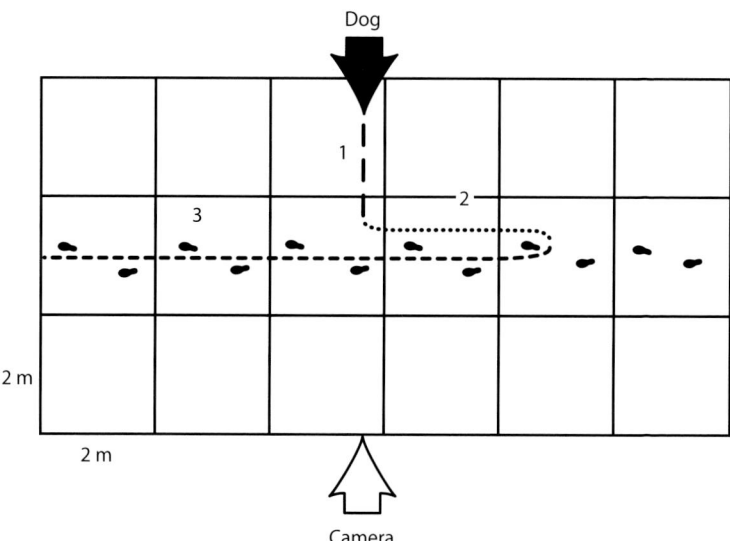

Figure 3.10 The dog's ability to determine track direction was tested in 2.2-yard (2 m²) grids. Only 18 of the 40 squares are shown here. This is an example of one dog's route during the searching phase (1), the deciding phase (2), and the tracking phase (3).

During 10 tests on 20-minute-old tracks on grass, and 10 tests on 3-minute-old tracks on concrete, the dogs always followed the track in the correct direction (i.e., in the direction the track was leading). However, the dogs did not always turn in the correct direction when they first found the track. If the initial direction was wrong, the dogs turned abruptly and walked in the opposite direction.

In the deciding phase, the dogs moved at half speed and their periods of sniffing lasted three times as long as during the other two phases. Once the direction was found, they moved faster, suggesting that following the track (the third phase) is a simpler task than determining its direction. Thus, the deciding phase seems to be the most difficult one; it is certainly the most impressive one from a human point of view.

The dogs needed 3 to 5 seconds to smell between two and five footprints to decide which direction the track had been laid, regardless whether it was on grass or concrete (other dogs under different conditions may require more prints).

It is assumed that the dogs determine the track direction by perceiving differences in the concentration of certain substances deposited by the track-layer. This suggests that, in some of the tests, the dogs must have determined a difference in the concentration of odor in the air above two consecutive prints that were made one second apart, either 3 minutes or 20 minutes earlier.

This Norwegian test was confirmed in 2005 by Peter G. Hepper and Deborah L. Wells of the Queens University in Belfast.[14] Their study examined how much olfactory information from an odor track left by a human is required by dogs to determine direction. Six dogs able to determine direction were tested on a 21-footstep track laid on 21 individual carpet squares, one footstep per square, by the same individual wearing the same shoes.

Dogs brought in at right angles to the track at its center were able to correctly determine direction at a rate better than chance. Dogs were unable to determine direction when the order of the footsteps was randomized by rearranging the order of the carpet squares. When the individual scent cue was removed, but ground disturbance left, dogs were unable to determine direction, indicating that it was the scent of the individual that was used to determine direction.

In the final experiment, the number of footsteps made available to the dog was reduced from 21 to 11 and then to 9, 7, 5, and finally 3. Dogs were able to determine direction from 5 footsteps but not 3. It took the dogs 1–2 seconds to figure out track direction by determining how much scent was present in a sequence of steps (with more scent in more recent steps, and less scent in older steps). These findings were consistent with the 1993 tests by Thesen et al.[15]

To a human, this feat may appear unrealistic. The dog's ability to determine track direction in such a short period of time must rely on a remarkable sensitivity for human scent substances. But as Neuhaus suggested in 1953, a dog's detection threshold for fatty acids, an important constituent of human skin secretions, may be 100 million times lower than a human's threshold.[16]

Alternating Nostrils

Human nostrils alternate every few hours. They are closed by a light swelling and the closed nostril lets less air pass than the other nostril. According to Noam Sobel et al. of the University of Berkeley, these changes in air current also have consequences for odor discrimination.[17] He gave 20 human test subjects a mixture of carvon (found in caraway seeds and the rind of mandarin oranges) and octane (which smells like petroleum) to smell.

Seventeen of the 20 subjects thought the mix smelled more like carvon than octane when they smelled with the active nostril, and the opposite when they used the inactive one. After a few hours, as the nostrils alternated, the same happened, with the active nostril smelling carvon. These types of alternations also happen in the dog's nose, suggesting one reason why a dog may miss some odorants on the track.[18]

4

Odor Processing

What is an "odor"? A simple definition is that an odor is something that can be smelled. But does that mean something that we, humans, can smell? Or what a butterfly can smell? Or what a dog can smell? What does it mean if we say something is "odorless"? In everyday language, that usually means something humans cannot smell. But different people have different sensitivities to odors, so what is "odorless" to one person may have a distinct odor to another.

Like the sense of taste, the sense of smell is a chemical sense. Odor prickles are molecules in liquid or gas form that exert their influence on the odor organs.

Odors

It is relatively easy to prove that something has an odor: if a person can smell it, or if you can train an animal to react to it based on odor, then it has an odor. But it is much more difficult to prove that something has no odor at all. Maybe a person with a very sensitive nose could smell it, or maybe the animal you trained was not trained correctly to smell it.

And there is another problem. Research has shown that people display certain brain wave patterns when they smell an odor.[1] The research shows that sometimes a person's brain reacts in this characteristic way to an odor even if the person says they do not smell anything. So is an odor something you physically respond to (as in the case of the EEG pattern), or is it something you are conscious that you have smelled? There is no answer to this question.

However, there are a few generalizations we can make. First, all materials are made of molecules, and some molecules have odor. Of the odorous molecules, we can say the following:

- Odorous molecules are relatively small: they must be light enough to float in the air.
- Some odorous molecules are *volatile*, meaning they quickly evaporate, making them easy to smell.
- Odor molecules do not dissolve well in water. This suggests that if you try to remove odor from an object, rinsing or boiling it in water is not enough. It is necessary to use (non-perfumed) soap or other fat-dissolving products.
- Odor molecules dissolve in fats. The perfume industry once used this characteristic to produce perfume: odorous plants (like lavender) were laid between sheets soaked with an "odorless" fat and left there for some days. By dissolving the fat later in alcohol, the lavender odor was released into the alcohol, which was then used to make perfume.

Most of the material dogs are trained to find are combinations of different kinds of molecules. Some of these molecules are light, volatile, and odorous, while others are not. The chemical identity of a material — essentially, what it is made of — is therefore not automatically the same as the "olfactory identity" of the material. For example, leather articles on the track have the same chemical identity, but all will smell different depending on the type of leather, the manufacturing process, what they've come in contact with, and so forth. To prevent confusion, in this chapter we will use the term "an odor" as meaning a material consisting of one type of odor molecules.

How Odors Reach Odor Receptors

Odor molecules float in the air, and as you learned in Chapter 3, the odor receptors that can react to these molecules are deep inside the nose. The main route for odor molecules to reach these receptors is through the nose, but odor molecules while eating can also travel from the mouth and throat to the nasal cavity.

When sitting calmly, a dog breathes in and out approximately 15 times per minute. When walking calmly, the frequency rises to 31 times per minute. During ordinary respiratory breathing, most of the inhaled air goes to the lungs. The odor molecules in the air do not reach the odor receptors in the olfactory epithelium, deep inside the nose, because the pressure difference between inspiration and expiration in the rear space of the nose is too low to transport odor molecules to the deepest parts of nose. Odor molecules

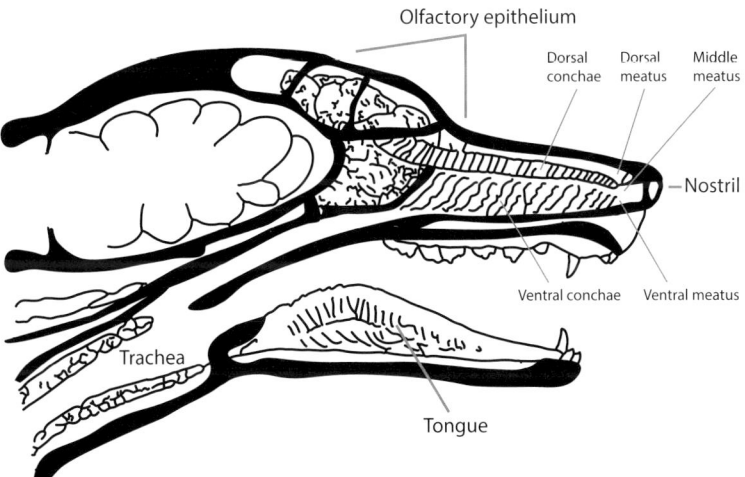

Figure 4.1 The nasal cavity has three main passageways: the dorsal, middle, and ventral meatus. During active sniffing, the dorsal meatus moves air primarily to the olfactory epithelium, bypassing the respiratory airways of the middle and ventral meatus. During normal breathing, only a small proportion of air (<15%–20%) travels through the dorsal meatus to the olfactory epithelium.

will only reach this area if their concentration in the air is very high. This means dogs have to actively sniff in order to smell odors at low concentrations.[2]

When a dog sniffs, its inhalation/exhalation frequency rises to 140–200 times per minute. The sniffing leads to differences in air pressure in the nose.[3] The total result is that the air, with the odor molecules in it, enters deeply into all the nasal cavities.

With Open Mouths: The Tests of Karl Zuschneid

People watching tracking dogs at work often stare with their mouths hanging open at their accomplishments. However, as soon as a dog is tracking with an open mouth, many handlers believe that the dog is no longer tracking, because a dog tracks with his nose, right? Even many instructors and judges believe a dog can't track with his mouth open.

However, the tests of Karl Zuschneid from Berlin point to a different conclusion, and also explain why dogs can breathe, uninterrupted, while sniffing.[4] In his 1973 dissertation on the smelling ability of the dog, Zuschneid used small plastic tubes in the dog's nostrils to measure air respiration patterns, which were printed on paper as waves interrupted by exhalation gusts through the nose. This helped researchers determine a sniffing frequency and sniffing period. The sniffing period is the duration of uninterrupted sniffing inspiration between exhalation gusts via the nose.

First Zuschneid did tests without equipment to determine how long tracks were perceptible to dogs under certain weather conditions. He also wanted to clarify whether fatty acids and fatty acid mixes (without the odors of the track-layer) formed a smellable track for the dog. He used a variety of fatty acids and fatty acid mixes, such as butyric, proprionic, formic, acetic, and caprionic acid.

In total, five German Wirehaired Pointers were tested on 60 tracks with lengths from 765 to 1093 yards (700 to 1,000 m). The research showed that, with tracks under different conditions, the

Figure 4.2 A military working dog tracks with an open mouth during a long and difficult training track.

shortest time that a track was perceptible was measured on a dry, dusty field, while the longest perceptible time, more than 22 hours, took place in a deciduous wood in autumn with a relative humidity of 70%–90%.

Furthermore, all the dogs showed great interest in fatty acids, although their level of interest depended on the concentration and composition of the fatty acid mix. The dogs could follow a 24-hour old track of 1/40 mol dilution (1/40 g mol/L) butyric acid without problems.

The registration of the dog's nose respiration during tracking showed a characteristic picture, which was more or less the same in all dogs. Four basic patterns were determined:

   1. For simple tracks (e.g., 30-minute-old tracks of the handler under favorable conditions) the picture is one of regular sniffing inhalations. The waves of the pressure differences are often

small, which means that the speed of air movement in the nose is low. The exhalation gusts via the nose are powerful and regular. In almost all simple tracks this respiration picture was consistent from beginning to end.

2. The above respiration picture fades away as the track increases in difficulty. The waves of exhalation gusts via the nose become smaller and the time between them increases. In other words, the dog sniffs longer, creating more air pressure in the nose.

3. The next phase shows the same picture as the preceding in principle. The sniffing periods are, however, still longer and there are short periods in which the dog is obviously breathing through mouth and nose. It wasn't unusual to see some dogs exhale via the nose in double gusts.

4. Finally, in the most difficult parts of tracking, the respiration picture showed the dog was almost continuously sniffing. A female dog showed the longest period, with a respiration pattern over 80 seconds long.

Exhaling via the nose probably performs a sort of cleaning of the olfactory cells in the nose mucous membrane, which is apparently less necessary for lower odor concentrations. It looks as though dogs breathe during sniffing the same way they do when panting in warm temperatures. But unlike panting, which is mostly ventilation without breathing, here the high frequency of sniffing contributes to the inhalation.

On simple tracks, dogs succeed easily in combining breathing and scanning for odors. The inhalation takes place during the sniffing and the exhalation happens gustily via the nose. When the odor of the track decreases, then the dog solves this problem in two ways: The speed of the air current in the nose increases, by which the capacity of inhaled air grows. The dog also extends the total duration of the sniffing period. The delayed exhalation then takes place partly via the nose and partly via the slightly open mouth of the tracking dog. The inclination to delay exhaling is a disadvantage for breathing. However, it creates an advantage in getting, by longer sniffing periods, more information about the incoming odors.

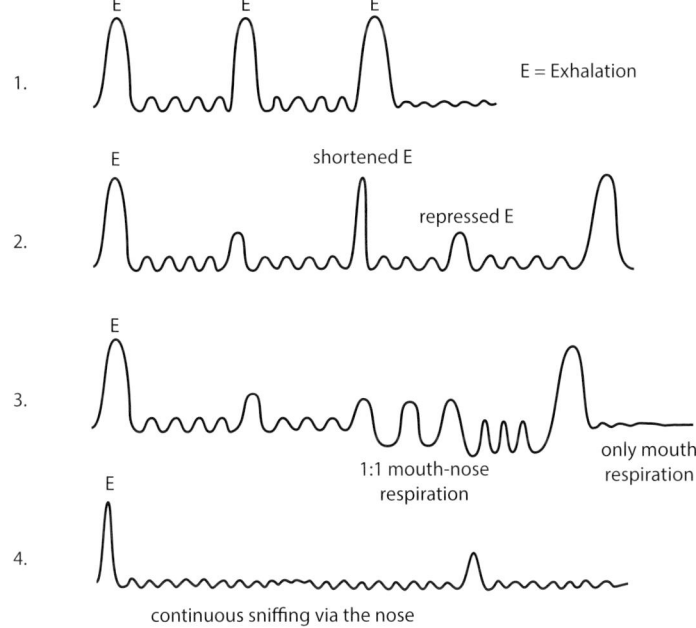

Figure 4.3 Zuschneid identified four types of sniffing pattern, from simple tracks at level 1 and the most difficult at level 4.

When the difficulty of the track increases due to extreme conditions, exhalation via the nose is suppressed altogether. During tracks with a minimum of odor, exhalation more often takes place via the mouth. The lesser resistance and the larger opening of the mouth allows for greater air volumes to pass than by exhalation via the nose. Because of that, exhalation takes less time. Indeed, tracking with an open mouth is an advantage, insofar that it saves time, for the sniffing and scanning of odors!

Odor Receptors

Odor receptors are located on the cilia of the olfactory sensory neurons. These cilia can be found in the mucus of the olfactory epithelium (see Figure 3.5 for the structure of the olfactory epithelium). Every olfactory sensory neuron has several cilia with receptors. There are probably around 1,000 different kinds of receptors. Research done with dogs has shown that there are no differences between breeds on this point.[5]

Researchers suspect that the cilia of a single olfactory sensory neuron all have the same kind of olfactory receptor. The olfactory sensory neurons that carry the cilia, and therefore also the receptors, live for 30–60 days. After this they die, and new neurons are made.

At some stage during the development of a new neuron, the type of receptor for the neuron is determined. If a neuron with receptor type A has died, this does not automatically lead to a new neuron with receptor type A. The determination of the receptor type is partly triggered by the odors the animal often smells. Animals that are systematically trained on certain odors develop more receptors for those odors.

The odor receptors are located on cilia in the watery mucus that covers the olfactory epithelium. To reach the olfactory receptors, the odor molecules must first dissolve in this watery mucus. The mucus contains agents that cleanse the air, such as antibodies for bacteria and detoxifying enzymes.

However, a characteristic of odor molecules is that they do not dissolve well in water. The mucus therefore contains olfactory binding proteins (OBPs) that help the odor molecules reach the receptors.[6] The odor molecules attach to these proteins, which allows them to dissolve in the mucus and to be transported to the olfactory receptors on the cilia.

The cilia contain molecular components that ensure we can perceive and differentiate between more than 10,000 different odors, even in small concentrations. The chemical odor gets converted to an electrical cell signal, which is conducted by nerves to the brain.

Each olfactory sensory neuron reacts to different odors. Every odor stimulates different kinds of odor receptors. It is likely that each type of receptor reacts to a certain part of an odor molecule: a certain shape or chemical group. However, the precise mechanism behind this reaction is not fully understood.

To simplify things, we will assume that part of different kinds of odor molecules may be the same, and as a result will stimulate the same kind of receptor. However, each odor molecule also has a number of different parts that stimulate different receptor types. The combination of the two leads to a single odor stimulating a specific group of receptor types. Each odor stimulates a different group. Figure 4.4 shows how four different odor molecules can stimulate four different kinds of odor receptors. The "part" illustrated in the figure must not be taken literally: perhaps it is not a physical part but instead some chemical or magnetic characteristic. In this way, about a thousand different kinds of odor receptors can differentiate clearly between a large number of odors.

Odor receptors are not spread evenly over the olfactory epithelium and are divided into at least four zones.[7] This is similar to other sense receptors: the taste buds (receptors) for bitter are located in a band across the back of the tongue, the receptors for

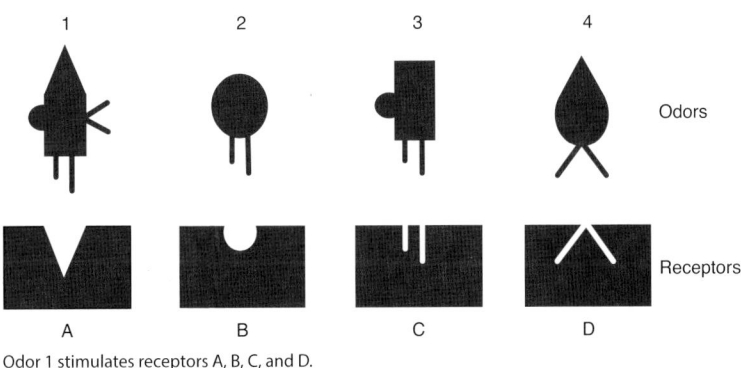

Odor 1 stimulates receptors A, B, C, and D.
Odor 2 stimulates only receptor C.
Odor 3 stimulates receptors B and C.
Odor 4 stimulates receptors A and D.

Figure 4.4 Schematic example of the relationship between odor molecules and odor receptors.

sweet on the tip of the tongue, and receptors for sour and salty are on the sides.

The precise way in which the odor signal triggers a reaction in the odor receptor is unknown.[8] Somehow this odor signal leads to the firing of an impulse, which can be compared to an electric current that is transmitted through a nerve to the brain.

The Bulbus Olfactorius

When the receptor reacts to an odor signal, the olfactory sensory neuron fires and an impulse is carried through the nerve to the bulbus olfactorius in the brain. The bulbus olfactorius is the olfactory center of the brain.

The connection between the receptor and the brain is short: the sensory neuron that has the receptors on cilia at one end is the same neuron (or nerve) that delivers the impulse to the brain. This is unique for the olfactory system: in all other sensory organs, the signal is first passed on to another nerve (sometimes several nerves) before the signal reaches the brain.[9]

The olfactory nerves converge to 1,000–2,000 nerve knots called *glomeruli* in the first layer of the bulbus olfactorius. The nerve ends of sensory cells that have the same kind of olfactory receptor all come together in the same glomerulus. Sensory cells

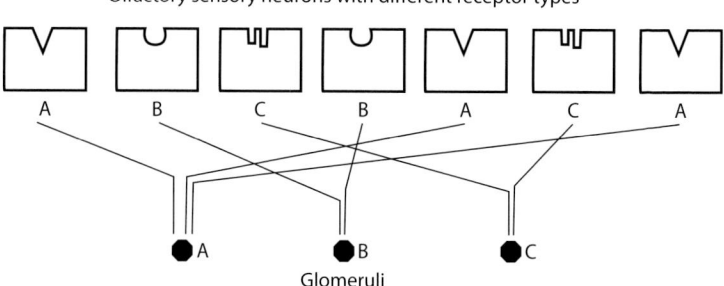

Figure 4.5 Schematic example of the relationship between olfactory sensory neurons and glomeruli in the brain.

of a certain receptor type therefore have a matching glomerulus in the brain.

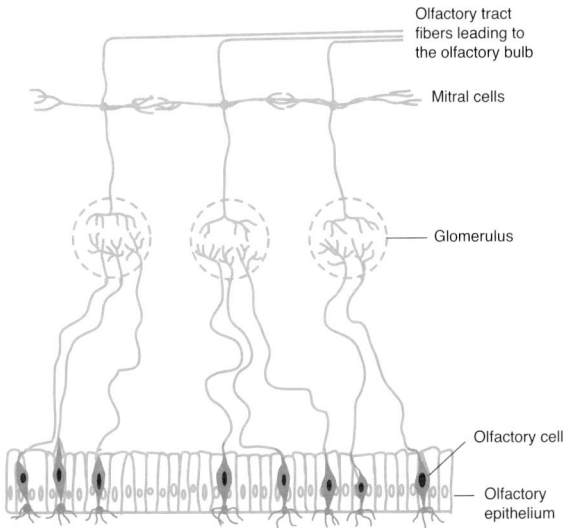

Figure 4.6 Schematic example of the relationship between olfactory sensory neurons and glomeruli in the bulbus olfactorius in the brain.

Because the information from many olfactory sensory neurons comes together in a single matching glomerulus in the brain, the signal is amplified. Even if only a few sensory cells are triggered by an odor, the information is bundled in the first layer of glomeruli in the olfactory brain. This layer projects a clear signal to the second layer of glomeruli, which are deeper in the bulbus olfactorius. The glomeruli in this second layer are interconnected, which leads to a better perception of small differences.

COMBINATION ODORS

Every odor stimulates a characteristic spatial pattern of glomeruli in the brain.[10] For example, fragrances such as flowers or perfumes are made up of hundreds of individual chemical fragrance components. When inhaling a complex mixture, of the approximately

350 different types of olfactory sensory cells, only those with receptors for the various components of the fragrances are activated.

When you smell a mixture of several chemical components, several types of sensory cell receptors are activated accordingly and with them the associated glomeruli. The result is a characteristic activation pattern of glomeruli that, in turn, shows which odor mixture we smelled.

The activation pattern for the odor of a rose is clearly different from the pattern for the odor of an orange. If certain chemical components are present in both fragrance mixtures, the patterns of activated glomeruli can overlap. In psychology this could be described with the term odor shape or shape recognition. Once we have learned an odor, we can recognize it again, even if some of the information is missing. One makes use of this, for example, when smelling artificial rose or orange odors, when tend to be greatly reduced from the natural odors.[11] When tracking, we see the same thing happen when a track-layer known to the dog wears rubber boots instead of shoes one day, and as a result the total odor complex in the track changes.

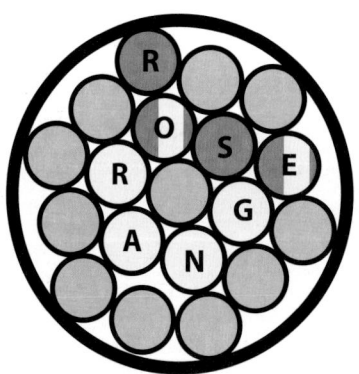

Figure 4.7 Odor shape. This model shows the activation of the glomeruli after stimulation with rose or orange odor.

GLOMERULI AND TRAINING

The development of the glomeruli in the bulbus olfactorius is partly determined by which odors an animal comes across. Training a young animal on an odor will help it develop more olfactory sensory neurons for that particular odor. The matching glomerulus also becomes more developed.

Cognitive Processing

The signals from the bulbus olfactorius follow two paths for further processing in the brain.[12] One path leads to the brain *cortex*, which is the outer part of the brain. Here the animal becomes "aware" of the odor: it "knows" it has smelled something, it "recognizes" the odor and, based on experience, reacts or does not react. This process is called the *cognitive processing* of the information.

Non-cognitive Processing

The other path leads deep into the brain to an area called the *limbic system*. The limbic system is responsible for many autonomic processes (independent processes we are not conscious of, such as breathing). The limbic system influences different physiological processes, emotions, and sexual behavior. The limbic system receives odor information through the main olfactory epithelium and the vomeronasal organ. Experiments with humans have shown that even though a brain reacts to an odor, it does not mean that

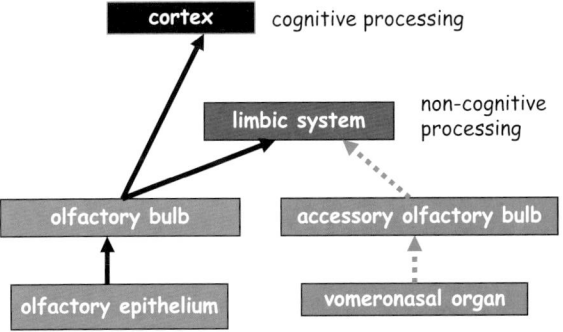

Figure 4.8 Schematic overview of the paths that olfactory information follows from the olfactory epithelium and the vomeronasal organ to the brain.

the person is conscious of smelling something.[13] The processing of olfactory information by the limbic system is called *non-cognitive processing.*

Odors can trigger significant effects on an animal through the limbic system. For example, the odor of lemons counters depression in rats.[14] The scent of a human male shortens the menstrual cycle of a human female. The odor of a strange male leads to a spontaneous abortion in a rat that has just become pregnant by another male. Some odors stimulate animals; others slow them down.[15]

The processing of information by the limbic system is fast: it takes place before processing in the cortex. This means non-cognitive effects of odors through the limbic system may interfere with cognitive processing in the cortex. A good example from police practice is the reaction of a dog to the odor of the kennel staff.

Using members of the kennel staff to create cross-tracks for training dogs often leads to mistakes. This can be explained by the direct positive association the dog has with the person's odor: food, being taken for a walk, attention, and so on. The dog can react to this odor before he "realizes" he is actually looking for a different odor, and thus the mistake is made.[16] The reverse problem can also occur: maybe an odor the dog finds difficult to track is an odor he has negative associations with, leading to avoidance behavior.

Another example is the reaction of a male dog to the scent of a female in heat. This odor initiates a sexual response through the limbic system. Even though a dog can be taught not to pursue this instinctive response, his first reaction to the odor will always be there, resulting from the procreation drive.

Motivation in Olfaction

The words *motor, motion, motivation,* and *emotion* are etymologically related to *movere,* which means "to move" in Latin. They all have a neuropharmacological connection as well: dopamine, which plays a role in the overall "reward" system of the brain.[17] This excitatory brain neurotransmitter is of great importance in both cognitive and non-cognitive brain processing.

Some dog breeds have higher baseline dopamine levels than others.[18] Border Collies and Huskies have high dopamine levels; livestock guarding dogs' levels are lower. This holds the intriguing possibility that individual differences and breed differences in baseline dopamine levels may have a direct impact on cognition, motivation, learning, and overall olfactory behavior and performance. Think of Border Collies, with their high dopamine levels. The words *hyperactive, obsessive,* and *compulsive* are frequently used to describe individuals of that breed.

Gadbois and Reeve write about how dopamine levels may impact dog performance:

> Our "dopamine hypothesis" essentially highlights the possibility that "software"-level characteristics (neurochemical and neural-level mechanisms and processes) are more important than the often-touted "hardware" characteristics.

Figure 4.9 The work ethic of high-dopamine breeds in tracking, like the Malinois here, is remarkable.

For example, we never had any luck with Bloodhounds and other hunting "scent dogs" mostly because of motivational issues, resilience, ability to work long hours or consistently, and overall performance and energy levels. By contrast, the "work ethic" of high-dopamine breeds, like the Belgian Malinois, Jack Russell, and Parsons, is remarkable.[19]

Remembering Odors

Memory for odors is, as we all know from our own experience, very good. This starts earlier than most people think: animals (and people) may remember odors from before birth. While they are in the uterus, animals learn the odor of the fluid they are in (amniotic fluid). This was proven by letting newborn lambs and babies choose between the odor of their own amniotic fluid and that of another, equally old conspecific.[20] Both lambs and human babies prefer the smell of their own amniotic fluid, demonstrating that the amniotic fluid of different individuals smell different and that the youngsters learned this odor before birth.

This type of memory can be manipulated. Researchers have demonstrated this by feeding pregnant rabbits and sheep different diets. The young rabbits and lambs reacted differently to the diet of their mother than to other food: more evidence that memory for odor was formed prenatally. In the rabbit study, it was demonstrated that not only did animals behave differently in response to the food odor of their mother, but also that there were differences in the olfactory epithelium that allowed for a stronger reaction to the odor.

It is well known that dogs also have a good memory for odors. A dog will recognize the odor of its mother, and the mother will remember the odor of her young, even after 2 years.[21] Odors that the dogs learn when young, especially those associated with mother-care, are memorized particularly well. In laboratory studies, odors dogs had been trained on were remembered after 3 months without training, and there is evidence that they can remember them for considerably longer.[22]

Factors Affecting Olfaction

Many factors can affect a dog's ability to perceive an odor. Some factors stem from the item it is trying to find. Other factors are from the condition of the dog itself. Discussion of a few of the key issues to be aware of follows.

TEMPERATURE

Temperature plays an important role in the perception of odors. Warm substances (or articles) give off more odor in cold surroundings than warm substances in hot surroundings. Cold articles are more difficult to find in cold surroundings.

Substances or articles that already give off a recognizable odor under normal circumstances smell stronger when they become warmer. For example, warm food smells much stronger than cold food.

Extreme cold can cut back the concentration of smellable gasses to hardly perceptible amounts (like the difference between a hot steak or a frozen one). But all frozen things give off *some* recognizable odor; minute amounts of gas are released, which are warmed up in the nose and penetrate the receptors in the olfactory epithelium.

ADAPTATION

To be clear: both humans and dogs do not smell with the nose. The olfactory epithelium is merely an organ to scan the environment. The "prickles" coming in via the cilia turn into signals, which are brought to the olfactory bulb in the brain. The brain "reads" these signals and tells us what they are. We are, in fact, smelling with our brains.

But the olfactory bulb adapts quickly. After spending some time with an odor, we will no longer be aware of it. Our nose still scans and receives the odor molecules, but the brain *adapts* and does not send us an odor message anymore. That's why an odor we strongly perceive at first will, after a while, not be noticeable anymore.

For example, you will notice immediately, coming into the kitchen, the strong odor of cooked cauliflower. But after being in the kitchen for a while, you will hardly be able to smell it anymore. If you go outside to get a breath of fresh air, then come inside again, you will again smell the cauliflower.

When working with dogs, you can come across many situations where adaptation plays a role:

- The density of narcotic odor in a room where a large quantity of a narcotic has been hidden, or where a smaller amount has been hidden for a long time, can be very high. In this situation, a dog may have problems finding the source of the odor, especially if he has been in the room for some time. This can be explained by adaptation: the sensory cells of the dog have been stimulated so much that they no longer react to the smell. Lack of a gradient in an odor-saturated environment can also explain why the dog cannot locate the source.

- Because of adaptation, tracking dogs that work out longer tracks will instinctively, from time to time, put their nose beside or above the odor field of the track to get a breath of fresh air. Directly after that they can perceive the odor of the track again and follow it. Punishing the dog's effort to clear his nose will lead to a decrease in the dog's performance. Or he will put his nose to the ground and act as though he is tracking, without doing so!

CROSS-ADAPTATION

Another aspect of adaptation is "cross-adaptation." This means that once adapted to a certain odor, it becomes impossible to smell certain other odors. Although not all cross-adaptations are known,[23] research has shown that certain chemicals can block a large number of olfactory cells or push aside other scent substances. Examples of this are acetone and xylol. If you first smell acetone and then smell xylol, both odors can be clearly perceived. However, if you smell the xylol first, the acetone cannot be perceived for some time after.

Handlers of tracking dogs and detector dogs, like drug and explosive detector dogs, have to be aware that other substances, such as ether or petrol, can more or less block the dog's nose for several minutes. Determining lighter odors becomes very difficult in that period.

IRRITANTS

The dog's ability to smell can also be disturbed by irritants and strong or abnormal odor prickles, such as fertilizer.[24] A handler should train the tracking dog with a wide variety of odors but should avoid irritants as much as possible. A common problem is attempting to train a dog to track on a field covered with fertilizer. On such ground, a dog will have problems, and some will refuse to track at all.

ODOR AMOUNTS

When training dogs on odors, be aware that differences in *amount* of odor appear to be perceived by the animals as differences in *kind* of odor. In other words, a lot of one odor smells different than a small amount of the same odor. This phenomenon is also known from hearing: a very loud C-tone sounds different from a very soft C-tone. Differences in amount of odor lead to qualitatively different processes in the brain. Therefore, a small amount of an odor does not lead to a less strong reaction than a large amount, but instead to a completely different reaction.[25]

This means that when training a dog on an odor, the amounts of odor used in the training must vary because a dog may think that a large amount of an odor is a completely different thing than a smaller amount of the same odor. When a dog is used only to find small amounts, he may not "recognize" a large amount of the same substance. It simply smells different from what he has learned.

COMPLEX AND SINGLE ODORS

Training animals to discriminate between odors is more difficult when the odors are complex (combinations of different odors) than when the odors are single odors.[26] If an odor is presented alone, an animal is much more sensitive to the odor than if the same odor is presented as part of a complex.[27] This is something to be aware of in training: if a dog is capable of finding a very small amount of a "pure" material, it may still have problems when it has to find this same small amount as part of a complex material.

Complex odors are generally learned as a unit. However, if an animal has previous experience with single components in the complex, they will learn these complex odors faster.[28] Beginning the training of a dog with single odors therefore leads to faster learning of the complex compounds that contain the single odors. But we cannot say that a dog, trained on the single odors, will always recognize these odors in complex compounds. A dog must also be trained on the complex compounds.

THE DOG

As we've noted, the olfactory organ is not static. It is continuously regenerated and it reacts to differences in the environment. When an animal is confronted with a certain odor often, its olfactory organ changes physically. These changes can be seen on all levels: more sensory cells with the right kind of receptor, larger glomeruli, and permanent changes in the brain. Conversely, when an animal never comes into contact with certain odors, this leads to a poor development of the olfactory organ for those odors.[29] Besides brain development, many other factors can affect how well an individual dog perceives odors:

- In general, females of a species have a more sensitive sense of smell than males,[30] and overall sensitivity decreases with age.[31] But there are large individual differences: not only in people, but also in other animals such as dogs.[32] A single individual may also be more sensitive at one time than at another.[33] This can be the result of hormonal variation, as well as other factors, such as illness.
- An individual can also be "odor blind": some people cannot smell certain odors. This is partly genetically determined.[34] Researchers think this may also be possible in dogs.
- Dehydration of the nasal mucosal membrane results in a tracking dog having significantly lower odor detection capabilities.[35]

- Albino dogs often have a significantly diminished ability to smell. This may partly be why albino animals in the wild don't often survive: their decreased ability to distinguish odors lowers their ability to find food and avoid danger.
- Physical stressors, including strenuous exercise, lack of conditioning, and high ambient temperature impact dogs' olfaction abilities directly and indirectly.
- Dietary fat content, amount of food per meal, and timing of meals have also been demonstrated to impact olfaction in dogs. Gastrointestinal microbiota likely impact olfaction via communication between the gastrointestinal tract and brain, and the microbiota is impacted by exercise, diet, and stress.[36]
- Short-nosed breeds sometimes experience problems with tracking because of respiration problems. However, boxers can track as well as other working dogs, but on long tracks they need more stops to rest.
- Smaller breeds are thought to have a disadvantage because they have a smaller olfactory area. In practice, however, it has been shown that small breeds can easily perform as tracking dogs.

Figure 4.10 Boxers can track as well as other working dogs, but because of the breathing problems, they may need more stops to rest on long or difficult tracks.

Figure 4.11 The problems some dogs encounter when tracking could be connected to adaptation.

HEALTH

In some cases, it will be difficult or even impossible for a dog to perceive odors due to health problems. For dogs, the most important illnesses affecting the sense of smell are the common cold and influenza virus. Research has shown that dogs have a lower olfactory sensitivity even before they show normal symptoms of influenza.[37]

Inflammation, changes in blood flow and hydration, and various systemic diseases can also affect olfaction and may impact the working efficiency of detection canines. Other illnesses that can diminish the olfactory system include renal failure,[38] Cushing's syndrome (an adrenal hypersecretion),[39] and hypothyroidism.[40] Certain medications, such as steroids, anesthetic agents, and antibiotics can also affect the ability to smell,[41] as can problems in the upper teeth, like a root infection.

Hyposmia, defined as a decreased sensation of smell, is characterized as type I, II, or III. Type I hyposmia is the inability to recognize odorants correctly. Type II hyposmia is a quantitative decrease in the ability to recognize odorants, seen in working canines as a change in threshold or persistent failure to alert to previously trained odorants. Type III hyposmia is a decrease in estimation of the magnitude of odors; this type of hyposmia is only recognizable in humans.[42] The causes of hyposmia can be broadly categorized as conductive disorders, sensory losses, or neural causes.

- **Conductive hyposmia** results from the failure of odorants to reach the olfactory mucosa. This can be caused by nasal inflammation, excess mucus production, and physical obstruction by masses (e.g., polyps, neoplasia).
- **Sensory hyposmia** is caused by damage to the olfactory mucosa (e.g., viruses, exposure to toxic chemicals).[43]
- **Neural hyposmia** is caused by lesions in the central or peripheral nervous system, specifically the olfactory cortex, olfactory bulb, and cranial nerves, as from a head injury.[44]

Tracking Problems

As discussed in this chapter, when your dog encounters problems with scent identification, either not identifying a scent or identifying a scent that shouldn't be there, you will need to consider a variety of causes. Always remember that many substances are odorless for humans but can be perceived by dogs. An objective state of "odorless" doesn't really exist. Furthermore, certain porous substances can absorb and retain odor, sometimes for a long time. Many dog handlers have made the mistake of punishing their dogs because they thought there was no odor present, only to discover later that there may have been an odor there after all. You can never be positive that an odor isn't there.

SUMMARY OF ODOR PERCEPTION PROBLEMS

Caused by the condition of the dog
- Common cold or influenza, or other illnesses
- Medication
- Genetic predisposition

- Dental problems
- Hormones
- Dehydration
- Albinism
- Physical stressors (e.g., long track, high temperature)
- Short-nosed breeds
- Small breeds
- Adaptation (nose-fatigue)

Caused by external circumstances
- Influence of chemicals
- Irritants and strong odor prickles
- Animal or human feces on or near the track
- Failure odors

Practical Advice

Although there is much we don't yet know about the sense of smell, we can give some tips for training dogs on odors. Most points below are valid for all types of odor training.[45]

- Check if your dog is able to work at the moment you need him. The physical ability to smell varies over time, and the motivation of a dog to work can also vary. It is sensible to check the capacity of your dog: either shortly before, during, or immediately after a practical case.
- Be aware of adaptation and cross-adaptation. Either may make it impossible for your dog to locate the source of a smell. Adjust your training and search method to these phenomena.
- Remember that differences in amount of odor can be perceived as differences in kind of odor. Train on small and large amounts, and do not expect immediate success: if a dog can find a small amount of a substance, it does not automatically mean he will also be able to find a large amount.
- For odor perception, practice is especially important, both physically and mentally. Regular exposure to training odors leads to physical changes in the olfactory organ that increase the sensitivity for these odors.

- Learning things young makes life easy. Odors learned when young are remembered extremely well. Begin odor training early (perhaps even in the litter).
- Training dogs first on single odors, then on complexes of odors speeds up the learning process. This method takes longer in the beginning, but in the end the training goes faster.
- It is not possible to prevent mistakes. The influence of an odor on the behavior of a dog through the limbic system and possible interactions of an odor with memories can lead to unpredicted effects. Try, where possible, to find out *why* mistakes happen and then use this information in training.

5

The Odor Complex of the Track

In Chapters 2 to 4, we looked at the physical process of smelling –
how the dog's anatomy helps it perceive odors. Now it is time to
turn to the track itself. What are the odor components of a track?
In 1936, dog researcher Konrad Most distinguished 12 odor components in a track:[1]

1. General human scent
2. Individual human scent
3. Odor of the footwear
4. Odor of shoe polish
5. Botanical odor
6. Odor of the soil
7. Added odors (e.g., manure or fertilizer)
8. Different animal odors
9. Blood trails of game
10. Game tracks
11. Artificial odors
12. Tracks of tires

Although there will always be many odor components present
in a track, the most important for us are artificial odors, soil damage, odors of footwear, and the individual human scent.

THE FOUR KEY ELEMENTS OF TRACK ODOR

1. **Artificial odors**, which we lay on the track during training, such as sausages, cheese, and dog cookies

2. **Soil damage**, caused by walking, kicking, or shuffling over the ground, creating physical changes and bringing out specific odors of plants
3. **Odor of footwear**, such as the odor of shoes or boots, shoe polish, and items ground into the soles of the footwear
4. **Individual human scent**, body scent, and foot sweat

1. Artificial Odors

Artificial odors are any odor deliberately added to or used to make a track for a dog to follow. For sport tracking, trainers often use various meats (e.g., tripe, sausage), cheese, dog cookies, or dog-food pellets to get the dog's attention and entice it to work out the track.

Some instructors will advise you to start with meat for your first track because dogs searching for meat use their natural hunting drive. This is, however, a misconception. Wild canines never hunt meat, tripe, or cheese; they hunt living animals, which is completely different.

It isn't the dog's hunting drive that is employed on a track with meat odor, but rather the drive to acquire food, just as a ball on the track employs the dog's prey and bring drives. A family member hiding at the end of a track evokes the pack drive (i.e., the drive to stay together).

CHEMICAL ODORS

In the 1930s, Konrad Most used artificial, chemical odors such as bergamot oil, rose oil, sandalwood oil, and menthol to train messenger dogs used by the military. In training, these dogs were first led over the route they had to work out later on. The dogs had to have confidence in their ability to orient themselves: following a human track was impossible because of the many soldiers walking over the route.[2]

This training was complex. The tracks of the infantry and the artillery often crossed each other, and the messenger dogs of the

Figure 5.1 This photo from the 1930s shows a messenger dog in training working on a chemical track over the road.

infantry often entered the area of the artillery, and vice versa. To prevent confusion, Most chose a different odor for every army section, and after that the dogs were trained to follow this specific odor, even if various tracks crossed each other. He succeeded in a reasonably short period of time: dogs trained for just 14 days showed that they were able to work out their chemical tracks with confidence.

Today, chemical odors are used in gun-dog training. Various artificial game odors are, for example, dripped on dummies (canvas retrieving bolts) or used to drag or drip tracks. Pack hunting hounds are trained by a trail laid with an artificial odor or with a drag, a bag filled with animal odor (often straw out of the cage of a tame fox) that is dragged over the ground. Bloodhounds will more commonly be "hunted" on a human track.

An artificial odor that often gives problems to tracking dogs is artificial fertilizer. Dogs have a strong aversion to this chemical odor (although they like the smell of manure). Dogs may refuse to track across a field covered with fertilizer, which may actually interfere with their ability to smell.

Figure 5.2 In pack hunt training with Bloodhounds in Europe, the dogs follow an ordinary human foot track.

2. Soil Damage

When we walk over any type of terrain, our footprints make changes. Sometimes we can observe these changes ourselves; for instance, when we walk across a meadow in the morning dew, we leave a visible track behind us where the dew disappears. If we come back when the dew has dried, the visible track is gone. However, the odor of the track is still there, which a tracking dog shows us by easily following the track with its nose to the ground.

PHYSICAL CHANGES

In walking over that dewy meadow, more happens than leaving a visible track. For example, the weight of our body creates pressure on the ground, depending on our weight and the composition of the soil.

On bare soil, this pressure will cause visible changes to the ground surface, such as a depression in the earth. This pressure in a footprint may release humidity and biological odors from the earth. Bacteria from plants breaking down in the ground give a certain odor to the soil. The pressure of our footsteps causes this odor to appear, and our footwear takes on the smell, carrying it along the track if the terrain changes to something like plants or asphalt.

On ground with plants, our footsteps cause other physical changes. Some changes are visible, such as bent or broken-off parts of grasses, weeds, and twigs. But there will also be invisible changes as our footsteps disturb, damage, or kill insects and micro-organisms. Furthermore, the pressure of our body and the friction as we walk on the ground cause a small amount of warmth.

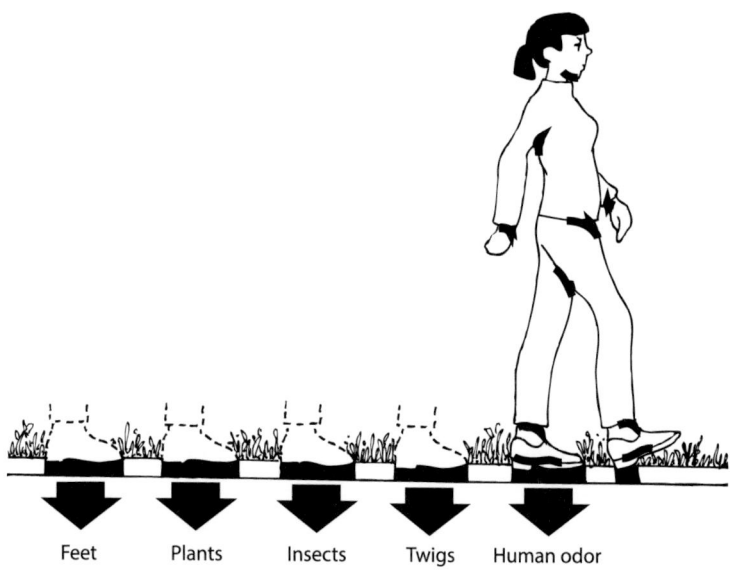

Feet   Plants   Insects   Twigs   Human odor

Figure 5.3 The pressure of our body compresses the vegetation and soil and damages grasses, plants, twigs, insects, and the like. In addition, individual human scent seeps out through the footwear.

ODORS OF PLANTS

Just as every soil has its own characteristic odor, plants, weeds, grasses, and flowers also have specific odors. Damaging parts of the plant sets free an odor of plant sap, which adds to the odor of the track. Everyone who has taken leaves off a geranium or mowed a lawn knows how odor can be released after damaging a plant. Humans need large amounts of odor before they can perceive it, but dogs can smell the plant sap resulting from the damage caused by one footstep.

Figure 5.4 Just as every soil type has its own distinctive smell, plants, herbs, and grasses also have specific plant odors.

The odors from damaged plants and grasses are, like soil damage, almost immediately set free and smellable, because the molecules from the plant sap change into a gaseous form (and by that into an easy-to-smell state). The intensity of this odor increases very quickly, but these odors also disappear rather quickly. The odor of plant sap, like the odors after soil damage, stops after a certain period of time, because all sorts of micro-organisms in and on the plants work hard to recover after the damage.

Figure 5.5 One footstep, which lasted only a fraction of a second, gives the dog enough information to follow the track to the next footprint.

BACTERIA

The wounds of damaged plants and grasses close quickly, just like wounds in our skin, and the dead or dying-off parts of plants are cleared away by bacteria that make things rot. And so the next change occurs on our footsteps. After a period of time, the odor caused by these bacteria becomes a clear smell for the dog, like a dung heap or the odor of a haystack for humans. Anyone who has ever smelled a pile of grass after one rainy day knows what kind of odor these bacteria cause. Dead insects or other small animals ground under our feet also leave specific odors on the track.

For bacteria to work at their optimum level, a certain amount of humidity and warmth is necessary. A part of that warmth is caused by the pressure of our feet on the soil and the friction of walking. Footsteps also release humidity from the ground, creating the optimal circumstances for bacteria to start their work of clearing off damage.

But when this little bit of warmth and humidity are used up, more has to be drawn from the surroundings. The strength of an odor therefore depends on the outside temperature and the relative humidity of the air. And although warmth encourages bacteria, a very high temperature has the opposite effect and delays their action. Extremely low temperatures also slow the work of bacteria.

Because bacteria also play an important role in human odors, we can partly determine the ideal weather conditions for tracking. For optimal microbe life and therefore optimal odor creation by bacteria, the humidity of the air has to be average to high, and the temperature should be neither too high nor too low. That means temperatures around 68°F (20°C) measured about 5 feet (1.5 m) above ground.

3. Odors of Footwear

Tracklayers can wear any type of footwear, but the rubber, leather, and any other materials used to make the footwear each have a specific odor, which together form the odor of the footwear. Added to the materials used to make the footwear are the chemical odors of finishes, protective coatings, and shoe polishes.

Walking wears off small bits of the sole of footwear, especially on a hard surface. These bits are left on the track, contributing to the odor complex. Added to this are the odors of things that are left in the soles (everything we walk on). These may be pleasant odors for the dog, or they could be repulsive odors, which would make the track more difficult for him to work out.

During tracking we have to take into account that as the terrain changes, some of the last type of ground walked on will be picked up and carried forward by the footwear. These odors will be brought onto the first few feet of the next ground surface to be walked on. For instance, coming from a meadow onto a road, some

Figure 5.6 Rubber, leather, and all materials used to make footwear have a distinctive odor that contribute to the odor of the track.

odors of plants (grass, weeds, etc.) will be picked up by the soles and left on the beginning of the road.

People with certain occupations, like butchers, carpenters, farmers, or humans working in labs or factories, may have specific occupational odors on their clothes and shoes that also can form a part of the track.

4. Individual Human Scent

All living creatures give off odorants by their metabolism, respiration, and glandular secretions. Through such processes, every living being acquires their own (individual) odor. These odorants can periodically be of a different strength and composition. The use of soap, foot powders, and certain medicines also have their influence on human scent.

Human scents result from four main sources, but not all influence a track:
- Body openings
- Human skin
- Perspiration (sweat) glands
- Sebaceous (sebum) glands

BODY OPENINGS

The odors from body openings (mouth, nose, ears, anus, and urogenital area) have no influence on the odor complex of the human track. These odors, however, can play a role with the work of search and rescue (SAR) dogs, which search for people under rubble and snow. In particular, the breath and sometimes urine lost from panic or excitement can be important odor sources for the SAR dog.

HUMAN SKIN

The skin is the cover that separates the individual from the outside world. This organ protects the body and consists of two layers:
- The upper, or outside layer called the *epidermis*
- The second layer called the *corium* (or dermis)

Underneath this is the *subcutis* and then fatty tissue, which both have important functions in heat insulation, energy storage, and as a physical buffer. In the skin we find the sebaceous glands, sweat glands, hair follicles (except for on the lips, palms, and soles of the feet), and the places where nails are formed.

In general, the odor of the skin is thought to be the sum of genetic influences, bacterial action, diet, and glandular secretions.

EPIDERMIS

The epidermis varies in thickness but is normally only some tenths of a millimeter thick, not more than a very thin membrane. On places where the skin has a lot of callus, like the palms of the hand and the soles of the feet, the epidermis is much thicker.

Epidermal cells are continuously renewed as cells develop within and move to the surface, while cells on the outer surface

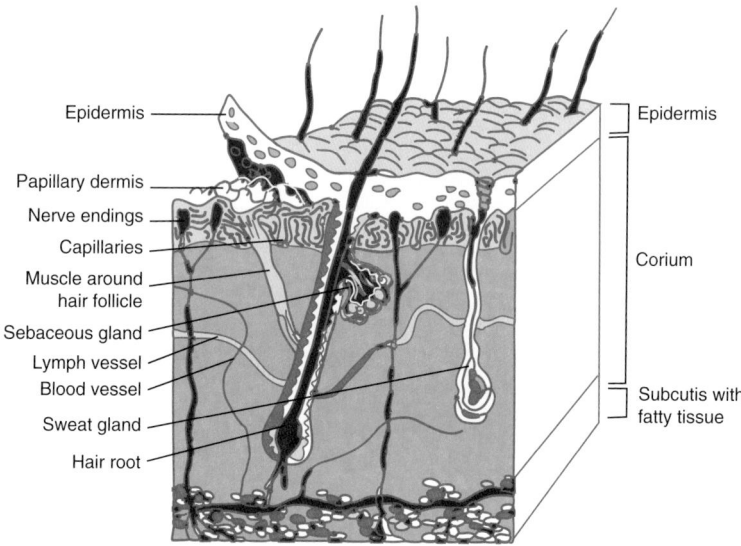

Epidermis

Papillary dermis

Nerve endings

Capillaries

Muscle around
hair follicle

Sebaceous gland

Lymph vessel

Blood vessel

Sweat gland

Hair root

Epidermis

Corium

Subcutis with
fatty tissue

Figure 5.7 A schematic representation of human skin shows the different layers, the hair follicles, and the sweat and sebaceous glands.

die and peel off at a rate of 0.5 to 1 grams of dead skin cells (rafts) per day.[3] In this way, the epidermis renews about once a month. The rafts that flake off from the outer surface are normally invisible, except on the scalp as dandruff and as a consequence of certain skin diseases (such as psoriasis). These rafts are also left on objects a person touches. If sufficient rafts and other material are left behind, DNA technology can be used to identify the owner.

The rafts also flake off into the air and are carried away with air currents. The theory of mantrailing is based on the idea that tracking dogs follow a trail formed by these rafts. However, as we discussed in the Introduction, this theory needs more time to be proven.

CORIUM

The corium is a very thin (less than 1/8 in., 1–3 mm) layer of connective tissue where the sebaceous and sweat glands begin. The corium begins immediately below the epidermis with the papillary

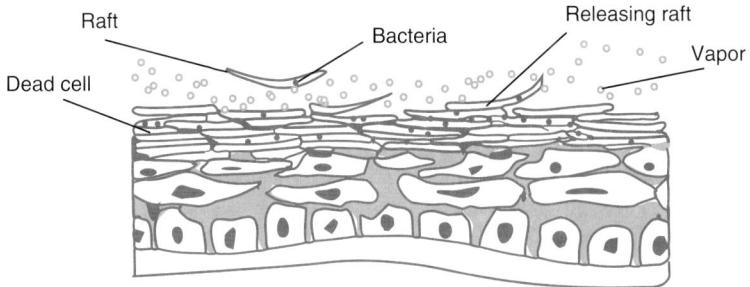

Figure 5.8 Dead cells called *rafts* flake off from the outside skin layer as new cells are formed and take their place.

dermis, which makes contact with the epidermis in a wavy, bulging pattern. The bulges are filled with many little blood vessels (capillaries) that provide food to the epidermis and transport waste products away.

Further down in the corium is the reticular dermis, which forms the bulk of the corium. The reticular dermis contains a network of bigger blood and lymph vessels, which supply the sebaceous and sweat glands and the muscles around the hairs. The reticular dermis is characterized by dense collagenous and elastic connective tissue.

The blood vessels in the skin are responsible not only for providing nourishment and oxygen to the skin, but also for regulating body temperature. In the corium there are also a large number of nerve ends, which control the senses of touch, pain, and temperature.

SKIN GLANDS

Three kinds of glands secrete directly onto the skin or into canals that lead to the skin surface. All contribute to the odor on the skin. Fingerprints on a glass slide are made of secretions from the skin glands. Such fingerprints are discernable to dogs for some weeks without specific preservation.[4] Two types of glands are typically called "sweat glands": eccrine and apocrine glands. The third type of gland are sebaceous glands.

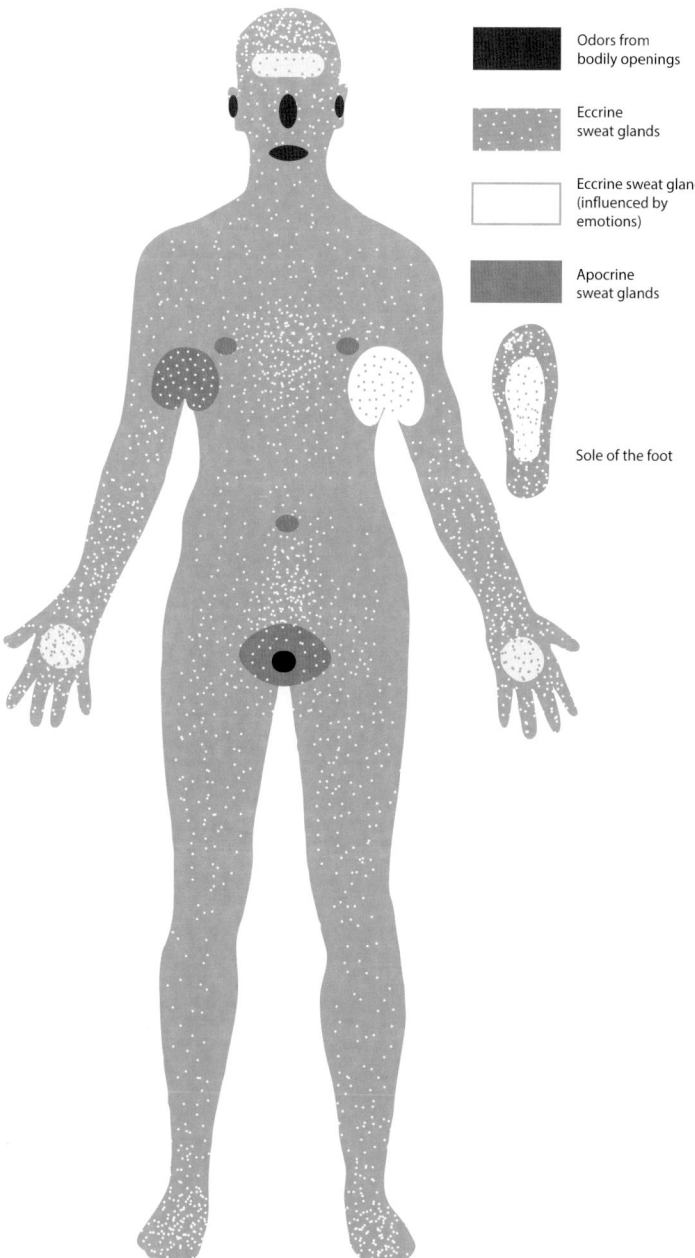

Figure 5.9 Distribution of sweat glands over the human body.

Eccrine glands: The human body has between 2 and 4 million eccrine sweat glands. They produce a clear, watery solution. For the most part (more than 98%), this solution consists of water in which numerous organic and inorganic components are dissolved.[5] Eccrine sweat plays a major role in thermoregulation of the body. Because of body warmth and air currents around the body, the sweat solution evaporates after it leaves the pores, which helps cool the body.

During heavy sweating, sweat will be absorbed by clothes that touch the skin. In emotional or nervous moments, the eccrine glands in the forehead, the palms of the hands, and the soles of the feet secrete a large amount of sweat. In healthy adults, eccrine sweat glands can secrete as much as half to one gallon (2–4 L) per hour.

Table 5.1 Eccrine Sweat Glands per Body Part*

BODY PART	AVERAGE NUMBER OF SWEAT GLANDS (PER CM², LESS THAN HALF A SQUARE INCH)
Sole of the foot	600
Forehead	360
Top of the foot	250
Forearm	225
Trunk	175
Upper arm	150
Leg	130

*From W. G. Syrotuck, *Scent and the Scenting Dog.*

Apocrine glands: Apocrine sweat glands are found in specific places on the human body, especially in the armpits and genital area. They produce a cloudy, viscous solution containing large amounts of cholesterol. Bacteria on the skin break down apocrine sweat into odorous molecules, in particular steroids, which play a role in attracting the opposite sex.[6] According to Spielman et al., the armpits, where the apocrine glands are abundant, are the source of pheromones, the major source of body odor as perceived by other people.[7]

Sebaceous glands: Sebaceous glands occur all over the body, except on the palms of the hands and the soles of the feet. They always lie beside a hair follicle where they discharge sebum, a fatty substance. Sebum seals the hair shaft, prevents the penetration of bacteria, and prevents a loss of fluid. Sebum also helps keep the skin pliable and protect it from dehydration. The products of the sebaceous glands are spread over the body surface by movement. Through movement, sebum also arrives at the palms of the hands and the soles of the feet.

On average there are about 100 sebaceous glands per square centimeter on the human body. On the middle of the chest and the back, and on the face and scalp, this amount increases to almost 1,000 glands per square centimeter. Humans with a high sebum production often have problems with greasy hair.

Table 5.2 Average Number of Bacteria Living on Human Skin*

BODY PART	AVERAGE NUMBER OF BACTERIA (PER CM²)
Armpit	2.41 million
Scalp	1.46 million
Forehead	200,000

* From E. Marples, "Life on the Human Skin."

Sebum is discharged into a canal in the skin as the gland cell breaks down. In the canal, the sebum and the remains of the cell are completely broken down and discharged to the skin surface. It takes 8–10 days from formation of the cell until the final breakdown products (including free fatty acids) are found on the skin.[8] These fatty acids are thought to form the olfactory signature of an individual. Support for this theory comes from examining scent-marking glands in other mammals: glands that are known to provide information about the identity of an individual produce fatty acids.

SKIN MICROFLORA

The products of both the apocrine and sebaceous glands are broken down into odorous compounds by bacteria living in skin canals and on the skin. Since we are interested in odor, let us look at these bacteria more closely.

Skin microflora include *Micrococcaceae, Staphylococci, Streptococci, Corynebacterium acnes, Pityrosporum ovale, Pityrosporum acne, Pityrosporum granulosum*, and *Propionibacteria*. Several studies have shown that treatment of the skin with antibiotics decreases bacterial populations, which results in a loss of fatty acids. However, some bacteria remain unaffected, probably because they are present in the hair follicles and out of reach of topical antibiotics. Different bacterial populations are found in different body areas, but in general the various populations remain quite stable over time.[9]

The consequence of these regional differences in bacterial populations is that different body areas of the same person have different odors. This is an important point for tracking training, which we will discuss later. The regions with the largest numbers of bacteria are the face, neck, armpits, and groin, but also the soles of the feet and between the toes. The differences in bacterial populations between individual people are quite large.

As people age, their skin microflora changes, likely due to shifting hormones and changes in sebum production. This means some elements of individual scent will change with age. For example, the *Streptococci* found in children disappear in young adults and Coryneform bacteria (mainly responsible for odor production) increase.

Only Coryneform bacteria are able to produce the typical axillary odor by decomposition of apocrine sweat. Coccis (*Streptococci, Staphylococci*, etc.), however, don't have this capacity. It remains to be more clearly established which substances participate in odor production.

LIPIDS

The lipids on human skin seem to be the prime contributor to people's scent, so they merit further attention. These lipids are, for the most part, created as sebum produced by sebaceous glands breaks down, although some lipids come from the epidermis and from contamination with touched surfaces.

Approximately 37% of the fatty acids found on the skin are "biologically significant"; the remaining 63% consists of more than 200 different kinds of free fatty acids ranging from very small to very large. Some of these are very unusual, for example sebaleic acid seems to be unique to the surface lipid of human skin.[10]

Individuals differ both in the lipid composition and amounts of different types of lipids. This individual difference can be huge: two individuals may have completely different lipid components, giving each person their own scent signature. Studies have generally shown that individual lipid compositions remain fairly stable over time, meaning it is unlikely that changes occur due to diet or metabolism.[11]

THE ODOR COMPLEX

What we think of as the track odor isn't a single odor, but rather a combination of many odors forming an odor complex. The odor complex of the track consists of the following:

SOIL DAMAGE

Physical changes
- Specific odor of the ground (type of soil or other material)
- Visible damage, like dew, broken off parts of plants, grasses, twigs, etc.
- Disturbed or crushed insects and micro-organisms
- Pressure, causing warmth

Odors of plants
- Specific odor of plants, weeds, grasses, etc.
- Plant sap from damaged plants
- Odors caused by bacteria on rotting plant and animal matter

INDIVIDUAL HUMAN SCENT

Footwear
- Odor of shoes and boots
- The wearer's scent and shoe polish
- Things stepped on or in

Human
- Scent of the feet
- Sweat from the feet
- Occupational odors
- Soap and/or medicines
- Particles falling off body and clothes

The Common Factor

As a result of regional differences in microflora on the skin, different body parts have their own particular odor. To humans, the odor in the armpit smells totally different from the scent of the genital area, and genital odor smells different from odor on the soles of the feet. In fact, Löhner found that for humans, the similarity between the same region of different people seems to be greater than different regions of the same person.[12]

However, in dogs, Löhner found that the similarity in different body areas of the same person was greater than similarity in scent between the same areas belonging to different people. This suggests that dogs have learned to distinguish a *common factor* in an individual's scent, for instance, the fatty acids, whereas humans notice a more regional odor. From his studies, Löhner described how dogs retrieved articles of clothing with scents of different parts of the body of a person whose track they had worked out shortly before. According to him, this illustrates the ability of the dog to find the common factor in the human scent that underlies the scent of different parts of the body.

Figure 5.10 Dogs can learn to search for the common factor underlying each human scent they track — an individual's scent signature.

Neuhaus commented on this ability:

> The ability of the dog to smell was in the beginning strongly underrated, based on the different threshold values for the perception of the different odors of the track. In the track of a mammal or human, the fatty acids play a key role; in a mixture of fatty acids, each odor has a lower threshold value than it would if it were separate. (Note: the lower the threshold value, the easier it is to smell an odor.) An equal mixture of 10 fatty acids corresponds roughly with the composition of the skin secretion in mammals and therefore with the odor of the track. This mixture can be observed by the dog when the concentration of the separate substances is only one tenth of the threshold values that would be necessary were the fatty acids kept separate.[13]

Of particular interest is the study of the dog's ability to discriminate between the scent of their handler and the scent of other people.[14] Three dogs were trained to retrieve dumbbells scented by the hand of their handler and to ignore those scented by the hands of other people. The dogs were rewarded with praise.

The researchers found that when the dogs were given a choice between a handler-scented dumbbell and an unscented one, the dogs chose the handler-dumbbell correctly in 93 percent of the trials, but when they were given the choice between two scented dumbbells, one by the handler and one by another person, the performance dropped to 75 percent correct. Taking into account the results in other choices in these experiments, it seemed that the dogs actively looked for the hand scent of their handler, choosing it over the elbow scents of their handler or a stranger. Their performance dropped to chance level when confronted with a choice without a correct, handler hand-scented dumbbell. After further study, the researchers concluded that systematic training on the handler's hand scent did not lead to an automatic generalization to handler scent.[15]

This is evidence that the capacity to focus on the common scent of an individual is the result of training: dogs trained to detect the hand scent of their handler had difficulty choosing between the hand scent of a stranger and a non-hand scent (e.g., crook of the elbow) of their handler.[16] Dogs trained to match objects scented in pockets to the hand scent of the same individual performed better in those trials than in trials where the hand scent had to be matched to another part of the body, such as the crook of the elbow.[17]

Stability of Human Scent

It is now generally accepted that there is a genetic base for unique human scent. Behavioral studies have shown that the difference between the scents of identical twins, siblings, or other genetically related people has been found to be smaller than differences between scents of non-related people. The stability of an individual's scent is also clear from these studies: siblings recognize each other's scent on a T-shirt after not having seen each other for more than two years.[18]

There is also evidence that the genes connected to an individual's immune system also influence individual human scent.[19] Recent theories are based on interactions between immune system antigens and bacteria. The antigens (or their breakdown products) influence an individual's bacterial flora and thus body scent.[20] This study area could be important for forensic scientists working with odors, since "scent profiles governed by [immune system antigens] could be more distinctive than fingerprints with respect to genetic identity, because the genetic component of fingerprints is uncertain."[21]

Recent behavioral studies indicate that women seem to prefer scents from men with distinctly different immune system genes than they themselves have.[22] This is explained in terms of sexual selection: by mating with such a genetically different person, offspring will have a broader spectrum of immune system genes and thus be healthier. In another study, it was found that women were able to identify people who had immune system genes similar to their fathers.[23]

All this evidence of genetic contributions to individual scent is evidence that an individual's scent is relatively stable. Although no experiments have been undertaken to try to specifically alter an individual's scent, it seems unlikely that such changes can occur easily. If a person's genetic makeup influences the microflora responsible for the composition of fatty acids on the skin, the only way to alter the scent would be to purposely change the individual's bacterial microflora. Minimizing axillary scent by modifying the microflora to produce less scent is a continuing source of income for the pharmaceutical and cosmetics industries, illustrating the difficulty of such actions. Application of antibiotics onto the skin does influence the bacterial population and can diminish their amounts. However, such antibiotics are usually only applied locally, and the larger part of the body continues to function (and smell) as before.

EFFECTS OF AGE ON SCENT

However, although an individual's scent is fairly constant, the chemical content of skin lipids does change somewhat with age. Ramotowski has summarized these changes, which include rates of sebum secretion and the amounts of certain fatty acids. For example, young children do not produce much sebum, and their lipid composition is dominated by those produced in the epidermis.[24] As hormonal stimulation increases in puberty, more sebum is produced.

Women have lower secretion levels than males, and people with acne have higher secretion levels than people without acne. The stimulation of the sebaceous glands results in a change in lipid composition on the skin: more endogenously produced lipids are found (created deeper in the body); the epidermal lipids remain relatively constant. Overall, the secretion levels and sebum composition remain constant from puberty until much later in life (males over 70, females over 50). The principle reason for the decline is diminished hormonal stimulation.

Although diet seems to have an effect on the scent of an individual, dietary lipids are only a small proportion of skin lipids, and the long turnover time of the sebaceous cells (approximately 8–10 days) prevents rapid effects. Washing minimizes the amount of lipids on the skin, but the effect is short term since the lipids are replenished quickly.

Stability of Odor on Articles

A tracklayer normally leaves one or more articles belonging to them along a track they set. In general, scents produced by sebaceous glands are quite stable. However, this is not to say they never change or fade. Direct sunlight, in particular, breaks down many organic substances, and some micro-organisms (bacteria, fungi) use organic components as a resource. In a study done by the Pacific Northwest National Laboratory, the chemical changes in latent fingerprint deposits were examined.[25] The research showed that saturated fatty compounds remain relatively stable over time. However, unsaturated lipids (such as squalene and some of the fatty acids) diminished substantially within the 30-day period, especially during the first week. With time, more saturated, low-molecular acids appeared, originating from the breaking down of the unsaturated lipids.

Another interesting point for scent on articles is what happens when scents of different individuals are superimposed upon each other, as could happen when there are several tracklayers using the same article without cleaning them in between (a practice we strongly discourage, especially in early training sessions).

Chemically, the odors from the various articles mix into a new compound containing the fatty acids from all individuals. Behavioral experiments with golden hamsters[26] and meadow voles[27] indicate that when two scent-marks are superimposed upon each other, only the top odor is perceived or considered important. How the animals are able to do this is not yet fully understood, but the term *olfactory occlusion* has been used to describe the ability to exclude some scents to focus on others. Anecdotal evidence from dog handlers indicates that dogs are capable of recognizing each of the two superimposed scents, but that this ability declines as the scents age.

Kalmus found that dogs are able to handle superimposed scents: one dog had been trained to pick out a handkerchief scented a few minutes in one person's armpit from among a number of other, similarly scented handkerchiefs. This dog was also able to pick out this person's handkerchief if the scent had been "overlaid" by scent from another person's armpit, or by an artificial odor.[28]

Löhner observed the same in a scent-matching test using human scents on pieces of wood. Even if the piece of wood was kept in hand for only 1 or 2 seconds, or if it was touched with a fingertip for 2 minutes, the dog succeeded in correctly matching it. The dog made the correct choice even if the wood had the scent of another person as well.[29]

In another study in Poland, Person A was given the worn trousers of Person B to wear, and then Person A sat in a car belonging to Person C. After this, a scent sample was taken from the car seat. Dogs were able to distinguish the scent of all three persons on the sample.[30]

However, although dogs are capable of discerning the scent of different individuals on an article, there is no need to make training difficult for the dog by reusing articles without cleaning them first. Clean training articles with unscented soap to dissolve the greasy products and then thoroughly rinse them with clean water.

Figure 5.11 Although dogs are capable of discerning the scent of different individuals on an article, in training dogs for clean-scent tracking, we recommend not making it more difficult for the dog by reusing articles without cleaning.

A Formula for Understanding Track Odor

Rudolf and Rudolfina Menzel created a formula to better understand the different odor components of tracks, which can be useful in understanding how to train dogs on different odors.

$S = C \times (T + P + G + F)$

S = the sum of the total odor of the track
T = the scent of the track-layer
P = the odor of the damaged plants
G = the damage to the ground
F = the odor of the footwear and the soles
C = the constant of the tracking conditions (humidity, temperature, ground surface, etc.)

If the track is laid in bare feet, then the direct contact of the soles of the feet with the ground leaves more human scent on the track by the peeling of skin cells off the foot and by passing fatty acids from skin secretions directly onto the ground. On the other hand, bare feet cause less damage to plants and to the ground itself, and thus their odor components will become less. The odors impregnated into the footwear will be entirely missing. So T becomes greater, P and G less, and F disappears completely.

The track will have more human scent, but in general the total intensity of the track odor will be less than a track laid with footwear because of the missing odor of the footwear and the weaker odors from ground and plant disturbance.

If the track-layer is wearing shoes or boots, then you get less of the fatty acids left behind, and as a result T will be less than on a bare foot track. On the other hand, the odor components P and G, caused by damage to the ground, will be stronger, because the sole of footwear is much harder than the sole of the feet. Furthermore, the odor of the footwear (F) will be added to the total odor of the track. Because of this increase of P and G, and the addition of F, the total intensity of the track scent will be more, but the portion of human scent in this complex less.

Under equal conditions, a track laid with shoes will be easier for the dog to work out than a track laid in bare feet, especially if the dog has less training. The clean-scent tracking dog, however, will work out the track laid with bare feet with a lot more pleasure because he will find more human scent.

Setting Up Clean-Scent Tracking

We assume, generally speaking, that the constant of the tracking conditions (C) doesn't change during a track. On the same type of ground, with similar covering, such as a meadow, the formula for the track of the handler, laid in shoes, will be:

$$S1 = C \times (T1 + P + G + F1)$$

and that of another track-layer, laid in rubber boots:

$$S2 = C \times (T2 + P + G + F2)$$

If we want to make it clear to the dog that he has to search for T (so that he is clean-scent tracking), we must change the variable odor components as much as possible during training. Therefore the track must be laid on different ground surfaces (P and G) and also be laid with different footwear, so that F changes.

If we compare the formulas of two tracks on the same ground surface laid by different track-layers with, as frequently happens, the same footwear (for instance, rubber boots) we can see that the differences in the tracks are minor, so dogs that are not clean-scent trained can easily make a mistake. In both formulas,

$$S1 = C \times (T1 + P + B + F) \text{ and}$$
$$S2 = C \times (T2 + P + B + F),$$

all the odor components are the same, except T.

To teach the dog the differences in these complex tracking odors, we initially use the familiar scent of the handler as T and a totally strange track-layer for the cross-track. Only when the dog is track-sure and clean-scent on the track of his handler do we start training the dog to compare the odor of a track laid by one stranger with the cross-track of another stranger.

6

Human Footstep Scents

Some trainers believe that in tracking, the individual scent of the track-layer plays no particular role. According to them, other factors determine the track, such as the odor of the shoes and a track-layer's shoe size and weight, which affect how much the track-layer disturbs the soil and damages plants in each footstep, and therefore the odor of the track. In their opinion, the scent of the track-layer is such a small part of the track that, even when this scent is present, it disappears under other odor components.

Other trainers believe dogs search for an individual human scent. Only by searching for such a specific, unique scent can a well-trained dog stay on track, even over hard road surfaces, and not be diverted by cross-tracks made around the same time.

So we ask: is it or is it not possible for the dog to perceive the human scent component in a track? A study by W. Neuhaus set out to answer this question by calculating human sweat production and sweat odors.[1] These he compared with the dog's very low threshold values for odors, which he had determined in earlier experiments. He concluded that the amount of human scent in normal tracks, even after several hours, was more than enough

Figure 6.1 Can a dog perceive an individual human scent component in a track?

to be perceptible for the dog. This conclusion was based on the threshold values for the individual components of human sweat.

But human scent is a mixture of odors. As a follow up, Neuhaus then investigated the threshold values for mixed odors. He found lower threshold values for such mixtures than if the different substances were offered separately.[2] His earlier conclusion that dogs could perceive human scent was therefore strengthened.

Even if a scent is surrounded by another, strong odor, Neuhaus found that dogs could observe small variations in the odor mix. This agrees with the observation that a dog can recognize the scent of a human and an article touched by that human, even when the article itself has a strong odor or has another strong odor on it.[3]

This finding has clear relevance for our work as trainers. Be assured that even when the other odor components of the track are about a thousand times stronger than the human scent, it is still possible for the dog to recognize the individual human scent.[4]

Sweaty Feet

The sebum and sweat secretions on human feet and soles play a big role in research on tracking dogs. The soles of the feet, in particular, are equipped with a large number of eccrine sweat glands that produce sweat, which has volatile fatty acids dissolved in it.

In addition, the many sebaceous glands on the sides and top of the feet, and bacteria in the sebum, also contribute to the presence of fatty acids on the feet. In 1931, by laying tracks with bare feet over an ice surface, J. Hansmann proved that the skin secretions of the feet produce a very good track for the dog to follow.[5]

In 1990, Kanda et al. compared fatty acids from the socks and feet of people with strong foot scent to those of people with weak or imperceptible (to humans) foot scent.[6] In people with strong foot scent, the fatty acids were found in larger amounts than in people with weak or imperceptible foot scent. One of the fatty acids, iso-valerianic acid, was present in all people with perceptible foot scent, but was not detected in those without.

Fatty acids are deposited by the soles of the feet onto any place touched by the feet. Even if there is no direct contact with the bare foot, as when socks or shoes are worn, these fatty acids are passed on from the foot to the track.

The footwear does not prevent this transfer of scent, and older footwear can increase the scent. Because of constant evaporation of the watery parts of sweat through the pores, and the fact that the materials of socks and shoes easily absorb fluids, the smelly substances accumulate. Worn footwear are fully drenched with the scent substances of the fatty acids.

Feet sweat all the time (often without us noticing). Sweat exits through the porous soles of the shoe and along the seams, creating a stream of moisture and scent substances. When the sole of the shoe touches the ground, these substances are precipitated and pressed out onto the ground. With every step, even when each takes only a fraction of a second, volatile fatty acids diffuse through the sole to be left on the ground.

This diffusion of the gaseous foot sweat through the sole of the shoe is increased by the movements of the foot in the shoe during walking. The foot scent substances in the shoe are pressed during walking and pushed out of the pores and seams by pressure on the ground.

HOW MUCH SCENT IN A FOOTPRINT?

In many studies, Neuhaus researched the sensitivity of dogs and humans to the fatty acids that are present in the skin secretions of mammals and humans.[7] In particular, he determined the minimum amount of certain odors that can be perceived. He found that dogs can perceive butyric acid, one of the elements of sweat, in concentrations of 1 to 100 million times lower than humans can.

Furthermore, he determined that only 1/1,000 of the fatty acids present in human foot sweat comes out of shoes by the sole and the seam between the leather upper and the sole. But he also found that the amount of fatty acids left on the track with every footstep is still 1 to 3 million times greater than the minimum amount dogs need to perceive that odor.

But shoes aren't rubber boots, some people might argue. Rubber forms more of a barrier for human scent to leave. So Neuhaus also researched how many odor molecules can come through rubber.[8] To that end, he put 1 mm^3 of butyric acid absorbed in a piece of filter paper in a rubber container carefully closed on all sides, which at the beginning of the test only smelled of rubber. In his experiments, he used three different thicknesses of rubber, and Table 6.1 indicates how long it took before the characteristic butyric acid odor was clearly perceptible for people.

Table 6.1 **Rubber Permeability Tests***

WALL THICKNESS	TIME**
0.17 mm	8 minutes
0.65 mm	50 minutes
2.00 mm	38 hours

* From W. Neuhaus, *"Die 'Fährtenreinheit' des Hundes."*
** Time needed for people to perceive butyric acid encased in rubber, with different wall thicknesses.

So people could smell the odor through the thinnest wall thickness after just 8 minutes, and through a thicker wall after 38 hours. This odor was perceivable for many days and then it slowly decreased. After 2 weeks, the thickest rubber wall did not smell of butyric acid anymore, but only of rubber. After opening the rubber packages, the inside of the container was free of the butyric acid odor, suggesting that all of the odor substance leaked out through the 2 mm thick rubber wall in 2 weeks.

The soles of rubber boots are usually thicker, about an eighth of an inch (3.5 mm), but the edges are usually thinner than the thickest rubber wall used in Neuhaus's research. Clearly, then, the odor of foot sweat *can* leak from rubber boots, particularly if they have been in use for some time.

Furthermore, the warmth of the feet, their pressure on the inside of the boot, and the movement of the rubber will speed up this process. Indeed, the tops of the boots are open, by which scent can escape, but the textile layer on the inside of the boots will absorb scent and by direct contact pass it on to the rubber. So even if the human scent substances located outside of the rubber boots are soon wiped off by grass, more human scent substances are constantly added from the inside, and are thus continually left on the track.

Table 6.1 indicates the perceptions of people; do not forget that dogs can smell butyric acid about 100 million times more easily.

In spite of this research, it is often still claimed that the individual scent of the track-layer is not what the dog is tracking. People point to such things as the size of the shoe, the track-layer's weight (and how deep one sinks in the soil), the manner of walking, and other factors as more likely objects of the dog's interest. But none of this applies for dogs tracking on a hard ground surface, and it has often been proven that dogs can work out a track on a paved road. The only odor they could perceive there is the individual human scent.

FACTORS THAT INCREASE SCENT

Clearly scent can leave shoes, and even rubber boots, and does so in amounts that can be easily perceived by dogs. However, the sweat accumulated in the footwear and the soles can be drawn from the material (leather, rubber, fabric, etc.) by fluid. Part of

Figure 6.2 The amount of fatty acids left on the trail with each footstep is 1 to 3 million times greater than the minimum amount required for dogs to detect that scent.

the fatty acids is readily soluble in water. If the shoe comes into contact with moist or even wet ground, the water dissolves some of the sweat stored in the shoe, and adds this further to the footprint.

The pressure of the footsteps on the ground transfers odor mechanically. With every step on wet ground, the sweat stored in the shoe will spread, be pressed out, and absorbed in the footprint, and therefore the track. This is why less scent transfer occurs on hard, dry surfaces. We can observe this in practice: a dog more easily follows a track on moist ground than on dry soil.

Figure 6.3 Old shoes become fully drenched in fatty acids, which are interesting scents for dogs.

THE FOREFOOT

The front part of the foot normally gives off more scent because it has more sweat glands. The front part of shoes therefore also has more scent. Besides, when walking, shoes touch the ground first with the heel and then with the front part; the middle part does not touch the ground every time. The heel contributes less to the scent left behind because it is thicker. The front part gives off more scent, for the following reasons:

- The front sole of a shoe is thinner and wears more quickly, so scent substances come out more easily from the pores.
- The front part of the foot smells stronger than the back.
- The front part of the foot sweats more because it is always flexed while walking. Furthermore, during walking, the flexing part of the foot rubs the sole of the shoe more (the toes also rub each other), which increases sweat and sebum production. The sebum between the toes is more quickly attacked by bacteria because the area has more heat due to friction of the toes.
- During walking, the front part of the foot stays on the ground longer than other parts of the foot. The whole weight of the body presses on this part, although only for a fraction of a second, which grinds the shoe harder into the ground.

WATER BEADS

We were interested in determining how much the sides and top of the shoe allow the passage of odor substances. To answer this question, we poured water into an old leather climbing boot that was waterproofed on the outside up to the place where the shaft begins. After half a minute, the leather at the sides was saturated and the outside showed moisture. As the boot was put on, beads of water formed on the outside, coming out through the invisible pores in the leather, in particular in those places where the leather was creased due to walking. With every step, the material flexed, the leather pressed together, and the outside became wetter. This simple test suggests how much power scent, which is mostly gaseous and therefore would come out even easier than water, is pressed through the pores to the outside of the footwear.

Influences on Human Track Scents

We've discussed in this chapter some of the evidence that indicates a human footprint includes fatty acids from eccrine sweat and sebum. By themselves, fatty acids don't change or disappear very easily. If, for example, sweat scent is caught in clothes or articles and

Figure 6.4 Tracking uses the better organs of another being to make up for our own, inadequate senses.

preserved in the right way (such as in a tightly closed glass jar), then a dog will be able to detect its scent for a very long time. However, like every substance lying on the ground, these fatty acids are subject to a variety of natural factors, some of which affect scent:

- Gases in the air
- Air movement
- Temperature and sunlight
- Surface type
- Water in the form of vapor, dew, rain, or snow

GASES IN THE AIR

Nitrogen belongs to the chemically "slow" elements, which means it doesn't combine easily with other elements. So although there is a lot of nitrogen in the air, it has little or no influence on fatty acids.

On the other hand, oxygen, which is present not only in the air, but also in water and earth, combines more easily with other elements. However, of the fatty acids, only formic acid combines very easily with air-borne oxygen. The other fatty acids remain fairly stable in the presence of oxygen.

Carbon dioxide, which is present in the air only in small amounts, does not affect fatty acids, even when the concentration of carbon dioxide increases (say, due to a large number of people in a small room).

Therefore, we should expect no essential changes to a track from the main elements of air. Elements such as hydrogen superoxide (found in grass) or ozone may influence fatty acids, but they are present in only minute amounts in the air.

AIR MOVEMENT

Although air itself doesn't greatly affect fatty acids, air movement does. Moving air over a track stimulates the evaporation and spread of fatty acids over a larger area. If a track is covered with sand or other material by the wind, this can, depending on the covering and of the age of the track, also make tracking more difficult.

TEMPERATURE AND SUNLIGHT

Fatty acids are stable insofar as temperature is concerned. Within normal temperature variations and limits found nature, warmth or cold will not change fatty acids chemically.

The influence of direct sunlight on a track, however, is not well understood. From experiments, we know that scents preserved in glass jars are not changed even after days of intense sun exposure. On the track, however, the *warmth* of the sunlight will increase evaporation, which is a factor that needs to be considered. The fatty acids are not changed by the warmth, but the scents of the track will dissipate faster.

SURFACE TYPE

Rich, humus soil changes sweat substances, and the scent gets lost. Live microbes, acids, and bases in decaying plant and animal matter are busy with a constant process of cleaning, including any fatty acids they encounter. Ammonia in the soil can also be important, as it easily combines with fatty acids to form fatty acid salts.

Dry wood that is not covered with paint or varnish (e.g., on bridges or planks over ditches) absorbs sweat with the fatty acids and keeps the solution, probably without changing it. Fresh wood contains all sorts of active chemical substances, etheric oils, and so on, by which the fatty acids of sweat are eventually changed. Other surfaces to consider include the following:

- Raw concrete, paving stones, and bricks absorb fluid, including sweat, very easily, making a clear track.
- Pebbles and sand are chemically neutral to the fatty acids and preserve scent well.
- Raw limestone, marble, and other carbonic acid minerals greatly reduce or change the scent from fatty acids.
- Asphalt and asphalt-concrete roads contain chemical substances with a disinfecting effect, changing and degrading the fatty acids of the track to a great extent. In older asphalt this effect is much reduced.

Figure 6.5 New asphalt and asphalt-concrete roads contain chemical substances that react to the fatty acids in the footprint, changing the scent.

WATER IN THE FORM OF VAPOR, DEW, RAIN, OR SNOW

The presence of and amount of water on the track is a critical factor to consider. Because some fatty acids are liquid at normal temperature, they will dissolve easily in water from precipitation (dew, rain, etc.) and soak into the soil on a track.

In soft or snowy ground, the pressure of the track-layer's body weight can cause wells or depressions in the ground surface, creating a scent-filled reservoir from which scent does not readily escape. Dogs can easily work out such tracks.

HUMIDITY AND TEMPERATURE

Although a moist ground surface means a clear track, this doesn't fully explore the influence of water on a track. It is a well-known fact that a dog can work out an older track better on a humid or dewy morning or evening than on a warm afternoon. Temperature and humidity (also water) play an important role.

Fatty acids evaporate in the air. They evaporate faster when the air temperature is higher, a process that is similar to what happens to other fluids like water, alcohol, and ether. If an air current (wind) is blowing over the fatty acids, the evaporation works faster than when it's calm at the same temperature. With evaporation, the fatty acid molecules change into a gaseous state without

Figure 6.6 A dog more easily follows a track on moist ground than on dry soil.

Figure 6.7 If rain or snow fell before laying the track, this favors the dog's tracking.

chemical change (see "Air movement" above). Like other gasses, they diffuse through the air and spread over the available room. The higher the temperature, the more the scent will dilute and become more difficult to perceive.

If evaporation takes place in a small, closed room, the fatty acids will produce only as much gas as the air in that room can hold, until the available air is saturated by the odor molecules. At the saturation point, evaporation stops. If evaporation takes place outside during calm weather, the air layer directly above the surface is saturated first. Only then, by slow diffusion, will the odor vapor move to the next air layer above. The presence of the odor vapor directly above slows further evaporation. If the temperature rises, then the air is able to pick up more vapor until it is saturated.

Key Points about Fatty Acids in a Footprint

The following points apply to the fatty acids in a footprint:

- Evaporation spreads fatty acids, but does not change them chemically.
- The more humid the air, the slower the scents evaporate from a track. As a result, a footprint's scent is retained the longest at low temperatures and high humidity.
- The higher the temperature, the faster a track evaporates and the more odor vapor the air absorbs (to the point of saturation). The gas molecules spread through air and, because of their greater dilution, are more difficult to perceive.
- With calm weather, the evaporation of the track will slow because the air layer immediately above the footprint will be saturated with odor substances first. It acts as a kind of cap on further evaporation.

Because of the above two points, we can deduce the following:

- In warm, dry weather, the odor of the track will dissipate faster. Air currents in these conditions further speed up this process. The odor substances will be dispersed and become so diluted that they escape the dog's perception.

This point is valid for dry air, but the air always contains humidity (water vapor). Though air saturated with humidity will absorb exactly the same amount of fatty acid gasses as dry air at the same temperature, the more humidity the air contains, the slower it absorbs the fatty acids. So humid air *delays* the evaporation of a track's odor substances. If, however, the temperature rises, the humid air will absorb more odor faster. With that, we come to the following conclusion:

- The moister the air, the slower the odor of the track evaporates.

To conclude, the odor of the track will remain the longest under the following circumstances:

- Low temperature
- High humidity

In other words, a track is best preserved when the air is colder and more humid. But as always, nature has her limits. The air has only to cool down a little (say, 1 degree) and it suddenly cannot keep a part of the vapor, which falls on the ground as dew! Dew is not damaging to the track, but if the temperature falls even lower, then rain or snow falls, making tracking more difficult.

In addition to the conditions already mentioned, retaining the track also depends on *the temperature remaining the same as when the track was laid.* When we take this factor into account, we come to the next deduction:

- The dog's tracking can be expected to be the most successful when, at the time of track-laying, the soil is moist, and until tracking is begun, the air remains cold, calm, and (almost) saturated with vapor, and the temperature of the air and the ground stay the same.

Figure 6.8 A dog follows an old track better on a humid morning or evening than on a warm afternoon.

ODOR ROOMS

There is, however, still another point to add. With high air humidity, the soil also absorbs fluid (water) as dew. How can we explain the well-known fact that dogs track better on moist ground than on dry soil?

For an answer to that question we worked out this experiment: filter paper drenched with foot sweat (obtained by laying filter paper in shoes) was dried in the air. Dry, it gave off almost no scent perceptible to us. But by misting some water over the paper with a plant sprayer, we immediately perceived strong sweat scent. This experiment was repeated with the same result. For this phenomenon, we found the following explanation: when the sweat-drenched paper dried, the odorous substances on the surface evaporated. The filter paper, filled with sweat fluid, shrank as it dried and closed off the deeper-lying scent substances with a firm, almost scent-proof seal. In this way, scent was stored in small "rooms" in the paper.

However, when the paper was misted, then these "rooms" swelled open. The stored scent substances (fatty acids dissolved in water) were brought to the surface by the liquid and became a solution of fatty acids spread over the paper surface. As the scent solution spread, evaporation increased, and we perceived a strong scent.

If the paper, however, is heavily moistened with water, the scent decreases, because the scent solution becomes highly diluted and the liquid film becomes so thick that the deeper scent molecules can only slowly reach the surface and evaporate.

MOISTENING

With this experiment, we also found an answer to our last question. When somebody walks over dry soil, the ground absorbs the scent substances coming from the feet. The evaporation of the scent substances starts immediately, and scent substances that have penetrated the soil more deeply are protected from rapid evaporation by the dry surface.

If the soil is now moistened a bit, for instance, by dew, a solution of dew and scent substances is created and the scent increases as evaporation occurs. This evaporation allows the dog's nose to easily perceive these scents. In addition, the moist air layer above the track saturates only slowly with these scent substances, and in the morning and the evening less wind blows.

It's also worth mentioning that the dog's nose is better able to scan odors in moist weather because their olfactory mucous membrane remains moist.

Conclusions

A track laid in dry conditions will be clearest if it has a thin film of fluid (dew) deposited on it shortly before the dog works it out. This moisture breathes new life into scent substance in the soil, as does a slight warming of the ground and the air.

If the track is laid in moist or wet weather, the best circumstances for the dog to track are when (in calm conditions and vapor-saturated air) the temperature rises slightly shortly before working out the track. Through that the moisture will evaporate, together with the fatty acid molecules in the bottom air layer.

7

Weather Conditions

In tracking, weather factors such as temperature, relative humidity, and wind are very important. Wind disperses the odor, the sun's warmth increases it, rain reduces it, and snow limits the odor but does not erase it altogether. If you can correctly assess the weather influences, you can also correctly assess how weather will influence your dog's tracking.

Human assessments of weather are often based on snap judgments about temperature and wind conditions as *we* perceive them. However, when you experience the temperature as 68°F (20°C), your dog's nose, just above the ground, may be in temperatures over 108°F (40°C)!

In this chapter, we cover many of the ways factors such as wind, snow, rain, and humidity can affect tracking conditions. In the remaining chapters of this book, we note many instances where you will be able to put this background knowledge to work in training or operations.

Wind Influences on the Track

To begin tracking exercises with a dog, most handlers start on calm days, if possible, especially when training first tracks and turns. Only later in training is it time to familiarize the dog with the treacherous wind and teach him to track taking the wind force and direction into consideration.

The wind can blow the odor of the track over large distances. Menzel and Menzel write that, on a 1.2 mile (2 km) U-track, an east wind with a force of 3.8 could blow the odor of the left track over 430 yards (400 m) onto the beginning of the right track.[1]

Wind-blown odors may cause a dog to overshoot turns in the track and miss articles. The dog has to learn not to be tempted by wind-blown odors; otherwise, he can easily be led astray by the deceptive and often changing wind.

Handlers must not imagine a wind-blown track as a straight line, as is often suggested in drawings. The changing wind and the lay of the land may cause the odor to be blown in a wavy pattern, creating an undulating edge to the wind-blown odor. Some dogs prefer to search at the edge of wind-blown tracks at the border between "track-odor" and "no-odor."

WIND DIRECTION

Handlers mostly measure the wind roughly, with a wet finger put up in the air to feel what direction the wind is blowing from.

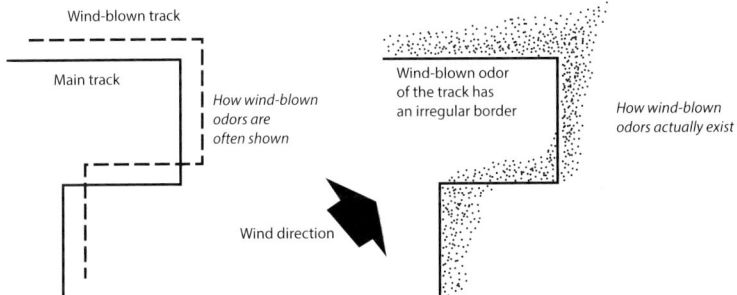

Figure 7.1 A wind-blown track should not be imagined as a straight line, as is usually indicated in drawings (left). The changing wind and contours of the ground may cause the odor to be blown in a wavy pattern (right).

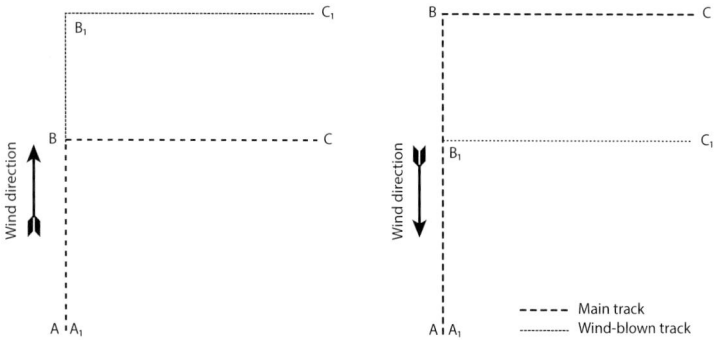

Figure 7.2 The influence of a tail wind (left) and a head wind (right) on a track with a turn to the right. The tail wind is generally thought to be an advantage, but the dog could overshoot the turn and lose his orientation.

This is a big mistake, as will be clear later in the chapter. Our rough measurement with a wet finger takes place at about 5 to 6.5 feet (1.5 to 2 m) high. But the area where our dog works is a lot lower. In general, the wind at our height blows harder than just above the ground because the ground surface inhibits the wind. A better method to pick up wind direction at the dog's level is to hold a thin plastic or paper strip at the dog's level to see what direction it moves.

Furthermore, the wind is redirected by ground formations and things growing beside the track, and by buildings or obstacles, behind which the air can be almost calm. Compare this with driving a car with a strong side wind. The car has to be corrected to stay on course, but when you pass alongside a building or a wood, there is a calm area and you have to again correct quickly. At the dog's level, this can happen on a smaller scale, with ground cover, grasses, shrubs, or depressions and ditches along the track.

Wind direction is the direction from which the wind is blowing — so a north wind moves from north to south. Wind speed may vary rapidly, with fluctuations in the order of seconds or minutes. Note that wind direction and speed change relative to the time of day. Just as tides have a daily rhythm, wind responds to the predictable, daily changes in solar radiation and temperature.

Changing wind conditions are mainly caused by obstacles that impede the flow of air, and these may be more numerous in one place than another. The surfaces of large bodies of water are fairly smooth, for example, so air flows freely over them, meeting few impediments. A grassy plain, however, has a much rougher surface than the lake it surrounds, jarring the flow of air over it. The plain has grasses and scattered single shrubs and trees, and wind must go over or around these — creating turbulence. The plain becomes a different landscape as it approaches the mountains. Here, there are dense clumps of shrubs and trees, and different sizes of vegetation (in height, width, and length) present in each copse. The airflow slows down among the groupings of trees and shrubs. The towns that dot the plain provide even more obstacles to obstruct airflow.

Wind almost always behaves erratically because of surface features: sometimes fluctuations are strong; sometimes they are weak. Vortices of different sizes give wind a whimsical character. The size of these swirls of air varies from a fraction of an inch to tens or even hundreds of yards. The speed with which the vortices move and rotate also varies. For the most part, vortices are caused by the wind encountering obstacles on the ground surface. The rougher the terrain, the greater and more volatile the vortices. Wind turbulence can also be encouraged by locally fluctuating temperatures. The greater the temperature differences over short distances, the more capricious the wind seems.

Wind at Earth's surface almost always fluctuates: the wind is gusty, but how gusty strongly depends on the nature of the terrain in combination with wind speed and the proximity of precipitation. Wind speed is measured in miles per hour and kilometers per hour, according to the Beaufort Scale, shown in Table 7.1. The table also provides descriptions of the effects of different strengths of wind.

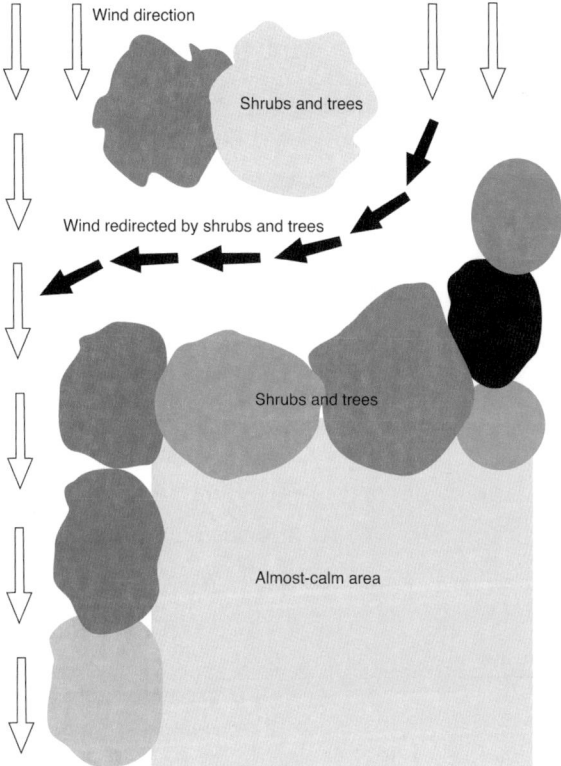

Figure 7.3 An aerial view of a hypothetical outdoor area. Air currents always follow the path of least resistance. Streets and roads, as well as natural features, channel the wind in different directions. Such air currents, of course, have a great deal of influence on the track.

WIND'S EFFECTS ON TEMPERATURE

The wind also influences the temperature near the ground. Wind mixes up the air near Earth's surface and can easily disperse the heat generated by solar radiation during the daytime. At night, when the ground surface cools down, the wind brings warm air to the surface, counteracting nocturnal cooling. If there is very little wind overnight, Earth's surface can cool considerably. This cooling process is exacerbated in an area with many obstacles that inhibit the wind.

Table 7.1. The Beaufort Wind-Force Scale*

BEAUFORT NUMBER	NAME	AVERAGE KM/H	AVERAGE MPH	CHARACTERISTICS
0	Calm	< 1	< 1	Smoke rises vertically
1	Light air	1–5	1–3	Direction of wind shown by smoke drift but not by wind vanes
2	Light breeze	6–11	4–7	Wind felt on face; leaves rustle; weather vane moved by wind
3	Gentle breeze	12–19	8–12	Leaves and small twigs in constant motion; wind extends light flags
4	Moderate breeze	20–28	13–18	Raises dust and loose paper; small branches are moved
5	Fresh breeze	29–38	19–24	Small trees in leaf begin to sway; crested wavelets form on water
6	Strong breeze	39–49	25–31	Large branches in motion; whistling heard in overhead wires; umbrellas used with difficulty
7	Near gale	50–61	32–38	Whole trees in motion; inconvenience felt when walking against the wind
8	Gale	62–74	39–46	Breaks twigs off trees; generally impedes movement when walking
9	Strong gale	75–88	47–54	Breaks branches off trees; slight structural damage occurs, such as roof tiles removed
10	Storm	89–102	55–63	Trees uprooted; considerable structural damage occurs
11	Violent storm	103–117	64–74	Extensive damage to woodlands and buildings
12	Hurricane	> 117	> 75	Almost nothing remains standing

* From National Weather Service, Beaufort Wind Scale.

Wind is a major factor in Earth's release of heat into the air. Air itself is a good insulator, so heat is not transferred if the air is not moving. But wind facilitates the transfer of heat (and moisture) from the soil into the atmosphere. The windier it is, the more effective the transfer of heat and moisture from Earth's surface into the atmosphere. During the day, when the sun warms Earth's surface, the wind carries heat off the surface, which means that the layers of air closest to Earth can heat up considerably. At the same time, the wind promotes evaporation, wicking moisture from the soil.

After sunset, the situation changes. Earth's surface cools by radiating heat upward, but the air above the surface remains warm. If the weather is clear and there is little wind, the temperature of Earth's surface drops quickly at night. In winter months in a cold climate, where the sun still warms Earth during the day (for a short period), the temperature of Earth's surface may be below freezing. But even during the winter, the air about 1 or 2 inches from the ground does not cool down quickly at night. The temperature at an altitude of 5 feet (1.5 m) or so is still up to 5°C warmer than the temperature just above the ground.

COASTAL WINDS

In coastal areas, the uneven heating of land and sea creates a local wind: during the day, a sea wind blows, but at night, a land wind blows. During the day, the air above land that has been warmed by the sun rises, creating an area of low pressure. The cooler air over the water, where there is higher pressure, then flows into the lower-pressure area over the land. This sea wind varies in strength, depending on temperature differences between land and sea. At night, especially when it is cold, the sea is relatively warm compared to the land, and the situation is reversed.

MOUNTAIN WINDS

Mountainous areas also have winds that follow this pattern: mountain and valley winds are local winds that occur as a result of changes in daily temperatures, and thus changes in pressure. The valley wind is a warm wind that blows uphill from the valley during the day. It arises because the air closest to the ground surface in the valley is heated more by the sun than the air layers above it. The warm air rises along the mountain slopes.

Mountain winds are the opposite of valley winds. A mountain wind is cold, and it blows downslope toward valleys during the

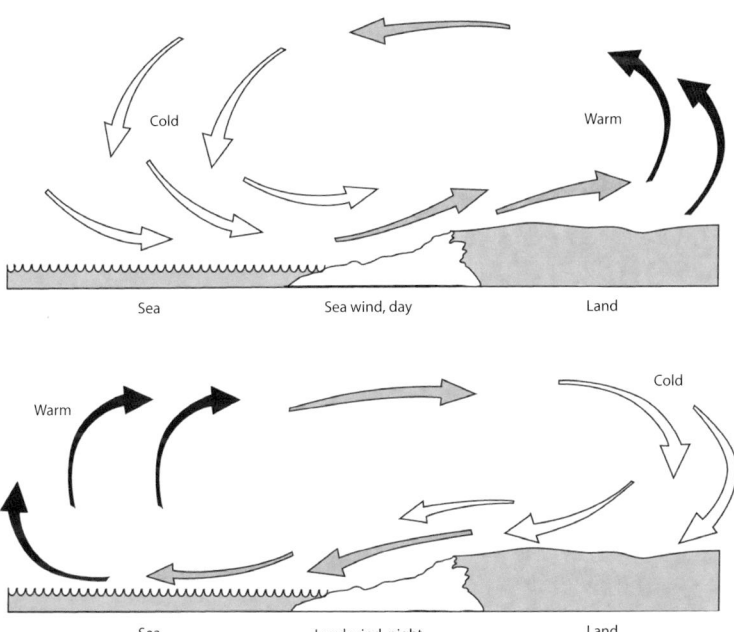

Figure 7.4 During the day in coastal areas, a sea wind
blows from water to land. At night, the direction of
the wind reverses.

evening, at night, and in the early morning. It generally occurs
on clear nights, when temperatures are lower. After sunset, the
air on mountain slopes cools quicker than the air at the same
height just above the valley floor because the air in the valley is
still warmer than that on the slopes. The colder air on the slopes is
denser than warm air in the valley bottom, so the air slides down
to the valley floor.

Mountain winds are often stronger late at night and early in
the morning: during the night, the air above the valley cools and
the temperature difference between the air in the valley and the air
in the valley exits increases. A relatively small area of high pressure
forms in the cold valley, and a small area of low pressure forms in
the valley exits. Air then flows from the high- to the low-pressure

areas — from the valley floor to the valley exits — resulting in an increase in wind.

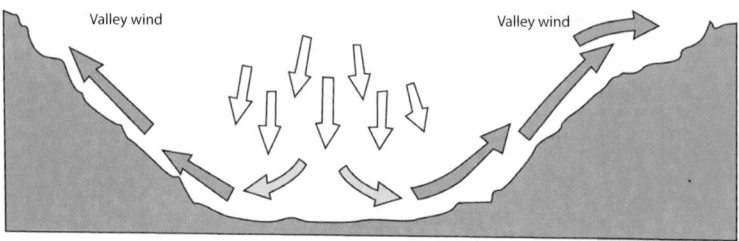

Valley wind created by heated slopes during the day

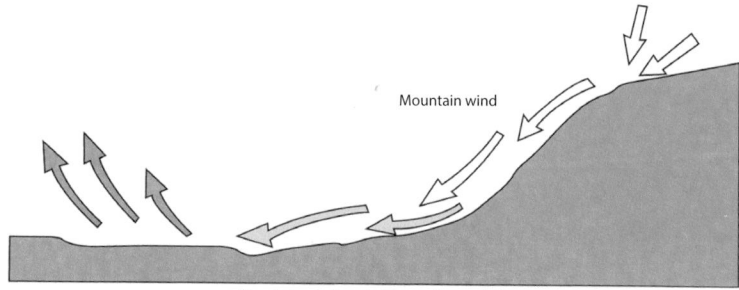

Mountain wind created by cooling at night

Figure 7.5 Mountain and valley breezes are local winds that occur as a result of daily fluctuations in temperature. When the valley floor warms during the day, warm air rises up along the mountain slopes, creating the valley breeze. In the evening, denser and colder air moves down the mountain sides and collects on the valley floor: a mountain breeze.

WIND AROUND BUILDINGS

Turbulence, where the wind constantly changes direction and strength, is partly a consequence of the wind moving at different heights and correspondingly different speeds above the ground. Right on Earth's surface, air does not move; as altitude increases, however, so does the wind's velocity because the influence of friction from Earth's surface is less and less the farther up the wind moves in the atmosphere. This is particularly true for air moving at roughly 33–67 feet (10–20 m) above the ground surface.

As a result of the above principle of air movement, an obstacle in the wind's path (a house or other building) affects the wind at altitudes higher than the top of the obstacle. When the wind blows against the front of the obstacle, a weir effect takes place. This can be seen in the winter when snow blows against the side of a house, for example — the wind causes snow to accumulate against the house. The house blocks the wind, so it is not as windy behind the house, but wind passing beside the house toward the back of it draws air away, forming swirls, so snow can accumulate in the area behind the house. The size of this area where snow can accumulate is about 15 times the height of the obstacle.

Have you ever walked or cycled through a street with apartments or other large buildings and just when you passed a large building, you felt a sudden gust of wind? It can be very windy at the base of large buildings. And if a storm is in progress, it can even be dangerous to cycle around large buildings. The wind always blows harder higher up from Earth's surface, and the closer to the Earth's surface a wind blows, the more it is inhibited by surface friction. Tall buildings contend with more wind than low buildings do. When the wind at high altitude blows against a high building, the building stops the air and forces it to gust in different directions, including down. This explains why it is often gusty at the base of tall buildings. The windiness around these buildings is even more intense if open areas such as parks or squares — places through which the wind can zip — are located adjacent to the buildings.

Breezes and strong wind gusts that play between neighboring high buildings are also strong. The air, after being redirected downward by the building, is then pressed through a kind of funnel between the buildings, and wind speeds pick up as more air is forced into that funnel. This translates into strong winds. Wind gusts moving through the narrow passages between tall buildings is called the Venturi effect. Keep this effect in mind if you need to follow a track around tall buildings, and consider the possibility of

wind-blown tracks. As well, consider the less dramatic up-winds
and down-winds, as described in the next section.

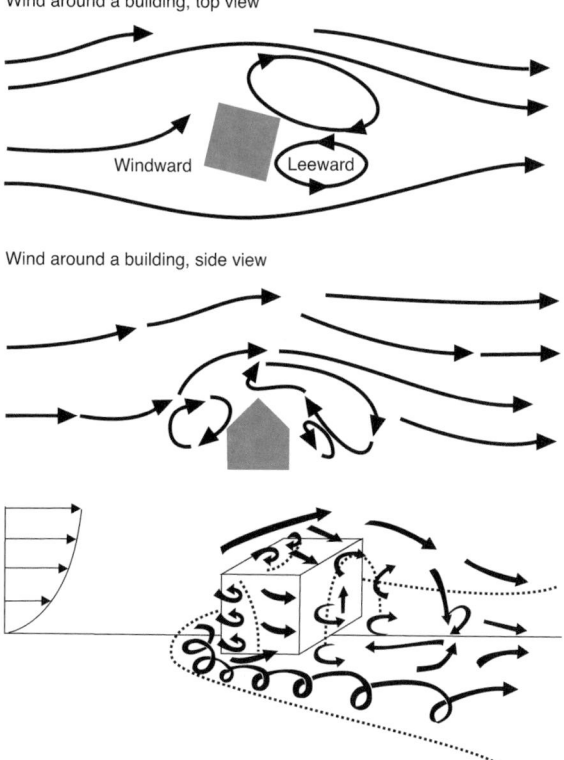

Figure 7.6 The movement of wind around buildings
complicates tracking in the area. The dotted lines
represent areas where turbulence is likely.

UP-WINDS AND DOWN-WINDS

At the same temperature, dry air is heavier than humid air because
water vapor molecules are lighter than oxygen. Therefore, dry air
sinks and humid air rises.

At the same humidity, cold air is heavier than warm air and,
therefore, cold air sinks and warm air rises. As a result, there are
upward and downward air currents.

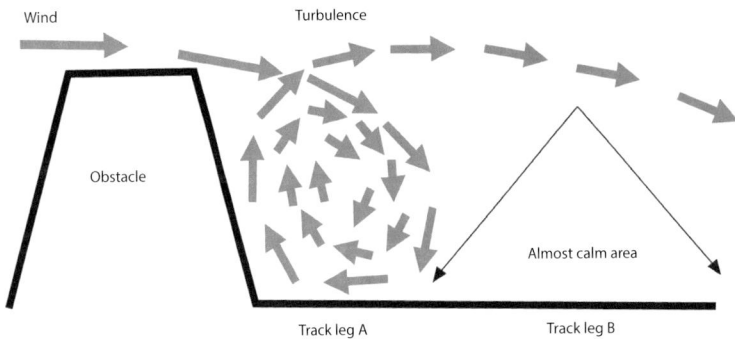

Figure 7.7 Wind speeds over 5 or 6 miles per hour (9 km/h) create turbulence behind obstacles such as walls and houses. Beyond the turbulence, there will be an almost calm area. Therefore, the conditions during track leg A are different than for track leg B.

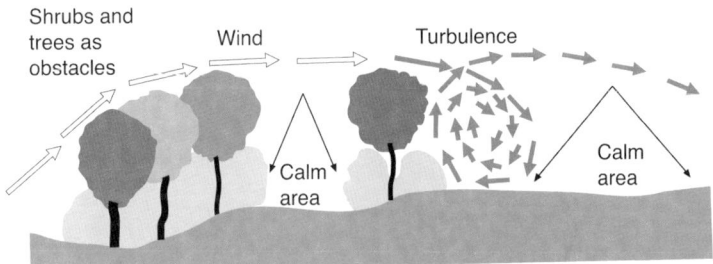

Figure 7.8 The first shrub forces the air up and over the second, beyond which turbulence occurs. Calm areas occur between the bushes and after the turbulence. Tracking conditions will vary in each area.

Sunshine heating Earth's surface will result in soil heating the air layer directly above it. Because warm air is lighter than cold air, this process leads to up-winds. When air cools, it becomes heavier, and that process causes down-winds.

If the temperature of a wall surface is higher than the temperature of the air surrounding it, an upward airflow (buoyancy effect) will result. If the wall's surface is colder than the air, a downward airflow results. So on the sunny side of a wall or a building, there

Figure 7.9 The wind is deflected by vegetation next to the track, but also by houses, buildings, or other obstacles. There can then be almost no wind behind buildings or bushes. Such sudden changes in circumstances around a track can sometimes cause problems for a dog.

is an up-wind, and on the backside of the same wall or building, in the shade, there is a down-wind. Remember to take these effects into account for tracks laid close to buildings or near walls.

Influence of Moisture on the Track

Some handlers greatly underrate the influence of wind, temperature, and humidity on the track, and on tracking generally. These circumstances change all the time. Humidity is highest early in the morning and early in the evening. High humidity influences both fatty acids and bacteria in the ground surface. See Chapter 6 for a discussion of these influences.

THE THREE CATEGORIES OF RELATIVE HUMIDITY

Dry	0%–30%
Normal	30%–60%
Moist	60%–100%

Relative humidity is the percentage of moisture in the air compared to the highest possible level of moisture in the air at any given temperature.

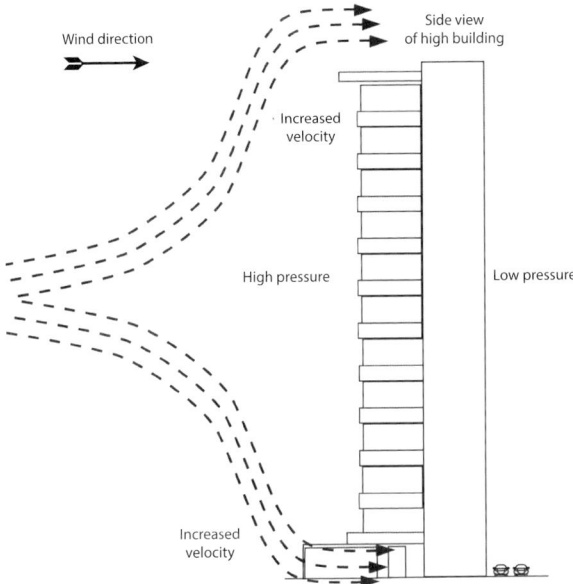

Figure 7.10 When the wind blows against a high building, here seen in side view, the airflow is impeded and forced to take different routes in many directions with increased velocity.

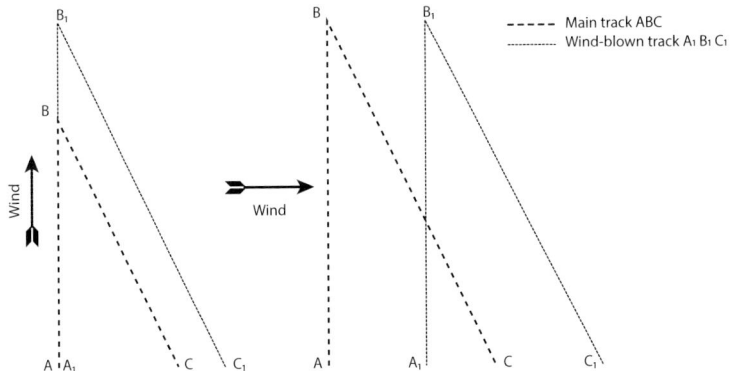

Figure 7.11 Wind influences on a track with an acute-angle turn. With a tailwind (left drawing) the dog works out the angle correctly. In all other wind directions (right drawing) the dog is almost compulsively tempted by the wind to cut the turn. Objects on or near the turn will almost certainly be missed.

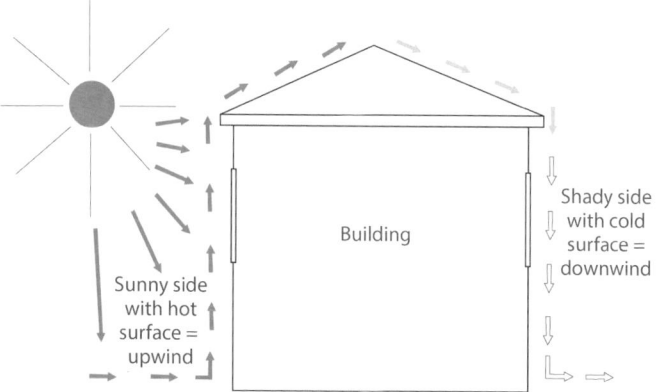

Figure 7.12 The effect of the sun on the outside walls of a building.

Humidity and air temperature have a significant effect on search strategy. Jinn et al. summarize these effects as observed in their study:

> As air conditions became cooler and more humid, dogs searched significantly closer to the experimental track. Dogs also modified their speed and head position according to their search location distance from the experimental track. When close to the track, dogs searched with their head up and ran quickly, but when their search took them farther from the track, they were more likely to search with their nose to the ground, moving more slowly.[2]

A low-humidity environment can influence your dog's nose. While searching under extremely dry conditions, the mucous membrane in the dog's nose gets dry sooner than usual, which will translate into poorer-than-normal search performance. If you and your dog are working out a track in very dry conditions, bring along a wet towel in a plastic bag that you can use to gently clean and moisten your dog's nose during the search.

RAIN AND SNOW

Another important consideration is rain, which prevents odor from rising. Water absorbs the odor of the track, so rain on the track can strongly dilute its odor. At the same time, the rain cools the ground surface, resulting in the air around the track becoming heavier and preventing the diluted odor from rising.

If rain or snow falls on the track, the odor substances are going to be diluted, washed away, or covered, leading to more difficult tracking conditions. However, if rain or snow falls before the track is laid, this is favorable to tracking. Moist ground helps spread the odors from the feet and footwear.

Odor can be frozen in ice and will keep; when the weather warms up and the thaw begins, the frozen odor emerges and becomes more noticeable, as described in a report of a major of the former East German (DDR) Volkspolizei (police force), who described conditions in which a dog worked out a track that was 6 days old and almost a mile (1,500 m) long:

> A woman missing since March 1st was found dead on March 5th in a stream between the towns of D. and H. Her jacket was about 30 meters from where the body was found in the stream. The corpse had probably been moved a result of the water current. Investigations had shown that the missing woman had attended a disco event in H. on March 1st, where she was last seen. It was necessary to clarify how the missing person got to the place of discovery. A tracking dog began work on March 6th.
>
> First of all, two odor preserves were made in the apartment of the deceased woman, which were used for a scent check for the tracking dog to find the track. The tracking dog started after a scent check at the place where the jacket was found. There he took up a track that led along the stream to a cobblestone street. Since this road is heavily used by pedestrians and cars, the dog had many difficulties working out the track, which were overcome by taking the scent from the odor preserve again. After about 50 meters along the road, the tracking dog turned sideways onto a cart road that led to a wooded area. On this cart road as well as in the forest, no fresh shoe marks were detectable.

After about 1,000 meters of forest, the dog ran to the village street and stopped at the entrance door of a restaurant. The tracking was ended at this point. With a high degree of probability, it could be assumed that the missing woman had taken this route.

It was now necessary to clarify whether it was actually the path of the missing woman. The following facts spoke in favor of this:

- The tracking dog picked up the track and ran to a point along the stream that was clearly identified as the point of entry for the missing woman.
- If the woman had used another route, she probably would have been seen by other citizens.
- The detectives present and the tracking dog handlers had no knowledge of the area. So "driving" or "helping" the tracking dog was therefore completely ruled out.
- No person authorized to be at the crime scene or any other person had previously used the route shown by the tracking dog.

Since it nevertheless appeared unlikely that the tracking dog could still smell a six-day-old track, the weather conditions between March 1st and March 6th were checked. Here it was found that these were extremely beneficial for the durability of the track odor.

It is known, for example, that frost preserves a track odor and the onset of thaw releases a track odor. An inquiry into weather conditions found that during this time the track was covered with a light snowfall 1 to 2 centimeters high. On the following days, there was mostly frost.

On March 5th, the weather changed, resulting in mild sea air. The daytime temperatures on March 6th rose to 3°C to 5°C.

It was fortunate that the thaw occurred at the same time the tracking dog started work. Although temperatures were positive for a few hours during the day between March 1st and 5th, the ground remained frozen. The track was therefore only odor-active for a few hours each day. The thin blanket of snow offered additional protection.[3]

The theory of the preservation of the track odor is not new and can also be confirmed by working with other service dogs. If, for example, odor preserves are frozen, they can be fully used at any time after thawing. Working out tracks is therefore possible under the circumstances described.

KEY POINTS ABOUT MOISTURE ON THE TRACK

When a track is laid in moistened grass (less so in sand or moistened soil), then the human scent and footwear component of the odor will be stronger, leading to a better chance of working out the track successfully.

When the track is moistened after it is laid, depending on the amount of rain, the track odor will be diluted and may be absorbed into the ground.

Snow retains and transfers individual human scent very well. Warmth occurs from the pressure of a footstep; some snow melts under the soles, and the melting water spreads out (as with tracks in moistened grass). Snow doesn't include plant or ground surface odor, but there may be a characteristic snow odor to contribute to the odor complex.

When a track passes over moistened, sticky soil (clay, loam, clumps on plowed land), the soles of footwear may acquire a layer that allows less odor to pass. The individual human scent on the track may then be weaker. As a result, clean-scent tracking may not go well, or will sometimes not succeed.

Influence of Temperature

Like humidity, temperature is also important to the work of the bacteria on the ground surface, which with warmth multiply to optimal numbers and perform their clearing work the best. When the first rays of sun warm the ground early in the morning, the slumbering, less-active bacteria start their activity. This activity decreases later in the day when it becomes hot, but in the evening their activity will increase because of the lower temperatures and the higher humidity.

Some compelling facts about temperature come to us via micrometeorology, the science that investigates the atmospheric influences directly above Earth's surface, especially temperatures in the first 5 feet (1.5 m) above the surface — the place where the tracking dog conducts his search work.

Table 7.2 shows how much the temperature varies at different heights above Earth's surface. It is vital that handlers understand this and remember that their dog works much closer to the ground surface than humans do. On a sunny day, dogs perform tracking work in temperatures between 86°F and 104°F (30°C and 40°C).

Table 7.2. **Air Temperatures Near Earth's Surface***

HEIGHT ABOVE EARTH'S SURFACE	TEMPERATURE DURING THE DAY	TEMPERATURE AFTER SUNSET
4 ft (1.2 m)	± 68°F (20°C)	Not recorded
12 in (30 cm)	80.6°F (27°C)	84.2°F (29°C)
1 in (2.5 cm)	93.2°F (34°C)	Not recorded
0 in (0 cm)	111.2°F (44°C)	55.4°F (13°C)

* From New York Academy of Sciences, "Marvels of Mini-Weather."

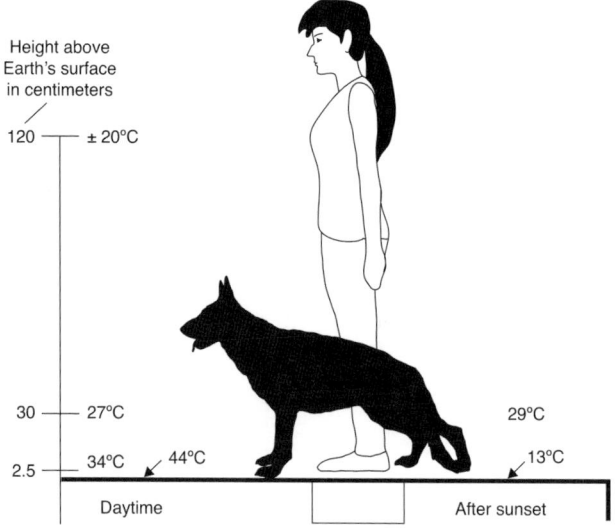

Figure 7.13 Air temperatures on Earth's surface.

The Sun's Influence

The solar radiation that reaches Earth's surface is partially absorbed by the surface terrain and converted into heat.[4] The extent of absorption depends on the nature of the terrain. Overgrown and dark areas, such as forests and asphalt, readily absorb radiation; white areas, such as snow and ice fields, bounce much of it back into the atmosphere. Of the radiation absorbed by the terrain, a small part slowly heats the deeper layers of soil. The rest of the absorbed radiation contributes to evaporation and heats the air just above Earth's surface. The most solar radiation reaches Earth around noon, when the sun is at its highest relative to the area receiving sunlight.

Air temperature has a daily routine, reaching its highest value (maximum) in the afternoon and the lowest (minimum) shortly after sunrise. Closer to Earth's surface, however, the influence of incoming and outgoing radiation is greater. The temperature close to the ground, therefore, has an exaggerated daily routine compared to that at 5 feet, especially in clear weather. In the afternoon, the air closer to the ground is warmer and at around sunrise colder than it is at 5 feet.

Also keep in mind that temperatures mentioned in weather reports and weather forecasts are not always representative of temperatures in urban areas. Especially in large cities, the difference between the weather forecast and the actual temperature can be significant. Stone and concrete buildings retain much of the sun's radiation during the day and only slowly cool down at night. In addition, people produce a lot of indoor heat in urban areas — by heating buildings, cooking, using computers, and so on — which may leak outside and delay the fall of air temperatures at night.

Trust the Dog

An accurate assessment of weather influences on the track is necessary to judge whether a dog is tracking correctly. We often think we know better than the dog does, and our assessments are

Figure 7.14 In cities, stone and concrete buildings retain much of the sun's radiation during the day and treacherous wind influences must be taken into account during a search.

usually based on the temperature and wind at our height. Knowing that a dog has to work out a track under much more difficult circumstances than many people think also makes the dog's work an even more impressive achievement.

Because of high temperatures during the daytime, warm air will rise from the track and bring up the odors of the track. That's why in such a situation the dog will not put his nose as close to the ground and will often amaze the handler by working out the track very well with a high nose. But what is more amazing is that many trainers (and judges!) actually insist that the dog, against his will, put his nose close to the ground surface, because they believe a dog only tracks correctly with a deep nose.

8

Equipment and Laying a Track

Buy good quality tracking equipment that fits well and that doesn't irritate you or your dog when you use them. As a minimum, you will need a tracking harness, a tracking leash, a tie-out stake, and a stake or flag to mark the start.

Tracking Harness

Starting with the first time you track with your dog, use a well-fitted tracking harness. The ritual of putting on the harness before tracking helps the dog know what is expected of him. Good tracking harnesses are made to cause a dog the least possible hindrance during tracking and yet allow the handler to keep a line on him.

A tracking harness is made of flexible leather or nylon and has a clip for the tracking line on the dog's back. The tracking harness must not be too tight; you should be able to put your flat hand between the body of the dog and the harness. If you have more than one dog, then we recommend having a separate harness for every dog, adjusted to the right size.

With young dogs, as with dogs with a gentle character, don't use a choke chain to teach them tracking. The chain collar is sometimes used in obedience exercises as a way to correct the dog.

Figure 8.1 A correctly fitting tracking harness gives the dog the necessary freedom of movement while tracking.

Figure 8.2 When using this type of tracking harness, the pressure caused by pulling is evenly distributed on the dog's chest.

However, by jerking the collar, even by accident, the tracking dog will think he is being punished. With tougher and highly agitated dogs, it sometimes may be necessary to have them track with a chain collar.

There are also tracking harnesses with a ring in front of the chest or the throat, as well as Böttger tracking harnesses with a groin line. These types of harnesses allow the handler to put more pressure on the dog. In these cases, the tracking line is attached at the chest and then pulled between the dog's legs to the handler walking behind the dog. These harnesses keep the dog's head — and nose — under pressure close to the ground, but they are definitely not our preference.

Figure 8.3 A Böttger tracking device with a groin strap, which can be used to coerce the dog. The tracking line is attached in front of the dog's chest and then passed between the dog's hind legs.

Tracking Leash

Use a long tracking leash with the harness, perhaps 33 feet (10 m) long. Tracking lines are made of various materials, such as nylon, cotton, and leather. Nylon tracking lines are lightweight but have the disadvantage that a dog's sudden jerk can pull the line through your hand and cause injuries. You can also buy wider synthetic belts, but they have almost the same disadvantage.

A cotton tracking cord is much better to hold, although it is a bit heavier. If it becomes wet and dirty, cotton lines become tough and inflexible.

A tracking leash of thin chromium leather is attractive and pliable. There are also tracking lines of thin, round leather, which also work very well. However, leather tracking lines are more expensive and require more maintenance. Tracking lines made from mountaineering rope are also pleasant to work with and less expensive than leather.

Figure 8.4 Tracking lines of thin round leather work very well, but need more maintenance.

Always take care that the tracking line is not too heavy, which can hinder the dog. Place a knot in your tracking line about 3 feet (1 m) before the end. When your dog walks away from the start and you play out the line through your hands, you'll know that the end of the line is 3 feet (1 m) after the knot.

Figure 8.5 If you have problems with a tracking leash that tangles, try wrapping it around a small wooden board. Tracking requires concentrated work, so the dog should not be hindered by things like a bad tracking harness or a tangled leash.

According to some examination regulations, tracking without a harness and tracking line is allowed. But in teaching your dog to track, it is better to use a pliable tracking leash and a correctly fitting tracking harness so you can better control him while teaching.

Tie-out Stake

A tie-out stake, which looks like a big corkscrew, can be useful where there is no place for you to tie your dog while you lay the track in the field. The stake has a ring to fasten the dog's leash to, which allows the dog to move around without becoming tangled.

As you are fastening the dog, don't pressure the dog with grim commands. Instead, start in a quiet way. The dog may sit, lie down, or stand on the tracking field, but he should always be calm, and

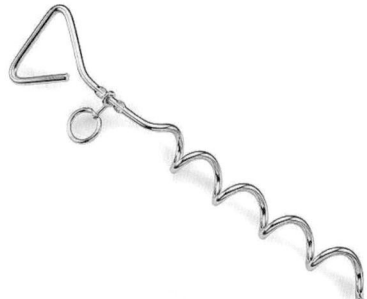

Figure 8.6 A tie-out stake can be useful while you lay the track in the field.

when you walk away from him to lay the track, he should not show frantic, excited behavior. If he does, return to the dog and calm him down by talking to him. You will need to teach your dog to stay alone for a while in later exercises.

Tracking Log

Make a drawing of every track you work out with your dog, and write a short report in a log. Keep notes on aspects such as the following:

- Weather conditions
- Terrain and name of the track-layer
- Wind direction with respect to the track
- Length of the track
- Details about time (e.g., how long the track took, time of day)
- Number of articles and the results of indicating
- The way the dog worked out the track

Such notes show you and your instructor details about your progress and any weak points that have to be trained for or changed.

It may seem a bit cumbersome to record all these details, but if you don't keep track, after some weeks you will not know what kind of mistakes you made earlier and what the causes were. If you keep a tracking log, you can also see if certain problems are occurring more often under certain circumstances (e.g., type of surface, track-layer, or weather influences like wind or rain).

Laying the Track

When laying a track, it is important to walk normally over the ground and not shuffle or kick down the ground. The human scent does not become stronger on the track because of kicking it in, as some trainers say. Instead, the kicking brings up more of the strong odor of the upper ground surface. In addition, shuffling causes more damage to the ground surface. By laying a track using normal steps and a normal pace, we prevent the addition of too much superfluous and disturbing ground odor intermixed with the human scent.

A dog is able to discriminate fresh tracks from older ones. This is logical, because otherwise the animal in nature might track away from his prey instead of toward it. Under normal conditions, a dog will walk from the older, weaker odor, to the newer, fresher odor. This gives the dog the ability to walk the track in the correct direction from the start of the track to the place where the track ends.

Figure 8.7 In tracking, a dog will naturally want to walk from the older, less strong odor to the newer, stronger odor. As a result, a track is always worked out in the correct direction.

However, this is not completely correct, because after laying the track, we continue to move: normally we walk back to the place where we can pick up the dog, and so the track continues from the official end of the track. The dog knows the track is done because he finds his toy, but in reality, the track would normally continue because the track-layer has to get back to the beginning.

After we finish laying a track, we normally walk on to the end of a terrain and walk back along the side, or we make a wide arc away from the track in order to return to the dog. We don't want wind to blow a confusing scent from the track we take back to the start. If you were to enter a car or hop on a bicycle, your natural track would ends and would be taken over by the artificial track of the tires.

TRACKS FOR A DOG NEW TO TRACKING

When a dog is first learning to track, try to make conditions as ideal as possible. For instance, the conditions of the terrain on which we track will affect how well the dog can work out the track. As an example, grass-covered terrain, a bit moistened by morning dew, keeps more odor than terrain with dry dirt or a sandy surface.

It is also very important that the tracking field is fresh and that there were no people or animals present shortly before. Short grass is also key. In long grass and in plowed fields, the dog can see the track, and it is not necessary for him to use his nose to follow the track.

Wind Considerations

In tracking we have to consider conditions like wind speed and wind direction. When it is calm, the track we lay will stay very still on the ground. The dog will walk exactly in the same place that the track-layer did. However, even when it is calm, the strength of the odor will decrease over time. The surrounding air will dissolve the odor of the track. How long a dog can work out a track after it was laid depends mostly on the weather conditions (humidity, temperature, wind).

But real calm is very rare, and so wind will move the track. Trainers then say that the track is "wind-blown." The odor will be blown from the track and will lie, depending on the direction of the wind, beside the original track. In such cases, the dog may not always walk on the main track, but may walk beside it and work out the track very well.

How long ago the track was laid also matters. With a light breeze, a track laid a short time before will not be blown very far. But a track laid a quarter of an hour before can already be blown away by a strong breeze. This is very important. An inexperienced handler may think their dog is not working well and possibly punish or correct him. But wind-blown tracks are very common.

The easiest track to follow is one where the wind is blowing toward the dog, so a track laid in head wind. The dog barely has to put his nose to the ground, because the odor is already blowing in his direction, especially the odor of articles on the track. Too often, training this way can cause the dog to search with a high nose and not track intensively with his nose close to the ground. The other way around, tracking with a tail wind, forces the dog to bring his nose closer to the ground.

The most advantageous weather conditions are those in which the early morning dew is disappearing and there is little or no wind. Strong squalls place the dog at a disadvantage for the track, especially on older tracks.

Laying the First Track

Begin training with a straight track. Choose a point in the far distance and walk towards it. That way you can, if necessary, find the track again. As a point of orientation, choose something that will be easy to identify later. Choosing a cow in the meadow nearby or a tree in a forest will, without doubt, cause problems with identification.

Landmarks such as a tower, a building, a tree standing alone, a fence, a sign, or another easily identified point are better choices. The points of orientation have to be at a distance and not on the track itself. To walk really straight, choose two points in line with each other. However, in determining the direction of the track, factors such as wind direction, the sort of terrain, presence of other tracks, and orders of the instructor should be your first considerations. Once you know which direction the track has to be laid, then choose an orientation point or points.

Figure 8.8 A point in the distance that can easily be recognized later, such as a chimney or a side of a building, should be chosen as an orientation point.

Keep your head up while laying the track and look at the orientation point as you walk. People who look at the ground as they lay the track will, without doubt, change direction and leave a track twisting all over the terrain. A wandering track will make it more difficult for the handler to assess how well the dog is tracking, and during an examination the judge may think that the dog is not secure on the track.

FINDING YOUR OWN TRACK

One of the first things we teach our tracking dog handler students is to find their own track. That is, if they had to lay a 300-pace track by themselves with two 90 degree turns and at least three articles on the track, after a half-hour break, we ask the handler to search for and work out the track again, finding the turns and articles with an accuracy of five steps.

Sometimes we let handlers function as "dogs" for each other, who then have to follow the instructions of the track-layer. At the start, the "dog" gets information about the handler's chosen points of orientation. The "dog" then walks in this direction with the end of a 33-foot (10 m) tracking leash in their hands. The handler follows behind the "dog" and gives only commands like "Stop: here is an article" or "Stop: now make a 90 degree turn to the left or right." All this must be done without tools such as GPS or sticks or iron pens to mark the track. This exercise teaches handlers how to remember their tracks. After all, how can you judge your dog's work correctly if you don't remember exactly where you laid the track and the articles?

Figure 8.9 A strange sight in the tracking field for outsiders: The "dog" — the person on the right — was commanded to turn to the right, and the instructor in the middle checks whether this corresponds to the orientation points previously specified by the handler.

The advantage of a good orientation point, especially in the building-up phase of tracking, is that it allows the handler to determine that the dog is on the right track. Without that certainty, a handler can't know whether they are assessing their dog correctly. In the building-up phase, a handler has to know exactly where the track is laid; otherwise, they may praise their dog while he walks far from the track, which is a big error. If it occurs more than once, the dog will begin to walk with his nose to the ground without really tracking. This is a problem we see all the time.

On the other hand, be careful not to correct the dog too quickly. Always take wind influences into account. Don't assume that we, with our poor sense of smell, know better than the dog does. It is important to have confidence in the good nose of the dog.

The Start

For teaching the dog to track, as well as in sports training and for examinations, we make a clear place where the track begins. To mark that place, you can use a stake, such as a colored dowel or a flag. The start is where the dog needs to pick up the odor of the track. The track-layer (in the beginning, normally the dog handler) should cover the ground surface at the start with their scent very intensively by staying beside the stake for about 1 minute.

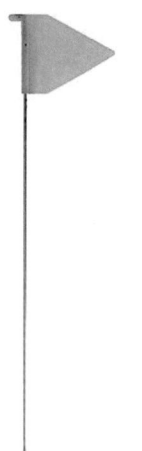

Figure 8.10 A tracking stake or flag at the start is used to mark the place the track begins.

Then walk forward about 16 feet (5 m) in a straight line in the direction you want the track. Take short steps so that they overlap, and keep your legs close to each other, so both footprints lie beside each other. Once you've covered the 16 feet, walk back over the track to the stake where you began. Stay for about another half a minute, and then begin to lay the track. First take short steps, and then begin to take more normal steps. With this method, there is a lot of scent at the start, which the dog can smell very clearly. The first 16 feet give the dog the opportunity he needs to pick up the scent of the track very well.

Some trainers say you need to give start a width of about 3 feet (1 m). In our opinion, this is not necessary, and in wind-blown conditions, it may make it more difficult for the dog to approach the track straight.

9

Dog and Handler Characters

Often we are asked how we train our dogs for clean-scent tracking (tracking on the individual human scent). For many handlers, this clean-scent tracking is a completely unknown area. However, to train good tracking dogs, both in sports and for professional use, clean-scent tracking is absolutely essential, and there are many conditions necessary for its success. Two that are critical are the characters of the members of the team: handler and dog.

The Handler's Character

Aside from the characteristics of the dog, the behavior and the character of the handler are critical to success in tracking. Whether or not a dog with ability becomes a good tracker or just a moderate tracker depends on the mentality of the handler.

The handler should know how to teach basic obedience exercises using positive reinforcement techniques. Positive reinforcement teaches the dog tracking using rewards when he is doing well. Positive reinforcement means immediately responding to a desirable behavior to make the frequency of the behavior increase. Rewards can be food, a ball, praise, or play with the handler — whatever the dog finds most rewarding.

Being able to work with the clicker is also useful. The clicker can be used to teach the dog to focus on the articles. For this training, the handler starts teaching the dog to lie down with an article between his forelegs and then rewards the dog with a click and food that we drop or place on the article. After lots of repetition, the handler can use the clicker on the track after the dog finds the articles and indicates. The handler can click and the dog will wait and stay focused on the article until the handler provides the reward.

It is the handler who has to mold the dog, and it is the handler who chooses the training methods that fit the dog. The chosen training method determines, to a great extent, whether the dog can learn to track independently or whether it waits every time for the handler's signals. The training method also determines whether a dog can learn to follow a human scent in the track even when it's covered by other odors.

Training clean-scent tracking dogs requires long, serious, and purposeful work. Handlers need a good knowledge of dog behavior in general and an even better understanding of their particular dog's emotional responses. Such training takes a lot of time, and people don't always want to invest that kind of time. Patience, creativity, and flexibility are also helpful qualities for handlers, as is the ability to handle stressful situations well.

Pressuring a dog will not result in success. Ever. A friendly understanding between handler and dog is an absolute necessity — the dog has to want to respond to the handler's wishes. Furthermore, the interest of the handler and the dog in each other must grow as far as the differences between them allow.

The Dog's Age

An important factor for success in clean-scent tracking is the age of the dog when he begins training. From the age of 8 weeks to about 7 months, pups and young dogs can learn without effort to

Figure 9.1 Searching and tracking requires close cooperation between human and dog. Neither can succeed alone, because the human lacks the sensitivity of the dog's nose and the dog lacks the human's interest in the things we usually want to train them to find.

use their nose. This is the ideal time to start tracking training. One drawback is that during this period, dogs lose their milk teeth, which makes them a bit sensitive (both physically and emotionally) for a few weeks. Then at the age of about 7 to 16 months, dogs go through their adolescence. That means they will have unstable periods with problems in concentration, so this is not an ideal time to teach a dog something new or to expect stability in learning. From about 16 months on, young adults and adults show steadier behavior, but patterns have already formed. Teaching new things will be more difficult now.

These stages are why you should start tracking with pups and young dogs. However, this doesn't mean you can't start training an older dog; just take the potential learning problems into account. This will prevent you from feeling disappointed, which can have a negative influence on teaching a dog to track. As teaching and training a clean-scent tracking dog takes time and effort, it is a good idea to be sure your dog has the characteristics you need to be a good student. Not every dog is capable of doing the finer tracking work.

Figure 9.2 Puppies and young dogs learn to use their nose in a playful way, as this Laekenois Belgian Shepherd puppy shows.

Figure 9.3 The puppy we choose for tracking training must always be from a good bloodline from dogs that have proven the necessary characteristics in searching and tracking.

CHARACTERISTICS NEEDED FOR A SEARCH OR TRACKING DOG

From a future search or tracking dog, we require 10 basic characteristics:
1. Willingness to work
2. Practical intelligence
3. Adaptive intelligence
4. Search drive
5. Tracking drive
6. Prey drive
7. Bring drive
8. Toughness
9. Obedience
10. Courage

1. Willingness to Work

The first thing a good tracking dog needs is a strong willingness to work. A couch potato (i.e., a dog you have to wake up before going to work) is not the right one to reach our goal. A dog that likes to work makes noise and shows a lot of interest when he sees that you're getting ready to go. The dog should show, both before and during work, an almost tireless willingness to work. He needs no encouragement to continue and concentrate on his work.

To have these characteristics, the dog must be in very good health, be in excellent condition, and have a great deal of stamina.

2. Practical Intelligence

Every dog has an instinctive intelligence, which means the skills and behavior determined by its heredity, such as the drive to acquire food and the hunting drive complex: every puppy runs after a moving object.

By practical intelligence, we mean the speed at which, and the degree to which, the dog conforms to the desires of the handler.

Roughly said, practical intelligence is how quickly and how correctly a dog learns the different exercises you teach.

3. Adaptive Intelligence

Adaptive intelligence can be divided into two abilities:

1. Learning proficiency: how fast the dog develops appropriate behavior in a new situation
2. Problem solving ability: the dog's skill in choosing the correct behavior to solve the problems he encounters

4. Search Drive

A well-developed search drive is needed for search dogs, such as detector dogs for drugs, explosives, cadavers, arson, and search and rescue. By search drive we mean the dog's natural interest in detecting an odor and then finding the source of the odor. For this he uses his nose with the support of his eyes and ears. In following the found odor, the dog uses air scenting, with a high nose, enthusiasm, and determination.

5. Tracking Drive

The tracking drive is expressed in the willingness of the dog to pick up a track, smelling the soil with his nose and striving to follow the track with enthusiasm and perseverance. When the tracking drive is decidedly present, then we speak of a passion for tracking.

TESTING FOR A DOG'S TRACKING DRIVE

The usual test of a dog's tracking drive is to have him work out an (interrupted) drag track (e.g., paunch or meat dragged over a track) or a track with bait, like slices of sausages, cheese, or dog biscuits. If the dog works out the track with a deep nose (close to the ground), the dog has tracking ability. However, merely showing an interest in a track of meat is not evidence that the dog can be trained as a tracking dog. It is nothing more than evidence that the dog likes meat, just as a failure to pick up that track may show nothing more than a lack of appetite at the moment. Nothing

Figure 9.4 Clean-scent tracking requires a dog with
a passion for tracking, like this shorthaired Dutch
Shepherd.

about the dog's interest in tracking a human is yet proven, because
that can be proven only by first working out his handler's track.

For this test, however, instead of having the dog search for the
handler, we recommend that the dog search for an article such as
a ball that the handler has hidden on the track. A very attached or
young dog can become so excited after the handler leaves his sight
that he will put his nose in the air and begin to search, which is not
a good approach for the tracking test.

6. Prey Drive

The prey drive is related to the hunting drive. Originally the prey
drive grew out of the attempt not only to hunt game, but also to
catch and kill it to satisfy both the dog's own hunger and that
of its young. This drive is also present in many dogs; however,
under influence of the play drive, it is usually focused on chasing
toys and other objects. The prey drive is generally expressed by
domesticated dogs by chasing, catching, and shaking such articles
to "death."

7. Bring Drive

In wolves, the forefathers of our dogs, the bring drive is expressed, under the influence of the pack drive, by the animal picking up prey or parts of it and bringing it to the lair, where the mother and cubs are waiting. The hunting, prey, tracking, search, and bring drives form a chain that takes care of securing food.

For our dogs, for whom the problem of food acquisition no longer exists, these drives can show up independently of each other. Then we see, for example, that the hunting drive can clearly be present without the prey, or that the bring drive has nothing to do with food. Given the lack of living prey, our dog's drive can be worked off by replacing prey with a toy, stick, ball, or, for greyhounds at a race track, a piece of rabbit skin.

RETRIEVING

Given the prey and bring drives and some focused training, dogs can be trained to pick up and bring such (replacement) prey, which is usually called *retrieving*. It is hopeless to start training a dog for fine search or tracking work if he has no bring drive. Great nose work requires a dog with an excellent bring drive.

Dogs that don't correctly retrieve can lose many points during an exam, so sometimes handlers choose to train their dog to indicate instead (to sit or lie down near the article upon a find). Many people find it easier to train indicating than to train retrieving, especially if the dog doesn't have a strong bring drive. However, commands like "Sit" and "Down" put pressure on the dog and aren't rewarding. Tracking dogs that have been trained to indicate usually show passive behavior upon a find instead of exuberance. They may seem depressed, which will certainly affect their tracking abilities later on. Putting this kind of pressure on a dog, even without realizing it, is the wrong approach.

On the other hand, a dog with a big interest in retrieving will track better and more intensively. The enormous advantage of

Figure 9.5 Dogs that are fond of retrieving get an instant reward when they find an article.

Figure 9.6 A dog taught to lie down close to the articles he has found will not display the level of happiness of a dog who is allowed to retrieve.

retrieving is that the dog immediately rewards himself for locating the article.

8. Toughness

A tracking dog must also be tough. By toughness we mean a dog that is barely affected by unpleasant prickles or events and can soon forget them. The opposite, a soft dog, is, for instance, a dog that once walked into barbed wire or a live wire fence and later creeps away whenever he gets close to a fence. A soft dog will quickly lose his tracking and bring drives and does not have the right character for professional tracking work.

9. Obedience

Without doubt, obedience is another characteristic we need for a tracking dog. The dog has to be happy to work with his handler and has to willingly and eagerly do what is asked of him. But the dog should be attentive without being dependent on his handler. He needs to stay independent to a certain degree, as he must often work on his own and has to solve problems himself while tracking.

10. Courage

Courage is the willingness of a dog to step into dangerous situations without pressure from outside. A frightened or timid dog will never become a trustworthy tracking dog, because changes in circumstances, such as guns firing, thunderstorms, traffic, or people who suddenly appear, will easily throw the dog off balance.

Puppies from Quality Stock

We require all the above characteristics to be present in a young dog chosen for training in clean-scent tracking. It's best to choose a puppy from parents who both have these traits, so the puppy is from a bloodline where these characteristics are deeply rooted.

What breed the handler chooses is of much less importance than that the dog be suited to the handler's character. In other words, select a dog that is able to please the handler. This is an important condition for successful cooperation in training and work. Nobody should be forced to work with a breed or dog they don't like.

The dog's bloodline cannot be disregarded in favor of beauty. In the past, only dogs that had proven to be qualified workers were used for breeding. Unfortunately, today it's more difficult to find good working dog bloodlines. However, the effort will always be rewarded, because you can only make a good start in training with puppies from quality stock.

10

Tracking Methods in Sports

Tracking as a sport is popular in many countries and with a wide variety of regulations. It is impossible to discuss all the different types of training programs for sport tracking, so in this chapter we will discuss four of the most common methods for training sport dogs to track:

1. Tracking with a toy (ball)
2. The drag track (meat)
3. The interrupted drag track
4. Tracking with bait (slices of sausage, cheese, or dog treats)

Common to all these tracks, the track-layer makes some turns and places a number of articles that the dog has to find.

1. Tracking with a Toy

Of the four methods discussed in this chapter, only this one could be considered clean-scent tracking. For this method, you need a toy the dog likes to play with, such as a tennis ball or an old leather glove. A tennis ball in a sock is also a good article to start with. This toy should be kept in your pocket for at least half an hour to adequately absorb your scent.

In the beginning, only track with a tail wind. Make the start of the track as described in the previous chapter. The first track you lay for the dog should be a straight track about 50 paces long, in a dewy, short-grass meadow (in the morning) with his toy at the end. Lay the toy directly on the track, hidden from the dog behind a bit of taller grass. After that, walk a few paces forward, and then with a wide circle far to the side of your track, return to your dog.

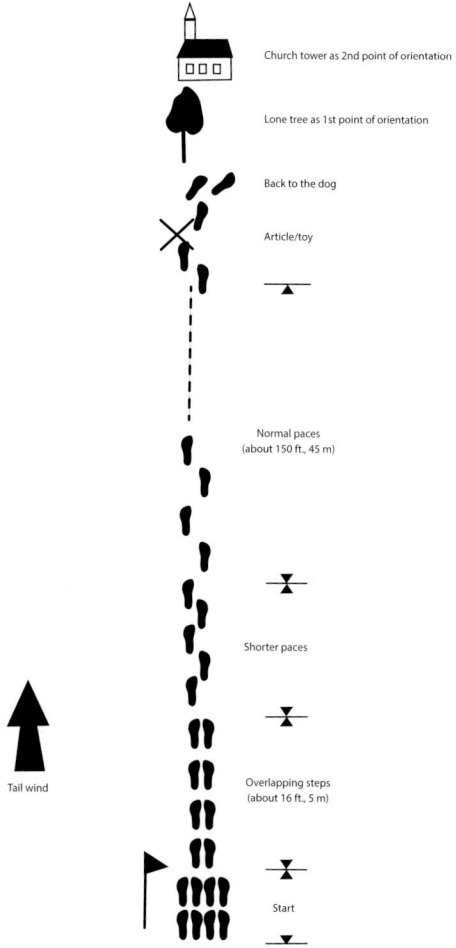

Figure 10.1 The first track with a toy.

If there are more tracks in the meadow, then walk to the end of the meadow and return to your dog via the terrain edges. By doing that you prevent walking diagonally through other tracks.

When you get back to your dog, praise him because he has been quietly waiting all this time, but don't make him restless by praising him too much. If your dog was restlessly jumping or straining at his leash, don't punish him, but pet him to calm him down. Restless dogs are not able to track correctly. If your dog is agitated, you may have to wait a bit before beginning to track.

Once your dog is quiet, take him with you up to a few yards before the start of the track. There put your dog into his tracking harness in a quiet way, and fasten his leash to the ring of the harness. It's best to begin training with his normal leash — later you can change to a long tracking line. As soon as your dog puts his nose to the ground to sniff at the start, tell him he is a "Good boy." Praising and rewarding good behavior is of utmost importance for learning to track. If your dog is obstinate, never punish or speak harshly to him, but try to encourage him to do what you are asking, just asking and not commanding. In a friendly tone, quietly say "Seek" in a drawn-out way without pressure in your tone.

At the same time, stand beside your dog, place your hand in front of his eyes, and make a movement toward the ground, pausing a moment above the start. With "Seek" you encourage your dog to follow your hand. Also make sniffing noises with your own nose. If he brings his nose to the ground, then he is a "Good boy." If he isn't doing that, encourage him once again with the movement of your hand and the friendly spoken "Seek." Slowly walk forward, bending beside your dog, stimulating him to use his nose. Don't touch your dog or the track with your hands, but walk on quietly and encourage him. Don't become impatient if your dog is not reacting and don't pull the leash. If he wants to bring up his nose, direct him quietly back onto the track again, repeating the encouragement "Seek" with your hand movement.

Figure 10.2 What you ultimately want is to get your dog with "Seek" and "Good boy" tracking with his nose to the ground.

As you approach the article, become quieter, without placing pressure on your dog. If he clearly smells, or sees, the toy, then let him move on, but don't let him loose. Follow him with the leash in your hand at a faster pace. If he locates the toy, then it is celebration time. Praise him exuberantly for locating the toy that maybe he retrieves to you. Sniff at the toy yourself clearly and audibly when you take it from him, as though to verify his "treasure" when you take it from him. As a reward, let him retrieve the toy again.

After that, release his leash from the tracking harness and fasten it to the collar. The dog will learn that tracking is over now. Don't immediately lay more tracks, but go off the tracking field to take care of your dog: letting him drink, relieve himself, and play a bit off the tracking field. Don't forget to take your starting and tie-out stakes when you're ready to leave.

THE BUILDING-UP PHASE

To begin with, only work on a straight track. If this is going well, increase the length of the track. In the beginning, you can track once every two days with your dog. Always make it interesting for him and, later on, take care to change the circumstances of the track.

Motivate your dog to use his nose by praising him and sniffing yourself. When your dog is using his nose more readily, it is no longer necessary to move your hand before his eyes to pick up the track. It is now important to get your dog to work with the word "Seek" and praise (e.g., "Good boy") so that he automatically puts his nose close to the ground to follow the track and to locate the toy he loves. Use "Seek" to encourage your dog to track and "Good boy" to praise him when he is using his nose well.

If your dog is tracking well, then you shouldn't say anything more; let him concentrate on his work. Sometimes a single "Good boy" can be used as he is locating his toy. Your dog has to learn to track with concentration, and you should not distract him. During tracking, walk behind your dog.

When your dog is succeeding regularly, you can exchange the short leash for a 32 foot (10 m) long tracking line. First use only 10 feet (3 m) of it and follow him quietly at that distance. If he stays correctly on the track, then you can slowly let the line slip to the full length. But be careful, with a 32 foot line, the dog could get far away from the track.

If this happens, then correct him with a calm "No" and immediately after that "Seek." If he comes back on the right track, then he is a "Good boy" again. Never jerk the line to keep him on the track, because the dog has to learn to track of his own volition and not in reaction to jerking and pulling on the line.

This is the difficulty in tracking. The dog has to work on his own, without influence from the handler. Tracking has to be built up slowly, so frequently remind yourself what your goal is: teaching the dog to use his nose to follow the track and locate the article or toy, and soundly work out the track all by himself.

If your dog is tracking very well, you can raise the time limit of the track slowly from 5 to 20 minutes or longer. The same is true with respect to the length of the track. Begin with 165 feet (50 m), and then raise it up slowly to a 650 or 950 foot (200 or 300 m) long straight track. Then you can also increase the complexity of the track with a second article. After laying out the first article, stand still for a moment to leave a bit more scent on that spot. That helps your dog start again after finding the first article. The second article, his toy, is then laid at the end of the track.

With the dog correctly tracking with a nose deep in the ground, you also can lay out a track in a side wind. Now and then, even tracking in a head wind won't be a problem, but don't start with that.

THE ARTICLES

Don't pressure your dog to retrieve if he stays at the located article, either standing, sitting, or lying down on his own. Drop the line, go to the dog, and praise him with enthusiasm. Don't use pressure to get him down if he is standing at the article. That can be corrected later when the dog is tracking well.

Some handlers think that a dog who retrieves will not, later on, indicate the articles by lying down. That is not true. By retrieving in the beginning, the dog will become more motivated to track for the articles. As soon as he tracks correctly, we can train him on the obedience terrain to go into the Down position quickly on command. In the beginning, we may need a bit of pressure and a serious command. However, as soon as the dog understands what we want, the command can be given in a soft tone. If you praise him enthusiastically when he immediate lies down, later on he will go down quickly on a whispered command. Then you can begin to add it to his tracking when he indicates an article.

If your dog wants to pick up the article when he lies down, you can use articles made of less pleasant materials, like metal. When he no longer wants to pick up the article, you can go back to the usual articles on the track.

THE TURNS

As soon as a dog can work out a long, straight track without deviation from it, we can offer him his first turn. Make the start as you did with the straight track. The first leg should be at least 50 paces

Figure 10.3 Articles as used in sports tracking (pieces rubber, carpeting, and wood). The articles should always be kept in the pocket of the track-layer for at least half an hour in order to absorb the track-layer's scent.

Figure 10.4 The handler is raising his arm, article in hand, to show the judge at an exam that his dog has found the article.

long, and you shouldn't place an article on the first leg. Near the spot where you want the turn, walk with shorter paces and make a square, 90 degree turn to the left or to the right into the head wind and begin to walk the second leg. Lay the article down after about 40 to 50 paces, at the end of the track.

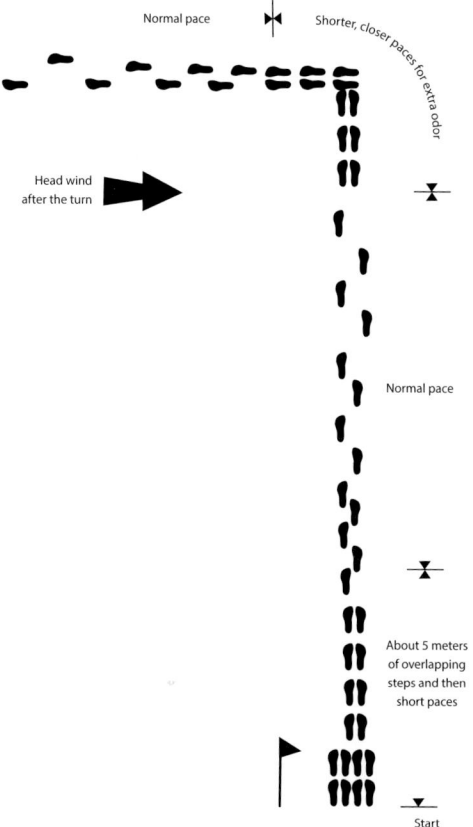

Figure 10.5 The first track with a turn.

Then get your dog, start the track, and walk quietly behind him on a 16 foot (5 m) long leash. As soon as he passes by the turn, he won't find the odor on the ground. As soon as you see this, stand still. Don't say anything, and let the dog work it out on his own. Eventually give him a bit more line, but don't push the line to send him in a certain direction. Stand still, and wait as long as the dog searches for the follow up of the track.

If he puts his nose in the air, then encourage him with "Seek." Your dog may circle in his search for the odor of the track. But never call your dog back to you or work him with the line. Let him search carefully; eventually, encourage him with "Good boy." It will take a while sometimes, but he will locate the second leg of the track and you will be rewarded for your patience. Praise your dog in a quiet tone and let him continue tracking in his search for the article.

The influence of the wind is often a great help for the dog in quickly finding the second leg, because in these first sessions you should lay the second leg into a head wind. If your dog hesitates on the turn, then he will catch the odor of the sideways track or the odor of the article. At the turn, walk as fast as possible behind your dog and eventually cut the bend, taking a shortcut across to the new direction the dog is moving. Then walk behind the dog on the track again.

Always lay the first turns with 90 degree angles. A more gradual bend can divert the dog because he has to cope with a series of small shifts in wind direction. A dog working out a straight track very intensively will not have any problem with a straight turn. He has the odor deep in his nose when the track ends in the direction he is moving, and he will have a busy search for the continuation of the track.

Once your dog works out one turn very well, then more turns won't be a problem. But you aren't there yet. First you have to try one turn a few times, every time at a different distance from the start: once after 32 feet (10 m), then another time after 350 or 650 feet (100 or 200 m). Not only can you vary the location of the turn, but also the wind direction, the number of articles on the track, turns to the left and to the right, and so on. Use variations to prevent the dog from becoming used to a certain track pattern. If possible, try to get your dog used to tracks laid under fences and railings, and also tracks that change terrain, such as from a meadow into a plowed field.

Eventually you can begin making turns with a curve or bend. Gradual changes in direction pose greater challenge to the dog as he needs to constantly adjust direction to keep to the track.

Figure 10.6 If possible, try to get your dog used to tracks laid under fences and railings and tracks that move from one type of terrain to another.

If at any time the dog is not working well, then go back to making a straight track with ideal conditions. It's okay to take a step back in training now and then. Good support and build-up are the most important things, and patience is essential.

2. The Drag Track

A drag track uses meat odor on a track to catch the dog's attention. Normally a drag track is laid with a piece of meat tied to a rope or line, or with a net or a nylon stocking with meat in it. With older dogs, their daily food portion will normally be rationed a few days before.

Many trainers begin by standing on the meat for several moments, ensuring the start has a strong meat odor. Then they drag the meat over the ground behind them as they lay the track. Sometimes track-layers push the meat forward with one foot, which creates a stronger meat odor on the track than dragging it because of pressure from the foot. The track should be laid with the wind at the trainer's back to prevent the dog searching with a high nose. A few pieces of meat are laid at the end of the track.

The working out of the track happens the same way as tracking with the toy, as described in the last section, except the dog is allowed to eat the meat at the end of the track as a reward.

Initially, this track should be no longer than about 32 feet (10 m). Depending on the interest of the dog, the team can work out about four to eight short tracks per day. As soon as the dog shows that he is able to work out these tracks correctly, he will get fewer, but longer tracks. The track will gradually be made longer until he can work out a 330 foot (100 m) track without problems. Then add turns on the track. Articles are laid on the track only when the dog shows that he is able to work out tracks with turns correctly.

3. The Interrupted Drag Track

Another common method, often used as a link from drag tracking to tracking without meat, is the interrupted drag track. For this method, use a piece of meat packed in a net or nylon stocking to drag with a rope or leash over the ground.

Begin with a straight track with a tail wind. At the start, stand on the meat for several seconds and then drag it the first few feet over the ground. After that, touch the meat to the ground every second step, then after some yards at every fourth step, until the end of the track, where you lay the pieces of meat as a reward.

At turns in the track, the first few times keep the meat on the ground and drag it around the turn. Later on, mark the turn by dragging the meat only briefly.

As soon as the dog works out this track very well, reduce how much the meat is dragged on the track. Then the meat is only

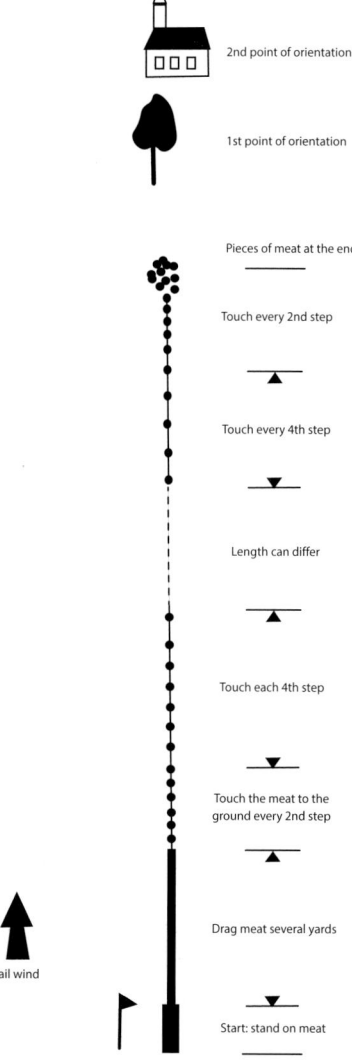

2nd point of orientation

1st point of orientation

Pieces of meat at the end

Touch every 2nd step

Touch every 4th step

Length can differ

Touch each 4th step

Touch the meat to the ground every 2nd step

Drag meat several yards

Tail wind

Start: stand on meat

Figure 10.7 The first interrupted drag track.

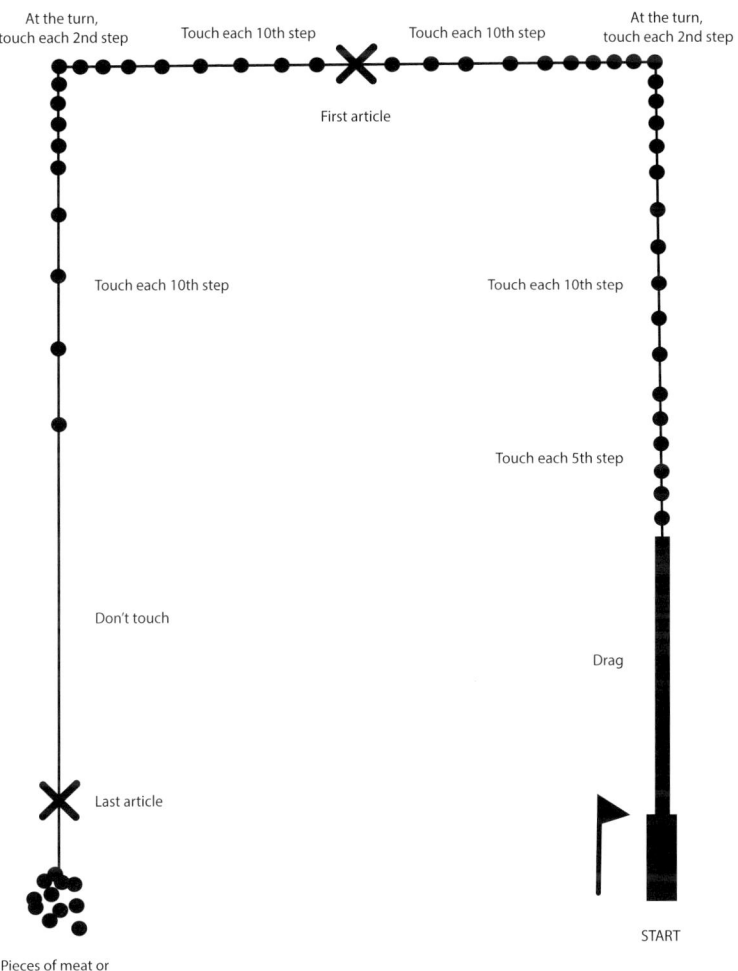

Figure 10.8 An interrupted drag track with turns and articles. The food should be about 16 feet (5 m) past the article at the end of the track.

touched to the ground with each fifth step, and later only with every tenth step, and so on.

As with the drag track, the interrupted drag track has no articles on the track in the beginning. They first appear when the dog shows that he can work out the basic track correctly.

4. Tracking with Bait

With this method, slices of sausage, pieces of meat or cheese, dog treats, or dog food are used to encourage the dog along the track. It is often recommended that you ration the dog's daily portion of food for a few days before, so that he is hungry enough to be interested in the bait. The first track is straight with a tail wind, to prevent the dog from searching with a high nose.

At the start, lay some pieces of the bait you will be using. To entice the dog in the right direction, a piece of food will be laid down every 8–12 inches (20–30 cm).

Once the dog is searching well, increase the spacing to about 15 inches, 20 inches, then at last about a yard (40 cm, 50 cm, 1 m). A bit of extra bait is also laid at the turns the first few times and sometimes laid right around the turn. Articles are placed on the track after the dog shows that he uses his nose correctly.

In another method, in the beginning bait is placed in every footstep. Trainers using this method say this very close association between food and the track-layer's footsteps will lead to footstep tracking.

Asking for Trouble

According to many trainers, especially those in sports tracking, using meat or other food to train tracking dogs should work for every dog. They argue that these methods easily get the dog to track deeply because they employ the dog's natural drive to find food. They explain a lack of success by saying the dog is not hungry enough.

In our opinion, such methods are, as they say, asking for trouble. As we explain in the next chapter, these methods are not always as successful as is hoped and instead create a distracting hunger in the dog. Perhaps the mistakes due to the use of meat or food on the track are not that bad in sports tracking — at the most this might

Figure 10.9 Praise and rewards are very important in teaching a dog to track.

cause the dog to fail an exam or to lose a title at a competition. But for professional tracking, these are significant mistakes that absolutely must be avoided. Clean-scent tracking is incompatible with food on the track, as will become clear in the next chapter.

11

Avoiding Trouble

At many dog trials, including international ones, it's a common sentiment that the final score depends on the results of the tracking phase: "The trial will be decided on the tracking field." Generally that's right, because many dogs will score "Excellent" one time and "Insufficient" another time in the tracking phase. However, when we hear, "It just wasn't the dog's day today" as the excuse for a poor showing, we absolutely disagree. Most failures in competition are preventable failures in training. In this chapter, we discuss some of the most common training issues that lead to operational issues. All can be avoided.

The Problem of Using Food on the Track

As we saw in Chapter 5, a track has two main odor components:
1. The strong odor of the ground surface damage
2. The less intensive human scent

Together these form the odor complex of the track that the dog has to work out. Dogs are easily able to smell the different odor substances of that complex.[1] Well-trained dogs are able to recognize the human scent component of the track, even if the odor of the ground surface damage is much stronger.[2]

Figure 11.1 At trials, the final score depends heavily on the results on the tracking field.

However, trouble begins when food is also laid on the track. It doesn't matter if this is an interrupted drag track or if there are pieces of meat, cheese, or dog food. After all, the odor of food is without a doubt much more intense than those of the ground surface damage or the human scent. By adding food, you change the intensity of the odor complex of the track into searching for the following:

1. The odor of the food
2. The damage to the ground surface
3. The individual human scent

The food's odor prickle on the track is a serious distraction for the dog. In the first place, the tracking dog will be focused on the dominant odor of the food, and with an interrupted drag track, he will also focus a bit later on the damage to the ground surface. But with these training methods, the dog doesn't learn to pick up the much weaker human scent in the track's odor complex. And now consider this:

- As a result of not noticing the individual human scent on the track, the dog will without hesitation move over to cross-tracks, game tracks, and artificial tracks (e.g., the tracks of tractor tires in the meadow).

• The connection between the odor of the track (the odor of food and the damaged ground surface) and the articles on the track (with the scent of the track-layer) is missing. The articles make no sense to the dog, and because of that he will likely walk over them.

Here then, you see two frequent causes for dogs "just not having their day today." If they were trained using food on the track, the handler has not clearly communicated what the dog is supposed to find.

We know the dog has the ability to perceive and distinguish individual human scent. As we explained in Chapter 6, human skin secretions contain variable amounts of different odor substances; these odors are caused by fatty acids. The relative proportion of these fatty acids differs from human to human, and sometimes one person lacks a fatty acid that is present in the sweat of someone else. Dogs can discover these differences immediately, and so they know which track they have to work out, for instance, in the case of cross-tracks.

Dogs are also well able to recognize odors that are covered with another odor. A dog can even recognize an article briefly held in the hand of someone he knows, even when that article before or after that is covered with a strong, strange odor. By the same token, dogs often have to track in situations where the odors change, as when a track moves from a meadow onto a plowed field. Even when the elements surrounding a track smell about a thousand times stronger than the foot scent of the track-layer, the dog is quite able to work out the original track.

In changing from one type of terrain to another, the odors of the first terrain are carried, at least in the first few steps, by the shoes (or boots) onto the next terrain, which will make the change easier. But the dog still has to adjust to a new mix of odors. This will be easier to do when the tracking dog is trained to search for the human scent in the track and recognize the other odors as *additions* to the key scent, but not the key scent itself.

The dog's ability to follow an individual scent in the track seems to contradict the experiments of K. Most and G. H. Brückner, which were discussed in Chapter 1.[3] Their tests employed a tracking wheel with porcelain and wooden shoes. Using this wheel, a track laid by a person was extended with an artificial track that didn't contain human scent. The tested dogs followed, without hesitation, the artificial track and so proved that they were following the odors of plants and ground surface damage.

Figure 11.2 If a dog follows the odor of ground and plant disturbance, how does a dog follow a track laid by someone in rubber boots on a paved road?

However, what likely happened with these tests was that the dogs got the human scent on the first part of the track. When it disappeared, they followed the "additions," expecting to meet the human scent again later on. After all, a dog will always work out a track from older to more recent odors to reach his prey.[4]

In nature, for instance on a game track, the individual odor of the game disappears under the perception threshold of the dog for a certain time (due to soil changes, weather, wind, etc.). But a dog that knows he tracks in the right direction will still follow that track, because he knows that the individual odor will be stronger again as he gets closer to the game at the end of the track.

Figure 11.3 On a game track, the odor of the game may fall under the perception threshold of the dog for a certain time, yet the dog will continue to follow the track. How is this explained?

However, it is also possible that the dog's observations were focused, by faulty training, only on the damage to the ground surface and the odors of plants. Focusing the perception of a dog on odors of plants or damage to the ground surface can happen, for instance, when a dog is taught to track with food used as a tempting (and distracting) odor. By distracting him from the human scent, we fail to communicate to the dog the key aspect of the track that we want him to follow.

Pressure

Another big problem in tracking training is when pressure is exerted on the dog. The following list ranks training methods in order of increasing pressure:

1. Clean-scent tracking (independent tracking)
2. The (interrupted) drag track

3. Bait in each footstep
4. Indicating the articles (command "Down")
5. Voice and/or line corrections
6. Forced-tracking with a special tracking harness (Böttger harness)
7. Forced-tracking with an electronic or a prick collar and/or a groin line

Figure 11.4 Training a dog to indicate during tracking puts pressure on him. When the dog is given the command "Down," it is usually pronounced with emphasis, and there are many somewhat unnatural requirements for the dog to follow. The goal is to have the dog lie down quickly and in a correct position (i.e., straight on the track and with the article between the front legs).

By using pressure in training the dog, we see the following types of results:

- Tracking or locating the articles becomes unpleasant for the dog (aversion).
- The dog's tracking drive (enthusiasm) decreases.
- Tracking becomes an obedience exercise.
- The dog's tracking condition decreases, which causes a decrease in the dog's mental and physical condition.
- The dog becomes extremely tired very quickly.
- The dog becomes highly nervous.

As a result of these problems, the dog will either refuse to track, or submissive dogs will pretend to track, nose to the ground without picking up odor. There are two key points to take away from this:

1. A dog that is trained using food and/or is taught tracking under pressure is not able to solve tracking problems on his own.
2. Such a dog can, if the track is laid exactly in the right pattern, and on familiar terrain, track "Excellent"; however, if he runs into a problem or a deviation from the normal tracking pattern, he will get the score "Insufficient."

Given these points, is it fair to say that a dog's lack of performance was because it "just wasn't his day today"?

Three Conditions for Optimal Tracking

Three interacting conditions greatly influence the achievements of the tracking dog, so you will want to ensure all are taken care of:

1. **Physical condition**: Well-trained muscles, optimal health, and a good diet all play a role in a dog's physical condition. When these are lacking, we see physical exhaustion after a brief exertion. With poor or insufficient feeding, hunger dominates the dog, which results in lack of concentration, intense nervousness, and insufficient energy to perform.
2. **Mental condition**: A dog with good mental conditioning will enthusiastically work out an exercise on his own, without any pressure or compulsion from the handler. When mental conditioning is lacking, we see apathy, stress, and physical tiredness.

3. **Tracking condition**: Tracking condition, achieved through regular training, is the ability to concentrate long enough to work out the track. When this is lacking, we see dogs that need a break after a short time because of concentration problems.

Figure 11.5 The physical, mental, and tracking condition of the dog affects his performance. Failing to look after any one of them can result in tracking failure.

Tracking Tempo

For a dog, tracking takes high concentration to retain the optimal tracking drive. Yet by nature some dogs are fast and some are slow. Slow dogs aren't necessarily tracking with more concentration, and fast dogs aren't necessarily tracking with less. Making a fast dog track very slowly creates pressure on him, with all the consequences described in the last section. Every dog has his own tempo of walking and moving. In trying to influence that, we often restrict the dog too much. With obedience training, we adapt our tempo to the ideal tempo of the dog for optimal results. So, why not with tracking?

There are four common tracking tempos. Following is an explanation of each and what it means.

1. Adapted to the circumstances
2. Highly uneven

3. Unnaturally slow
4. Extremely fast

1. ADAPTED TO THE CIRCUMSTANCES

When laying a track over a flat field, the track-layer walks about 2.5 miles per hour (4 km/h). The dog's speed of working out the track in simple conditions will be slightly higher, and in extremely difficult situations will be much lower. The tracking conditions can vary considerably and depend on many factors, such as the type of terrain, how old the track is, weather conditions, cross-tracks, and so on. Ideally the dog will work out a track only as quickly as will allow it to notice the slightest differences in odor. How well the dog adapts his tracking speed to the various circumstances can be seen as a good indicator of his training.

2. HIGHLY UNEVEN

We usually see a highly uneven tracking tempo in dogs with poor mental and physical conditioning. The first leg of a track will be done quickly, but the following legs will be done slower and slower. The longer the track, the slower the tempo becomes.

However, in other dogs we see at the beginning of the track a slow start, which a handler can improve with correct motivation, such as a well-timed "Good boy." After such motivation, and as the dog gains confidence in the odor of the track, these dogs may gradually increase their pace.

3. UNNATURALLY SLOW

Any unspoiled dog that is trained appropriately will be happy to track under all circumstances. The unnatural, slow, and hesitant working out of a track, despite the ample supply of odor on the track, is incorrect according to most examination regulations. The dogs present an image of uncertainty and nervousness. Dogs that track unnaturally slowly were likely taught to do so in order to avoid mistakes like walking over turns and articles. Dogs working under such strong psychological pressure may not be able to independently solve the problems they encounter on the track and may walk over turns and articles.

4. EXTREMELY FAST

In principle, the stronger the odor of the track, the easier the dog can follow it, which will therefore also increase his urge to move forward. However, the impetuous and unconcentrated search of a running dog and handler over the track is highly undesirable, as errors will inevitably result. For example, in addition to the restless, nervous search image such a team presents, they will more often get off the track, run over articles, and miss turns and then nervously circle to find them again. This form of tracking is

Figure 11.6 To encourage a dog to track more slowly, trainers sometimes put the tracking line under one of the front legs, or they use the Böttger tracking device or a groin strap. As a result, the dog is forced to limp and thus slow down. However, some handlers and instructors make it a habit and do this on all dogs. If they put the line under the hind legs, the tracking line can touch the sensitive parts of the dog. Not only is tracking with the line between the front legs pointless and distracting, but a line between the hind legs can also be painful.

energy draining because it involves many body movements, as well as mental excitement and constant restlessness. These demand an enormous amount of oxygen from the dog, which normal breathing cannot provide, so the dog may pant.

The widely used methods of the (interrupted) drag track and food on the track are aimed at quickly training dogs to become diligent trackers. These may be the easiest methods for the handler to learn, but for dogs with a sufficient track drive, who are pre-nervous in a state of hunger to track, they are also the methods that cause the most problems. Such dogs will nervously eat the first kibble at the start and then run to the end of the track as quickly as possible to eat the rest.

The fewer aids or motivation enhancers that are used in tracking training, the fewer unintended side effects you will need to get rid of later. Save yourself some future trouble.

Flawed Expectations

The biggest mistake made in many training methods is the expectation that the dog knows from the beginning what humans want. Some people assume that the dog will be instantly interested in any odor the handler wants him to be interested in and that he will concentrate automatically on that odor. They unconsciously think of it like an obedience exercise, that it is as simple as giving the dog the order to sit or to lie down. But the work of searching and tracking, unlike the simple command-response training required to get a dog to lie down, is the product of a longer, more systematic training that has to go in two directions at once:

1. The handler must bring the dog's attention and focus to sense impressions that the dog would never be interested by himself.
2. The second task is to train the dog to respond to key words, which can help bridge the gap between the handler's needs and the dog's understanding.

The training of clean-scent tracking dogs requires long, serious, and purposeful work. A good knowledge of dog behavior in general and an even better understanding of a chosen dog's emotional responses are required conditions for this job. Such training takes a lot of time, and in today's time-pressured world, people don't always want to invest that kind of time, so not everyone will reach their goal.

By using pressure, the achievements we just mentioned cannot be reached, ever. A truly friendly understanding between human and dog is an absolute necessity to succeed in clean-scent tracking. The dog has to *want* to respond to the wishes of his handler. Furthermore, the interest of the handler and the dog in each other must grow as far as the differences between them allow. Only in this way can human and dog achieve the close cooperation required for searching and tracking. Neither can succeed alone because the human lacks the sensitivity of the dog's nose and the dog lacks the human's interest!

Figure 11.7 The biggest mistake made in many general tracking methods is expecting the dog to know from the beginning what humans expect of him.

Serious Errors

A frequent and serious error we see in tracking training is if the dog is not required to search for a *specific* human scent and is instead allowed to retrieve items on which just any human scent is present. For instance, if a handler forgets their own dumbbell or ball, they may ask to use someone else's. Or they deliberately ask the dog to search for an article with someone else's odor on it. When we correct this practice, we sometimes get the response: "Yes, but my tracking dog has to search for every scent in the future." Doing things this way teaches dogs a retrieving automatism that can't easily be reversed. From this will come big problems in later tracking work.

Figure 11.8 Prevent retrieving automatism in (future) clean-scent tracking dogs. Train your dog to only retrieve articles with a certain scent and not everything that comes his way.

From the very beginning, we have to make it clear to the dog that he cannot bring whatever he likes, but only things with a certain scent. We start with the scent of the handler, and the dog must search for only this scent. Because of this well-known scent, the dog easily understands that he has to smell things before picking them up.

Some dogs naturally work clean-scent and will never pick up a dumbbell with a stranger's scent. However, if unwise handlers pressure them to do so, the dog accepts this and obeys by picking up the dumbbell. But by this they learn that for the handler, it doesn't matter what scent an article has. Of course, then the dog doesn't understand when, some months later, the handler's attitude changes, and he suddenly wants them to be interested in specific human scent.

We've often observed how seriously a clean-scent trained dog takes the concept of "scent" and makes choices instead of just retrieving; we share three experiences below. A study by Bräuer and Blasi from 2021 shows similar observations.[5]

The first incident involved a young female dog to whom "scent" meant the scent of the handler. One day on the training field, a box with new dumbbells was brought out, and without thinking, someone took one of them, waved it in the youngster's face, and then threw it for her. The dog, who was crazy about retrieving, chased as quickly as usual after the dumbbell, sniffed at it, and immediately kept searching for the article with her handler's scent. Fortunately, the handler saw what happened and corrected this error at once by dropping an article with his own scent, without the dog noticing. That way it became a correct exercise out of a serious mistake. If the handler had not provided an article with his scent, the young dog may have picked up the dumbbell as a solution when she couldn't find an article with the handler's scent. This response, while a reasonable solution for the dog in this situation, may have taught her a response that would be difficult to correct later.

Another error we observed with a different clean-scent working dog was less simple to correct. It happened in Austria during a test that included both a tracking and a discrimination component, during which the dog had to find the track-layer's article from among five other articles. After working out the track correctly, the dog was allowed to smell the scent of the track-layer and was then brought to the articles.

Because of an almost unbelievable mistake, however, two track-layers were exchanged, and so the dog sniffed at a different track-layer than the one who laid the track. However, the article of the original track-layer was indeed among the five other articles. The dog smelled all articles very intensively, stood still at the article of the track-layer, but didn't pick it up. The odor was, of course, still well-known from the track, but it didn't match the scent he had just smelled.

Although the handler encouraged the dog to retrieve, the dog refused and came back to the handler without the article but with signs of confusion. The handler couldn't understand his dog's actions. A confusion in the track-layers should have been impossible under correct testing protocols, but after further investigation, it was revealed that the unthinkable had happened and that the dog was right in not picking up the article!

A similar situation occurred at a search and rescue tracking test. The dogs had to work out a 1.2 mile (2 km), 3-hour-old track laid over different types of terrain (meadow, wood, heath, sand, roads, ditch). On this track, seven articles were to be found and, at the end, the track-layer had to lie down and be clearly indicated by the dog. So the track-layer didn't have to wait in a field for 3 hours, after laying the track he came back to the meeting place. Before the handler started working out the track, the track-layer went back to the place he marked at the end of the track. But at some point the track-layer had to leave the field and asked someone else to take his place, which was clearly against the protocols for the test. The clean-scent trained dog worked out the track very well, indicated all articles, but then ignored the person at the end of the track. And that was correct, as was proven later on!

Figure 11.9 The exchanged track-layer: The dog came back to his handler with signs of confusion.

Concentration

It is important to make sure the dog has eaten enough before tracking so that he can focus on the odors of the track and not on hunger pangs coming from within his body. Another tip that can help the dog learn to track calmly and with concentration is to approach the start from different directions. If you walk straight to the start, the dog may run on ahead. If you approach from a 90 degree angle, the dog has to slow down his tempo to find the track direction. Another tip is to bring the dog into the track with the right balance between an excited, heightened tracking drive and enough time to absorb the odor at the start. It is also advisable to avoid long, monotonous, straight track legs, as these promote the urge to run ahead. Therefore, make short track legs of different lengths with various types of turns, and later also curves and circles. This will help the dog to concentrate better on the track, which improves his mental and tracking condition and also slows his pace naturally.

By making the tracks and conditions more difficult, the dog will track more slowly. With age and experience, the dog will also become slower in tracking as he knows he needs to concentrate.

Variation

After basic training, introduce variety in tracks for the dog, including different track patterns and ground surfaces. As far as the latter goes, by tracking on increasingly solid or hard ground surfaces, the dog will track less on surface damage and more on human scent, which is ultimately what we're after.

It is only by letting the dog learn on its own, and by introducing some variety, that we get dogs that can independently solve all the problems they meet while tracking.

Figure 11.10 To correctly build up training, change terrain often and use small back roads when trying roads for the first time.

Figure 11.11 As soon as the dog has mastered the technique of tracking, the track-layer must begin to train the dog with all possible changes of soil types and terrains.

Handler Influence

Many dog handlers don't fully understand how much their own mental disposition affects their dog in tracking. This aspect of training is worth a lengthy exploration since it can help you avoid many common training errors.

Everyone who has ever tried to teach a dog something knows that dogs respond very well to handler cues. Most people also realize that dogs pick up cues that they were not specifically trained in. For example, if you put on your walking shoes, your dog will stick to you like glue because he expects to go for a walk. However, handlers may not appreciate how subtle the cues can be that dogs learn from — many are those the handler is completely unaware of. The results of these unconscious kinds of cues are called the Clever Hans effect, named after the apparent mathematic abilities of a horse called Hans.

THE CLEVER HANS EFFECT

Kluger Hans (Clever Hans) was a stallion that lived at the turn of the 20th century in Germany. His behavior confounded animal psychologists of his time, made a name for a pattern, and still is of importance in training dogs. The owner of this horse, Wilhelm von Osten, was an eccentric man who believed that a horse is at least as intelligent as a human. He was absolutely convinced that horses could count, read, and reason. To prove it, he set to work.

Figure 11.12 Wilhelm von Osten in 1902 training his stallion Hans.

The first thing he did was to give his horse Hans a certain "language." After careful consideration, he chose the tapping of the horse's front hoof as the mechanism for communication. All letters in the alphabet and every number were each represented by a specific pattern of taps. As he began training Hans in this language, von Osten took Hans's leg in his hands and tapped it for him. The horse eventually learned to move his leg without help, and after some time the animal seemed to understand this language.

On June 28, 1902, a newspaper advertisement appeared with the following text:

> I want to sell my seven-year-old, fine, docile stallion with which I do tests in order to determine the intellectual powers of a horse. The horse distinguishes ten colors, reads, knows the four main processes of calculation, and a lot more.
>
> Von Osten, Griebenowstrasse 10, Berlin

"A lot more" included spelling, as well as knowledge of musical notes, coins, cards, and how to tell time. But von Osten did not really want to sell Hans. His advertisement was meant to garner interest in his horse and gain popularity for his idea that animals are creatures with keen minds. To von Osten's great annoyance, nobody responded to his advertisement, as it was believed to be a late April Fool's joke.

A MIRACULOUS HORSE

Only after a second advertisement did von Osten receive a response. Now it was time to show off Hans's capabilities to a select group of invited guests, who were allowed to interrogate him. The horse proved to know a lot. Hans could name the date, tell what time it was, convert fractions into decimals, and add up, subtract, multiply, and divide in answer to guests' questions. Observers were amazed at the horse's abilities.

News of the Clever Hans event went around the country, and even the world press wrote about it. Many people thought Hans's performance was somehow fraudulent, but reports of his accomplishments were so impressive that animal psychologists became enthusiastic and wanted to examine him. All were astonished because von Osten did not wish to capitalize on his miraculous horse.

A committee of leading scientists tested the horse, after which they admitted they did not detect the kinds of tricks usually used in circuses with performing animals.[6] The hesitation of the scientists shows how deceptively real Hans's skills were.

MINOR MOVEMENTS

Animal psychologist Oskar Pfungst carefully observed the way the horse worked and also carefully watched von Osten. It was clear to him that there was no swindle — Pfungst himself questioned the stallion and the animal answered in the correct way with his tapping language. For a person without animal psychological training, there would be no doubt that the horse could indeed think and do math. But then Pfungst performed another experiment. He asked Hans questions that nobody present in the room knew the answer to. The stallion started tapping his hoof and did not stop. Pfungst wrote that "The animal seemed to be absentminded."[7] It became clear that the stallion was waiting for a cue to stop tapping. But this sign couldn't be given because nobody but Pfungst knew the answer. Pfungst concluded as follows:

> So far as I can see, the following explanation is the only one that will comport with these facts: the horse must have learned, in the course of the long period of problem-solving, to attend ever more closely, while tapping, to the slight changes in bodily posture with which the master unconsciously accompanied the steps in his own thought-processes, and to use these as closing signals. The motive for this direction and straining of attention was the regular reward, in the form of carrots and bread, which attended it. This unexpected kind of independent activity and the certainty and precision of the perception of minimal movements thus attained are astounding in the highest degree.
>
> The movements that call forth the horse's reaction are so extremely slight in the case of Mr. Von Osten that it is easily comprehensible how it was possible that they should escape the notice even of practiced observers.

Pfungst had stumbled across Hans's reaction to a small, unconscious movement with the head or the body of the questioner as soon as he reached the correct answer, and Hans used this as a cue to stop tapping.

THROUGH THE TRACKING LINE

The Clever Hans effect is one way the handler can unknowingly influence the "achievements" of a tracking dog. Another way the handler may influence the dog is through the tracking line, which provides contact between handler and dog. During the search, the dog notices every emotional nuance of his handler on the line. He may feel trust and security, or potentially doubt, irritation, and much more. This creates an interaction, so the more confident the handler is, the safer the dog works. The greater the handler's uncertainty, the weaker the performance in front on the leash. In the worst case scenario, uncertainty can build up so that the team can no longer perform.

A dog feels any movement of the leash when he is working. Whether or not you choose to work with your dog on leash depends on the dog's temperament and ability to handle pressure. By using a tight leash and loose leash deliberately, you can control your dog's speed and eventually increase his willingness to work. Tightening the leash can stimulate your dog to move on even through difficult situations. The dog feels tension on the line, which slows him down a bit, encouraging him to stay on track and get to the end goal and reward. A tight leash can also help the dog feel the support of the handler, giving him a sense of security and encouragement to persevere.

But a dog that pulls on the leash may respond to a tightened leash by pulling even harder; this type of dog will go much too fast when the leash is slack. Most of the time, such dogs require you to correct them with commands.

Conversely, you cannot hold the tracking leash too tightly on a somewhat unsure dog that tracks slowly, because the dog may feel the tight leash as a correction. In any case, too much pulling and

Figure 11.13 Dogs react with lightning speed to the slightest cues from handlers, often completely unconsciously given.

adjusting of leash tension will upset the dog's concentration on the track, leading to mistakes.

Another big mistake is to pull the leash tight at certain moments in training sequences, such as during tracking training when the dog is searching for an article on the track, or when the dog must make a turn to stay on the track. Some handlers will pull a sagging leash tight at these moments, or, if the leash is already taut, pull their dog backward. This may be done unconsciously or deliberately, but if this type of correction continues throughout training, the dog will connect pulling tight or back with an article or turn, and he will not search anymore. Instead, he will mimic tracking, head to the ground, waiting for his handler's signal.

Aiding and supporting the dog with the leash, as with other handler influences on the tracking dog, will be penalized during examinations. Therefore, it is important to teach the dog to track independently. We can do that by stimulating and motivating our dog during training sessions and helping him as little as possible, because everything a dog learns by himself, he will never forget.

THE IMPORTANCE OF TRACKING "DOUBLE BLIND"

The case of Clever Hans demonstrates the extent to which an animal is able to observe and respond to subtle human gestures. But since this famous stallion performed his "tricks," much knowledge about the use of human-provided cues by animals has become lost to dog handlers, even professionals, leading to many faults in both training and practice.

It is widely believed that the dog's success in becoming "man's best friend" was due to the dog's ability to adapt to human behavior and social organization. Humans continuously and unconsciously use gestures in their communication with dogs, and dogs seem to be highly responsive to these cues.

Researchers have proven that dogs are able to recognize a wide variety of human gestures — pointing, bowing, nodding, head turning, and glancing — as cues for finding hidden objects.[8] Dogs are also able to generalize, recognizing that one person — the owner — can perform the same gestures as another familiar person (e.g., the instructor).[9] All of these experiments are important because they illustrate how well dogs can learn to "read" us.

How can we prevent ourselves from cueing our dogs, then, if they can pick up on and respond to such minimal signals? The answer is obvious: handlers must work "blind." As soon as the dog understands tracking fundamentals and you begin to work on stranger tracks, it is critical that you do not know the position of the track and, preferably, have no one close by who knows it either, since that person may also unconsciously cue the dog. That is called "double blind" working.[10] Working double blind will greatly increase the tracking dog's independent, successful performance.

CONCLUSION

Handler influence on dogs is still a problem, not only in the world of professional tracking, but also in sports tracking. With inattentive judging, many dogs pass their tracking examinations after being led by their handler over the track. If professional search dogs get used to reacting to the slight signals of their handlers, the dogs will be unable to search independently, with sometimes life or death consequences.

Professor David Katz of Stockholm University stresses that professional and sports dogs will never reach a high level of tracking if we, the handlers, trainers, and instructors, do not understand the influence of the Clever Hans effect and continue to fool ourselves and cheat our dogs: "Tracking only makes sense if the handler does not know the direction of the track. Everything else is childish and fooling yourself."[11]

12

Preliminary Exercises for Clean-Scent Tracking

Dogs that will be taught clean-scent tracking need their training focused on that goal from the beginning. Both young and older dogs follow the same phases of training. However, older dogs sometimes take a bit longer at each step in training. If they were not raised properly as puppies, they may have behavior problems that first have to be resolved.

It is important to observe the dog's play and prey behavior and to see how strong a bond the dog has with his handler. If the dog's play and prey behavior have become connected with a sense of frustration, or if he has not bonded well with his handler, then the dog will be more difficult to train.

The Game

From the beginning, teach a young dog to play search games. The younger you get him started, the better. Search games can begin with puppies as young as 8 weeks, but at least by the time the puppy is 6 months old. For these games, use items you have worn: knotted socks, an old handkerchief, a rolled-up T-shirt, or another piece of clothing that's not too big. Just make sure it is an article with enough of your scent. An old leather glove and a tennis ball in a long sock can also be very useful. A tennis ball by itself is unsuitable for this purpose.

Figure 12.1 The first search games get the dog focused on the handler's scent.

Wave the article in front of the dog's nose to urge him to catch it. If he is willing to catch it, then throw it quickly, in his sight, into higher grass and let him immediately go after it. The key to this game is to allow the dog to play with the article any way that comes naturally to him. Young dogs may shake it, throw it up high, and carry it around. They consider the article to be prey they have caught while searching (in their opinion: hunting).

When the dog lets the article fall somewhere, immediately get the article moving again. The best way is by throwing the article low over the ground, which will activate the puppy's hunting and play drives. In this game, you have only a supporting role; the dog decides how the game is played. Avoid giving commands like "Keep it," "Bring," and "Out." Let the dog play as he wants to play. After all, it is a search game and not a retrieving exercise.

In this first phase of learning, the dog will effortlessly focus on the article with your scent. It is very important that this playing never become handler directed. The young dog expects to play with the article as motivated by his instincts, which then translates into training for life. The game allows you to introduce work using the play drive, but you should take care not to break into or change the game. If you interfere, the exercise becomes about obedience and the dog may lose interest. Observe and wait until the dog involves you in the game. Your role in this game is to keep the article moving and interesting to the dog.

Later on, you can work in the idea of bringing/retrieving. In doing so, we must not take the article away from the dog, but we can encourage him to bring us the article by walking away. When the passion for retrieving is obvious, the bringing can then be rewarded with a dog biscuit.

Young dogs do not always show that they are tired. Don't play too long, and give your dog the rest he needs. The amount of rest time varies greatly between breeds and individual animals. When the young dog has understood the game, give him a time-out, during which he can keep his article, and after the break, he will once again invite you to play with him.

A Moving Object

To make it clear to the puppy that he has to search for the article with the scent of the handler, we have to work with the dog in the right manner. An article lying there without movement will not be an object to hunt; a moving object, however, is immediately of interest.

With the dog's origins as a hunter, everything that moves fast will be recognized as prey and activate his hunting drive. When the article disappears in high grass, then his search drive will be activated. The search drive is an act of instinct that the dog has from his forefathers; it is not necessary for him to learn to search.

The growing dog will learn through this search and prey playing to use his sense of smell very intensively. At the same time, the handler has a great opportunity, while the dog works at searching and locating, to learn their dog's unique body language and search behavior.

Using the dog's innate drives, we introduce him to the behavior we require. We don't force him and we don't help him. This is important because the dog learns to search of his own free will. At the same time, he discovers the finer points of searching (like using air turbulence) by himself. By using different prey and search games, we can ignite the dog's passion for searching.

However, if we don't pay attention to the dog's behavior, then our attempts to train can cause big problems. For example, if a handler hides an article without letting the dog see and then expects an untrained dog to search for it, then the dog will not know what he has to do. His search drive was not engaged. He will do everything except search. We often see this behavior when a dog is expected to work out a track without preliminary exercises. If the handler, maybe impatient by now, then brings the dog to the article's hiding place and shows him where it is, then a misunderstanding between handler and dog is clearly going to occur. The dog has heard our grumbling before, and it's always accompanied by something unpleasant. To the dog it looks like this: the handler is grumbling because of the article. The dog may conclude that the article itself is a problem or that searching for the article is not allowed. With this conclusion, the dog will want to avoid the article and search as much as possible — clearly not the result you want to achieve.

With that we have, without meaning to, tossed up a barrier between the dog and the article, and by extension between the dog and the scent of the handler! It may be possible to overcome this barrier, but somewhere in the dog's mind there will always be a bad feeling, which may be why the dog will never reach his peak performance in searching and tracking.

Figure 12.2 By influencing the right drives, the dog can develop a real passion for tracking.

To avoid this scenario, throw the article in full view of the dog into the high grass and, immediately after it disappears, allow the dog to start searching. As soon as the dog has found his article, he will pick it up and carry it around, full of pride. For him this is real prey!

Normally the dog shakes the prey and fully expends his hunting drives on it. He has to do so; we would frustrate him if we tried to become involved in this.

PREY SHARING

In normal pack relations between handler and dog, the latter will bring the prey to the handler on his own. Why does he do that? Well, he still has the instincts of his forefathers, the wolves. They also carry prey back to the pack, allowing the prey to be shared out, exactly as our dog is doing now. As a pack animal, he expects us to share in the prey. During searching, and later on when the dog plays with the toy, the handler may not interfere. The handler must wait patiently until the dog brings the prey on his own.

However, react quickly if the dog lies down somewhere and begins to destroy the article. Loud and clear interference in this situation will communicate that this destruction, which is tantamount to eating the complete prey, is not right and anti-social.

However, if the dog merely chews on the prey as he carries it, do not react. This chewing comes from the dog's ancestors, who were allowed to press out the blood and body fluids as a reward for carrying it. This is no longer allowed for the modern hunting dog, for commercial reasons: the game would be damaged. Our future tracking dog, however, is allowed to chew. We have to accept that this "prey," in the dog's mind, is still living. The dog's chewing allows us to gauge how much the dog is getting into his hunting behavior.

After bringing the article to his handler, the dog expects the handler, as a member of the pack, to share the prey. In the dog's view, it would be anti-social if we took the article and simply put it in our pocket, in effect confiscating the complete prey. This prey-sharing, however, must not degenerate into an obedience exercise, sitting in front of the handler and offering the article. For the dog, the right approach in this phase of training is whatever comes naturally, which may be laying it in front of the handler's feet or presenting it with his mouth so the handler can take it. However, avoid playing tug with the article: many dogs conclude that they have to fight for their find, which should never be the case in this hunting ritual.

Prey-sharing is related to old hunting rituals. After the hunting dog has found the wild animal the hunter shot, such as a deer, he waits quietly beside the hunter, who takes over the carcass. After the belly is opened, the dog gets a part of the bowels as a reward, in the way of prey-sharing. We share the prey with our dog the same way. Take the article and hold a biscuit over it with your thumb and forefinger. Wait for a brief moment to increase the dog's excitement, and then allow the dog to take the biscuit. Repeat this once or twice, and always offer the reward near the article, because the reward has to form a connection with the article. After

Figure 12.3 How the dog brings the prey in this phase of training is not so important, but the exercise should always end with prey-sharing.

the prey-sharing, put the article, without showing it to the dog or paying attention to it, in your pocket; it only appears again for the next game.

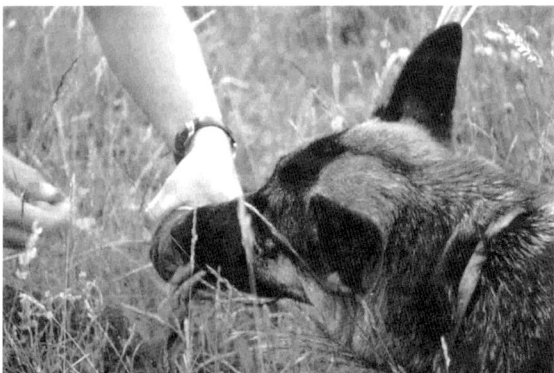

Figure 12.4 To share the prey correctly, the handler should always give a dog biscuit close to, but not touching the sock toy. The dog should make a mental connection between the two, but you don't want the odor of the biscuit contaminating the toy.

Only the Handler's Scent

In the beginning, allow your dog to search immediately after throwing the article; later on, make the dog pause briefly to focus him first. During this pause, hold the dog by his collar or, even better, with your both hands around his chest. Do not keep him in place by command. You want to develop his search and bring drive and shouldn't use obedience exercises that pressure the dog and take away his desire to continue working. Through this pause to focus, the future tracking dog learns to search for the article with your scent instead of senselessly running after any thrown article.

In normal dog training, an owner lets the dog retrieve everything, with or without human scent. Most dogs have such a passion for retrieving that it's no surprise when dogs begin a chain of retrieving automatism. Because of that, every random article will be retrieved during tracking, even if it has no track-layer scent. In the same way, the dog will retrieve all thrown articles without first smelling them. To prevent this, from the beginning use only articles that smell strongly of your scent. That way the dog becomes accustomed to searching for and picking up only articles with this scent.

Of course it isn't necessary to use a new article each time. After prey-sharing, put the article back in your pocket, so it can absorb your scent. If the article came into contact with the biscuits during prey-sharing, then wash and rinse it very well before imbuing it again with your scent.

We should warn you against another common mistake: during search games with future tracking dogs, never hide the articles in high places, such as on furniture or in a tree, because that teaches the dog to search with a high nose, which can cause problems later for tracking dogs. For detector dogs (drugs, explosives, etc.) this is not an issue; these dogs must not only learn to search over the ground surface, they must also learn to search for items placed high up, eventually on command.

Searching Without the Throw

After making the dog strongly interested in searching — ideally he's passionate about searching — you can now sometimes have a search without throwing the article. Use a wooded or overgrown area of land and engage a helper to hold the dog. After a short period of you and the dog playing with the article without searching, have the helper keep the dog in place. In sight of the dog, walk in a straight line over the terrain with the article in hand, visible or not, depending on the dog's interest. While walking, drop the article in a bush or clump of grass, without the dog seeing, and then circle widely back to the dog. If the dog is already looking toward the terrain with a great deal of interest and is full of "hunting fever," then let him go. At the same time, give an enticing and stimulating, but quiet and long-drawn out "Seeeek." If the dog isn't immediately watching and excited to begin, walk the terrain

Figure 12.5 The right approach. With one hand, the handler brings the dog's attention to the track and motivates him with "Seeeek." The handler's crouching posture adds to the tension.

and show him the article, moving it around and calling it to the dog's attention.

From this search exercise, without the article being thrown, you can see whether the previous exercises were done well and if the dog was searching mainly with his nose. If that was not the case, and if he was searching with his eyes, then he will now have problems. In spite of that, don't help him. The dog has to learn that the fastest way to his article is by following the track of the handler. This exercise ends with the dog's free play and the prey-sharing. Once the dog has the main idea, such search games have to be done in many different locations and situations.

First Tracks

Once the dog understands that it is a fun game to search for the article, we can start the first tracks. For this the handler needs a helper who knows the dog very well. Now there are two possibilities. We can start with tracking directly on a hard surface, such as a secluded and quiet street, and lay the track in the same way as described for the wooded or overgrown field with short grass (below). On a hard surface, you'll just drop the article behind an object on the surface. If the previous exercises were well done, you will see that most young dogs don't have any problems starting hard surface tracking immediately.

The other option is to begin with a field or other area with short grass. Have the helper keep the dog at the edge of a field that has not recently been walked on. Walk a few yards into the field and make the start by standing still and stepping back and forth for about 1 minute. While making the start, you can enticingly show the article to your dog. When the start is ready, walk forward, with the wind at your back, in a straight line into the meadow. Begin with small steps, but after a while you can change to normal paces. Use normal steps with no shuffling or foot dragging. Depending on the attention of the dog, if necessary, look back to the dog while walking and show the article a few times. After about 164 feet

Figure 12.6 Even puppies and young dogs can start tracking on paved ground immediately.

Figure 12.7 If the previous exercises were well done, you will see that most young dogs don't have any problems with hard surface tracking, as this Dutch police dog shows.

(50 m), lay the article in front of your feet in the grass, walk on a few more paces, and then circle back to the dog, which will be waiting with excitement.

Now put the dog in his tracking harness, fasten the tracking line or the normal leash, and walk to the start. There the dog will stand at your side while you show him the beginning of the track. To do this, hold the dog with one hand and use your other hand to point to the start. While doing so, encourage the dog with a long-drawn-out "Seeeek." As soon as the dog has smelled the start very well, loosen your hold on the harness and let the dog go ahead on his leash. Adjust the line length depending on the interest and temperament of the dog. Give more line if the dog is moving at a good pace, but if he's moving too quickly, shorten the line to slow him down.

Normally the attentive dog will follow the track immediately and search for his beloved article with his nose close to the ground. When he finds it, he may play with it as usual and, of course, you should show that you are satisfied with his work. Wait until the dog involves you in his play, throw the article for him a few times, and end with prey-sharing.

In the beginning, if the dog doesn't search with a deep nose, but simply runs straight to pick up the article, be patient. It may take time to teach him what you expect. If the dog does the track correctly, but too quickly, then lay the track in a curve. If the dog strays away from the track, point out the track in a quiet and friendly way. The curve requires the dog to bring his nose closer to the ground surface instead of running straight forward.

In the meantime, take care that your dog understands the command for tracking very well; now and then during tracking repeat "Seek" and "Good boy." Once the dog understands he has to work out a track with his nose to the ground, you can keep the dog out of sight when laying the track. Then he won't know the direction and has to trust his nose.

Tracking should occur on a tracking line, although with dogs that are quick to feel pressured (soft dogs) or with dogs that play with the line, the tracking exercises can happen without leash in the beginning. As soon as the dog knows what we expect, he needs to work on the leash again.

Figure 12.8. The handler must show great interest in the article the dog has found on the track and reward the dog for the good work.

We want to warn you emphatically against a frequent mistake, which is using someone else's tracking harness and tracking line, such as when a handler forgets their own equipment. Although this may not be so important with tracks laid by the handler, it may be a problem when the dog graduates to working with tracks made by someone else. We never work with strange equipment. If you do, the dog will get used to perceiving other (strange) scents on a track, which is a disadvantage in clean-scent training.

These tracking exercises can be done on different sorts of ground surfaces, but never in high grass; the grass must be short, otherwise the dog will be tempted to search with a higher nose.

If the dog is 5 to 8 months old and works out these exercises very well, you can prepare him further for his future clean-scent tracking with the exercises in the next chapter.

13

Basic Clean-Scent Tracking

After the search games and the first tracking exercises, the dog will now will be ready to learn clean-scent tracking. To begin, you will work in a quiet place using an article with your scent along with a similar article without odor.

Picking the Correct Article

Of course, articles without odor don't really exist, because in principle everything has a certain odor. By an "odorless article" we mean a clean article that is laid down with a pair of tongs. Such an article has its own odor, as well as the odor of the detergent it was washed with, the odor of the water it was rinsed in, and the odor of the surroundings in which it was dried and later transported. Maybe even the tongs will give the item a certain odor. Without doubt, dogs are able to perceive even such small amounts of odor. However, what is key is that the article doesn't have another human's scent.

To make early training clear for our dog, we want him to find only articles that are deeply imbued with our scent, which means we had them for at least half a day in our pocket. This prevents the dog from having a problem with scents, on top of the mental stress of learning to track. Only if he is track-sure and the concept of "scent" is absolutely clear in his mind, can he also manage problems like older tracks and articles that have been held only briefly.

Figure 13.1 An article with the handler's scent lies between the "odorless" items.

Lay the article with your scent beside or behind an odorless article in front of the dog and send the dog to search. If the dog (as will be the case almost every time) leaves the other article and picks up your article, give him exuberant praise. After that, let the dog play until he brings the article to you. Play fetch a few times, and end with the all-important prey-sharing. If you see that the dog first smells the articles and then picks up the right one, then the next time you can lay down an article with the scent of a person the dog doesn't know instead of the "odorless" article.

If the dog picks up the wrong article, which seldom happens, then say a quiet "No." Even better, ignore the mistake and begin to play with the correct article. The dog will then quickly let the wrong article fall and will take the article with your scent. What also works well is to pick up the right article and sniff at it audibly.

If your dog then does the same, reward him and let him take over the article.

We want to repeat that in no case should the dog be pressured to bring the article directly to you. The dog must have the chance to play with it. This is not a retrieving exercise; it is about teaching the dog what scent we want him to search for. Therefore we use all sorts of articles, but always only articles with our scent, such as tied socks or stockings, gloves, or rolled towels we have held for a long time.

Figure 13.2 The correct way to retrieve should be taught separately on the obedience training ground.

Once the dog picks up his handler's article without hesitation from an increasing number of articles, then we can connect this exercise with tracking.

On the Track

All the tracks we lay for our dogs are only footprints; we never use dog biscuits, pieces of meat, cheese, or some kind of artificial odor. As soon as possible, the dog must learn to recognize the handler's scent on the track and to only follow his handler's scent. In the beginning, lay the tracks with older shoes, ideally when it is calm and on fresh terrain, where you know there were no people or animals present shortly before.

In the beginning, lay a simple, straight track. At the end of this track, beside your own article, a helper lays other articles of the same sort. This can be done by having a helper walk from another side to the end of the track, but you can also take the other odor articles with you in a closed glass jar and use a pair of tongs to lay these near your own article at the end of the track.

Once you reach the end of the track with the dog, let him go to the articles. If he finds the right one, praise him. Gradually, it will be time to retrieve more correctly. That means don't give the dog time to play with the article, but entice him with "Apport" or "Bring." But don't use a lot of pressure, because the dog must continue to like tracking. There is no better way to keep the dog's attention on tracking than playing and having fun. The dog that doesn't find searching and tracking a fun game will never perform well in these areas.

The Important Start

To successfully track a human scent, it is very important to begin the track with a good start, as we explained in Chapter 8. At the start, which if necessary is marked with a tracking stake, the handler stands for 1 minute. Then the handler walks the first 16 feet

(5 m) with short paces and gradually with wider paces until walking normally.

At the start the dog must learn to take some time to fix the odor of the track in his mind. That means the dog is not allowed to walk over the start after just a brief sniff; instead, tell him with a long-drawn-out "Smeeell" or "Seeeek" to pick up the odor thoroughly.

Guidelines

By nature a dog has the inclination to follow certain lines in a terrain, like ditches, trenches, roads, fences, or the borders between two types of terrain, such as meadow and field, between two meadows, or the edges of woods and hills. If these "guidelines" coincide with a turn in the track or a cross-track, they form an extra difficulty for tracking dogs.

Figure 13.3 Fences and forest edges form a guideline for the dog in the terrain, which he will tend to follow.

If a track laid along the edge of a ditch or fence makes a sudden turn, that track is much more difficult for a dog to work out than a track laid diagonally in a field and that makes a turn there.

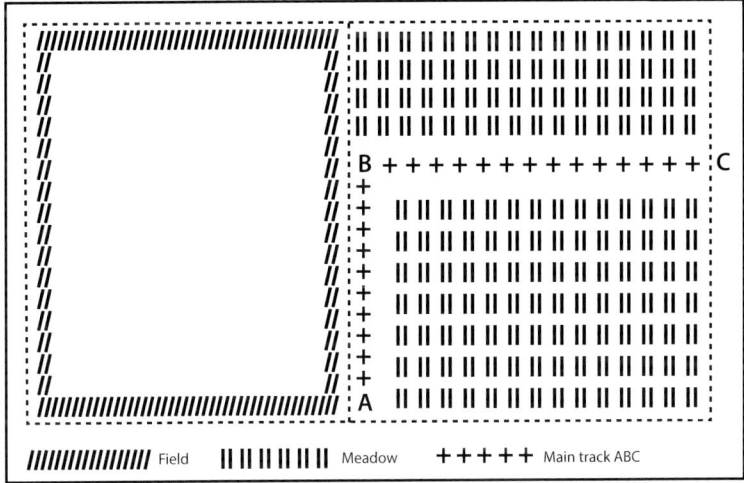

Figure 13.4 Borders between terrain types are also guidelines.

The dog will be inclined to stay at the edge of the ditch or fence and so he may overshoot the turn. Depending on his level of concentration and experience with such problems, he may conclude that he lost the track and will search for the correct direction. For

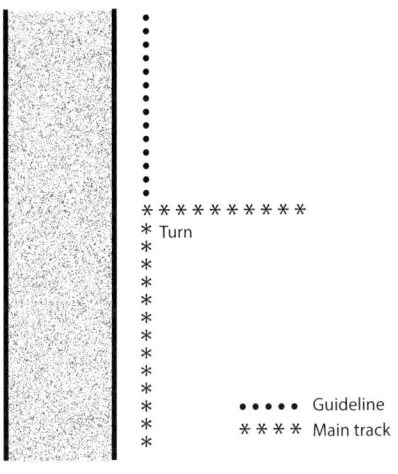

Figure 13.5 Although the track makes a right angle, the dog will be strongly inclined to follow the "guideline," in this case, the bank of the ditch. It is better to avoid such difficult situations for dogs just beginning their training.

beginning handlers, it is often difficult to assess whether a dog is really searching intensively for the continuation of the track or if he is just walking with his head down.

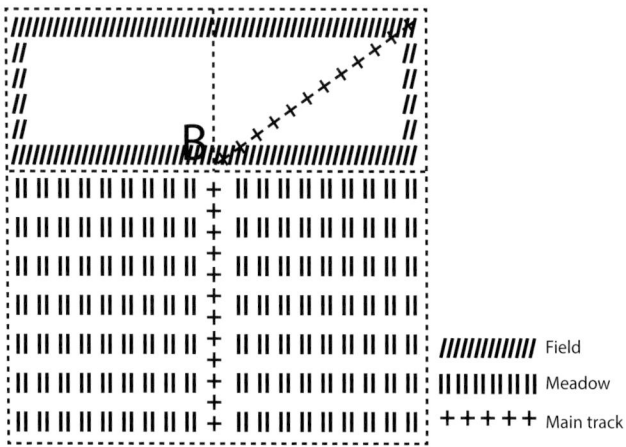

Figure 13.6 Here the dog is tempted to go straight over B or to take a right-angle turn along the edge of the meadow and field.

If the training was built up correctly, step by step, the dog's attention and tracking drive should remain strong. As soon as a dog understands an exercise, give him something with a slightly higher degree of difficulty that he can solve by himself. Taking too big (or irregular) a step in building up, making too high a demand and, as often happens, presenting more than one problem at a time (e.g., working out the first turn that is also laid along a guideline) will greatly decrease the dog's attention and interest in tracking.

Right-Angle Turns

If the dog has been able to work out a straight track for some weeks, you can proceed to give him a turn, normally a right-angle turn to the right or the left, without a bend or curve.

When the dog arrives at the turn, he will observe that the straight track ends and he will try to find the track again, most of the time by circling at that spot. The longer it takes, the more nervous a dog becomes, and the more difficult it will be for him to pick up the track again. For that reason, in the first sessions, we lay the turn in such a way that the part after the turn (the second leg) lies in a head wind. The wind coming from the second leg will lead the dog over the turn.

To make the first few turns easier, use short, close paces just before and after the turn, just like you did at the start. This ensures there is more scent around the turn. At first, use the short paces both before and after the turn; later on use small steps only a short distance after the turn. If this works well, then lay the turn with normal paces, the same way you would make a turn in obedience heel work.

Acute-Angle Turns

If everything is going well with right-angle turns, then you can progress to making acute- and obtuse-angle turns and then as many different turns as possible. We have to prevent the dog from learning a certain tracking pattern. Regular tracking patterns are boring for the dog, and they remove the dog's motivation to follow the individual scent in the track.

In the beginning, always lay acute-angle turns with a tail wind. That's the only way the dog can work out these turns correctly. All other wind directions tempt the dog to cut off the turn.

Acute angles also present a psychological block for dogs. The tracking dog is used to his handler always walking behind him. When searching for a lost scent at the turn, the handler is the dog's point of orientation, telling him what direction he doesn't have to search. Therefore, it is a victory for the dog to overcome this by tracking back towards the handler, as happens immediately after an acute-angle turn. However, once the dog understands this, he will have taken an important step forward in independent tracking.

Traps

Once the dog can consistently handle a variety of turns, slowly begin to make the tracks older. First wait 10 minutes after laying out a track, then 20 minutes, and then half an hour. Work up to tracks to 1 hour old or even older. In this phase of training, we can also build in certain traps for the dog. For instance, on a meadow lay a track more than 328 feet (100 m) long near the edge of a field (or another guideline), and then suddenly make a turn. Often the dog will briefly overshoot the turn because he's following the guideline in the terrain, but as long as he corrects himself, this is fine.

Another trap is to lay a track in a wooded area straight to a field, but then take an obtuse-angle turn once reaching the field. Here, the big temptation for the dog is to stay in the woods or to walk straight into the field. You can do the same at the intersection of paths or roads; instead of moving straight, make a right-angle turn or, even more challenging, make an obtuse turn off the path or road. This latter trap ensures the dog follows the scent and not the guideline provided by the path or road. These are important exercises for the dog, making him track-sure as well as clean-scent working in all sorts of terrain possibilities.

Variations

At first a dog will follow a total odor mix, which will include the human scent as well as plant odors and ground damage. Eventually he needs to learn to search only for the human scent in the track. The best way to achieve this is by changing all other parts of the odor complex except the human scent, which continues through all other changes as a sort of red line.

For example, walk a section of a track in shoes, then in bare feet or socks, and then again in shoes. This helps the dog understand that for him, the most important odor in the track is the human scent.

Figure 13.7 By gradually working more often on harder surfaces, tracking on the odor of plants and damage to ground surface will decrease and tracking on the individual human scent will increase.

Then lay the tracks over different sorts of surfaces: from a meadow into a field, from the field into a stubble field, from a clay surface to woodland soil, over paved roads and whatever else you can find to change the circumstances of tracking. Combine different possibilities, but still using the well-known track of the handler.

TYPES OF SURFACES

By gradually working more often on harder surfaces, tracking based on the odor of plants and damage to the ground surface will decrease and tracking on the individual human scent will increase. Surfaces to work into your training, from softer to harder, are listed as follows:

- Grassland
- Woodland
- Field
- Sand
- Cobblestones

- Paving bricks
- Flagstone
- Gravel
- Concrete
- Asphalt

Figure 13.8 Asphalt and asphalt-concrete roads contain chemical substances with a disinfecting effect that change the fatty acids of the track. This effect is much reduced in older asphalt.

Rewarding and Mistakes

For good work, the dog should receive praise, and for a mistake, he should be corrected with "No," but no heavy punishment. The latter can confuse the dog, leading him to refuse to track or to pretend to track.

The same will happen if we often pull the dog in a certain direction with the tracking line or prevent him from moving where his nose takes him. That also causes the dog not to track independently and to instead wait for his handler's instructions. This is definitely not what you want since it will greatly decrease your dog's effectiveness as a tracking dog.

14

Advanced Clean-Scent Tracking

In 1930, the Menzels wrote that "The world of odors and tracking is a closed book for us, people. Here, we are in the unpleasant situation that the dog has to teach us something, instead of the other way around!"

We shouldn't make training dogs more difficult for ourselves by not taking known influences, like tracks laid by other people, into account. At tests and trials, we may have to work out a track on terrain of unknown composition. But training and testing are completely different situations. This point is worth repeating: training and testing are different situations. A student lab assistant doesn't begin her studies by analyzing mixes of unknown composition. On the contrary, her study is carefully built upon increasingly difficult mixes and reactions. So it is logical that, when we first teach our dog to track, we should know exactly where other tracks or cross-tracks are. Only once our dog knows what to do should we begin to work double-blind in order to avoid influencing his work.

Assessment

In training, it is very important that you know exactly where you laid the track. This allows you to check your dog's work and assess his attitude at turns and terrain changes. In the beginning, it is also important that the track be laid in terrain where no people or animals walked shortly before. This doesn't mean that we don't get the dog-in-training used to cross-tracks. But in the beginning, when teaching the dog to follow your track, cross-tracks may be confusing. Even later on, when the dog knows what to do, only let him work on terrain where you know all the tracks and cross-tracks. This is the only way you can correct certain mistakes.

While the dog is following only your track, exact knowledge of the terrain is less meaningful, but for later training on tracks of other people, this knowledge can have decisive meaning. Otherwise, you may unknowingly praise your dog for taking the wrong track.

Cross-Tracks

When teaching the dog to ignore cross-tracks, the handler is still the track-layer. The dog is used to the handler's scent, and he will have few difficulties discriminating it from other scents. The people laying the cross-tracks should be absolutely unknown to the dog.

Keeping to the right track is a difficult exercise for a dog, especially if it has been crossed by other human tracks. The dog must stay attentive and concentrate for long periods. A brief fading of attention is all it may take to change to a cross-track. At that point, the dog may observe the difference and stand still, ready to search for the right track. However, if the handler at that moment tries to prompt the dog with the well-known command "Seek," the dog may feel pressured or encouraged to follow the wrong track.

It's not only a moment of inattention that can cause problems. A dog with a strong search passion can, in his enthusiasm, change over to a cross-track. Even if he notices his error right away, it demands great mental control to go back and find the right track. A dog isn't always capable of such control, especially if the handler pushes him all the time in training. For example, if the dog has learned that hesitation and back tracking isn't allowed, he may continue with a cross-track even if he realizes he's following a new scent.

Another problem is if the handler doesn't know where the track is laid and can't help correct him promptly (with a simple "No"). Not knowing the exact location of the cross-track is not always caused by carelessness in training. Because we cannot smell the track ourselves, it is impossible to know when our dog catches the scent of a cross-track by the wind. Such problems make correcting and rewarding the dog during tracking very difficult.

ADVANCED CROSS-TRACK TRAINING

Recall the formula created by the Menzels for understanding the odor complex of a track:

Sum of odor complex = Constant of tracking conditions × (Track-layer + Plant odor + Ground odor + Footwear)

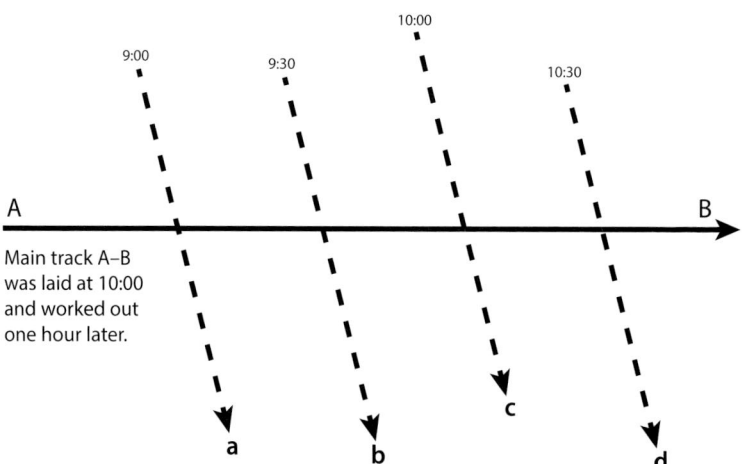

Cross-tracks: **a** laid at 9:00; **b** laid at 9:30; **c** laid at 10:00; **d** laid at 10:30.

Figure 14.1 Testing dogs on their ability to ignore different cross-tracks.

Adapted from a drawing by E. Stuchly in *Die Erfolgreiche Fährtenarbeit.*

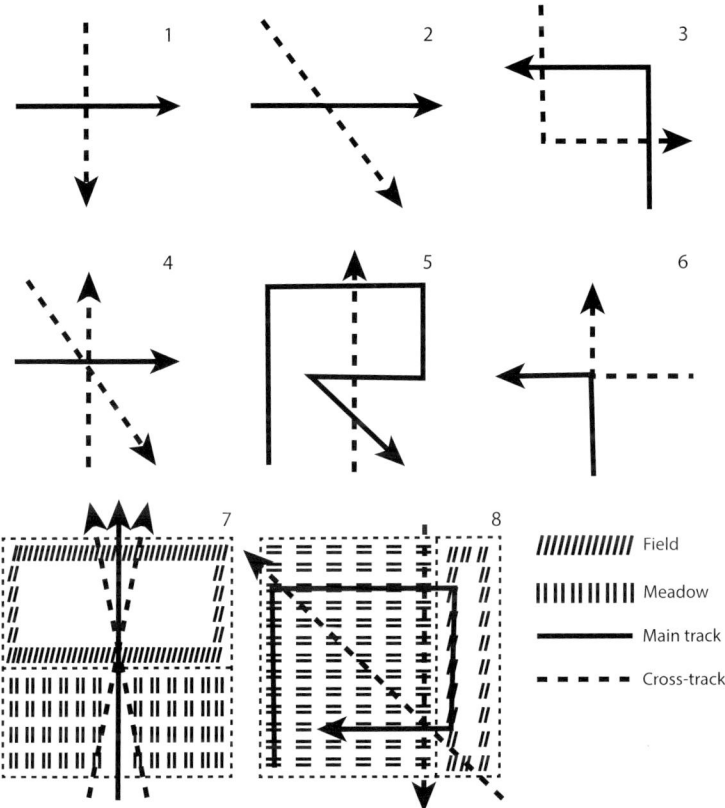

Figure 14.2 Cross-tracks in order of increasing difficulty (from 1 to 8).

Adapted from a drawing by L. Haberhauffe and G. Albrecht in *Schutz- und Diensthunde.*

For advanced training in searching for the complex track scent for T (in the beginning the handler), the cross-track should be laid where the formula of the handler's track changes:

From

$C \times (T1 + P1 + G1 + F1)$

to

$C \times (T1 + P2 + G2 + F1)$

and the formula of the cross-track should be

$C \times (T2 + P1 + G1 + F2)$

Figure 14.3 As the Menzels point out, the world of odors is one where dogs know far more than we do. Handlers need to train their dogs well and then learn to trust their dog's nose since it has access to a world of information we cannot access without their help.

That means, for example, that the handler's track goes over from grass to a field and the cross-track stays on the grass. The dog will be very tempted to go over to the cross-track.

The most difficult of all temptations is the combination of Most's tracking cross (see Chapter 1) with a change of terrain. In that case, the original track turns and goes over to another ground surface, while the cross-track turns and continues in a straight line from where the original track left off on the first ground surface. This challenging track results in two common errors:

1. Overshooting the turn and continuing forward
2. Searching on at the edge of where the ground surface changes

RESEARCH ON CROSS-TRACKS

TOHRU UCHIDA

In 1953, Tohru Uchida from Japan studied the influence of fatty acids on tracking.[1] He wanted to use the best Japanese tracking dogs (all German

Shepherds), so he tested them to work out tracks laid according to Most's tracking cross. He assessed the results of these well-trained dogs and selected the best. The selected dogs were not tempted to follow the wrong track at the cross. They correctly followed the original track, and so were clean-scent tracking.

For the next tests the tracks were polluted: track-layer A wore shoes with butyric acid (one of the fatty acids in human sweat) on them, and then he put on his own shoes (without butyric acid). The shoes of track-layer B were normal until the turn, and then butyric acid was added. All the dogs correctly followed the track of A, even at the turn, and were not tempted to go over to the track of B.

During a similar test, a mixture of fatty acids and other substances present in human sweat was used instead of butyric acid. In this test, the dogs followed the polluted track and went over at the crossing from track A to track B. Some dogs refused to work out the track at all.

These experiments proved that a well-trained tracking dog not only recognizes the qualitative and quantitative details of human sweat scent, but can also use them as a guide for tracking. The dog is not tempted from the track by a change in one sweat odor component. Only when multiple odor components are changed or used as a distraction can the dog no longer with certainty determine the details of the scent track.

The results of these tests also apply to the tracks of game or other animals. These odors are even simpler, because there is no shoe odor to complicate things. But mixed odors, such as cross-tracks of other game or animals, which dogs can perceive and which attract them, are a concern here.

JEAN HONHON

The ability of dogs to determine the differences in odors between the main track and the cross-track was tested in 1967 during the doctoral research of Jean Honhon from Paris.[2] Instead of Most's tracking cross, Honhon used a Y-scheme. At the branch of the Y, the dogs had to decide which track they should follow: the original track or the cross-track.

Honhon determined that the right choice depended on the following:

1. The length of the track between the start and the branch
2. The gap in time between the creation of the main track and the cross-track

In Honhon's study, if the first leg was about half a mile (800 m) long, then 75–85 percent of the time the dogs stayed on the correct track; if it was only 164 feet (50 m) long, then the dogs chose the correct way in only 45 percent of

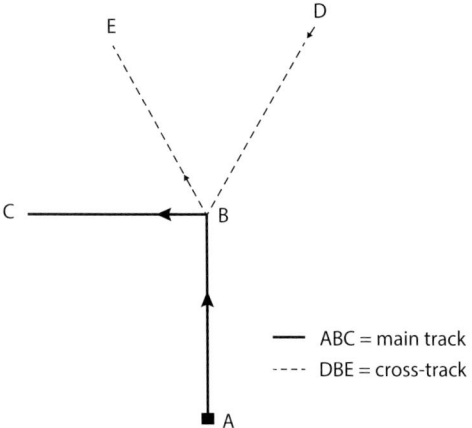

Figure 14.4 Honhon's Y-scheme. Staying on the track from A to C depends on the length from A to B and the difference in time with cross-track D–E. The greater these are, the more chance that the dog will track from A to C.

the cases. These results suggest that dogs need a longer time to fully commit to a scent on the track.

If the difference in time between the creation of the main track and the cross-track was 15 minutes, then in 65–75 percent of the cases the dogs made the correct choice. If this difference in time was 30 minutes, then the correct decision was made in 70–75 percent of the cases. And if this difference was 1 hour, then in 75–85 percent of the cases the main track was followed.

Interruptions

After the dog has learned to handle cross-tracks, you can build in short interruptions of the track, such as before fences and gates. On the command "Wait," the dog has to stay in place until you help him over the obstacle and he can continue the track. The first few times we create such obstacles, we should make another "start" right after the obstacle, so the dog has the opportunity to work his way into the track again.

You can also build in a sudden end to tracks now and then. That means, for instance, that the track-layer carries a bicycle and, after some distance, jumps on and cycles away, without leaving an article. Never allow a dog to follow this artificial bike track, because the clean-scent track might be forgotten. The artificial track contains no human components at all. On arriving at the break, if the dog refuses to continue, reward him simply with your voice and then give him a toy.

Figure 14.5 Dogs can learn to track on paved surfaces even in the beginning of training.

Figure 14.6 Tracking for too long (months) on one soil type (e.g., grass) can ensure that the dog does not want to search on another type of surface, such as a paved road. Such a dog will always go to grass to look there for the track.

We also have to stop the dog from back-tracking. Otherwise, the dog will learn that with tracking problems (e.g., brief interruptions due to difficult terrain), he can choose the easiest solution, which is to turn around and follow the track back.

TEAM TRACKING

Many dogs in dog sports work out the same track on the same field every week. Some dogs lose interest after a while, and they track with less quality.

Our club has found a way to make training interesting for our dogs and handlers. We often lay tracks many miles long through all sorts of terrain, such as woods, fields, plowed land, paved roads, sand, ditches, brooks, and so on. On these tracks, the track-layer leaves behind 20 or more scented articles.

After a few hours, we go to work out the track as a group; the first handler begins with their dog at the start, and the other handlers and dogs follow in a line about 65 feet (20 m) behind. When the first searching dog gets tired, or when he has found a few articles, this dog will be taken away from the track. He goes to the end of the group and the next dog in line continues the track.

In our experience, the dogs following the lead tracker dog become more and more enthusiastic to take the lead. The tracking drive of every dog that gets his turn to work on the track is very strong. Such long and varied tracks are positive for both handlers and dogs and help increase everyone's reading of the tracking dogs' behavior.

Tracks Made by Strangers

Until now, the human scent in the track was always the well-known scent of the handler. Once that skill is well in hand, it is time to train the dog to follow a different human scent. This is a major change for the dog. Do not make this change with any other complication or difficulty.

For the first "stranger tracks," we use a person who is well known to the dog and whom the dog likes. This will make the transition to real strangers easier. For the first tracks, this well-known person lays a long, straight track that begins with a "start" and ends

Figure 14.7 For the first "strange tracks," use a person the dog likes.

with an article well imbued with the person's scent (to match the scent on the track, not the handler's article). With this person, and later also people completely unknown to the dog, take your dog through the same stages of training that you did with your dog as he learned to track your scent. When problems occur, simply go back to a phase where the dog did well, and from there, once again carefully, step-by-step, build up the dog's tracking skills. Once the dog can track the scent of a familiar person, then move to the track of a person the dog has never met.

SUMMARY OF TYPES OF TRACKS

Eventually, you will want to use the widest possible variety of tracks for your dog. Following is a summary of some of the types of tracks you will want to expose your tracking dog to.

MAIN TRACKS

- Pure tracks: laid by a human in terrain where there are no other tracks.
  - Start with tracks made by the dog handler.

- Transition to tracks made by people the dog knows well.
- Last, transition to tracks of people the dog doesn't know at all.
- Tracks with a start: give the dog a lot of scent information
- Tracks with an article scented by the track-layer at the beginning
- Tracks without a start: the dog has to search for the track and decide on direction
- Warm tracks: less than 1 hour old
- Half-warm tracks: less than 2 or 3 hours old
- Cold tracks: older than 4 hours
- Snow and ice tracks
- Night tracks: worked out in the dark or with a flashlight
- Interrupted tracks, such as through a stream to the other side
- Broken-off tracks: end because the track-layer gets into a vehicle or on a bike

CROSS-TRACKS

- Cross-tracks: tracks that are near the main track, either in the same or opposite direction, or intersecting it
- Cross-over tracks: cross a main track that is just as old or older
- Cross-under tracks: tracks crossed by more recent main tracks
- Side cross-tracks: tracks laid parallel to main tracks, either in the same or opposite direction. Wind direction can be to or from the main track.
- Over cross-tracks: tracks laid upon main tracks, either in the same or opposite direction
- Under cross-tracks: tracks covered with main tracks, either in the same or opposite direction
- Artificial tracks: caused by vehicle tires
- Animal tracks: intentional, such as horse or dog tracks, or unintentional, by game, cattle, etc.

COMPLICATIONS FOR CROSS-TRACK TRAINING

- Difference in time between the tracks
- Angle to the track (right, acute, obtuse)
- Age of the main track
- Place where the cross-track occurs: in the beginning of a main track, a dog needs time to recognize human scent; near the end, a dog is more tired

- Occupational odor of the cross-track layer (e.g., baker, farmer, construction worker)
- Combinations with other difficulties (e.g., soil, temperature)

Final Note

Always make sure in training that the dog can pick up the odor at the start, especially on stranger tracks. Experience shows that, especially with older stranger tracks, it will be almost impossible for the dog to reliably recognize the track-layer's scent within the first 40 yards (37 m). Inside this distance, dogs frequently have trouble with cross-tracks, especially when they are at an obtuse angle to the track. Subjecting a dog to such exercises as a test or trial is asking for trouble. Such a problem cannot be solved even by an excellent tracking dog.

For clean-scent training with unknown track-layers, we have generally found that about 40 to 80 yards (37–73 m) will be enough for a dog to get an imprint of the individual human scent in older tracks or tracks under difficult conditions. Odor summation, as discussed in Chapter 1, helps in this situation.

15

The Limits of Tracking

At the end of Chapter 7, Weather Conditions, we discussed how high the air temperature near the ground is on a sunny day and how this adds to the physical stressors on the dog during tracking. Yet even tracking under normal conditions is extremely strenuous, and the limits of a dog's physical and mental stress are quickly reached.

Dog Athletes

Intensive tracking requires great mental and physical efforts by the dog, just like top-level athletes. Tracking demands high neurological and cerebral activity, as well as an abnormal body position and concentrated muscular movements because the dog must walk in a peculiar, tense way — stretched and bent. These movements cause an extra load on the joints and the muscle activity produces pyruvate and lactate (lactic acid) in the muscular tissue (a process known as acidification). The more intensively and longer a dog tracks, the more his muscles produce lactic acid. If insufficient oxygen is taken into the body, the lactic acid accumulates, causing the muscles to contract less well. This causes muscle soreness and may cause the dog to limp or stop tracking.

Figure 15.1 On a sunny day, a dog is tracking in temperatures much higher than at the height of the handler.

Figure 15.2 Intensive tracking requires concentrated muscle movements from the dog, especially because of the tense, slow walking in a forced, curved posture.

High demands are also made on the dog's respiration, heartbeat, and body temperature. Table 15.1 shows the effort the dog brings to tracking. The dog's body temperature, pulse rate, and respiration all reach top levels.

Table 15.1. **Physical Stresses of Tracking***

	MALE		FEMALE	
	BEFORE	AFTER	BEFORE	AFTER
TEMPERATURE (°F)	100.9	104.2	101.1	103.5
TEMPERATURE (°C)	38.3	40.1	38.4	39.7
PULSE RATE	92	142	94	130
RESPIRATION	41	145	36	125

Research before and after working out a track about 1,000 paces long. The male is 5.5 years old and the female 3 years old; both are experienced tracking dogs.

* From I. Briewasser, "*Fährtenarbeit, die Grenze der Belastbarkeit*

Because of these requirements, before tracking we have to take our dog through warm-up exercises, just like an athlete, which allow the animal to prepare itself mentally and physically. First, remember to give the dog an opportunity to recover from the car ride or time in the kennel, including the opportunity to relieve himself. After that, the dog's joints and muscles can be prepared for tracking by quiet walking alternating with short runs. This warm-up can be more or less intensive, depending on the outdoor temperature.

The dog also needs a cool-down period. In his research, Briewasser determined that it took 1.5 hours for a dog's pre-tracking temperature, respiration, and pulse values to be restored after tracking. This compares to studies in which the body temperature of a dog after a 1,312 yard (1.2 km) tracking exercise increased to 41.86°C and 10 minutes after the exercise was still 40.56°C.[1] For that reason, we recommend that you walk with the dog in a relaxed way for 5 to 10 minutes after tracking and then give him at least 1.5 hours rest before starting other exercises.

From a veterinary view, intensive (ball) playing with the dog, or other active games, is inappropriate after tracking: a top-class athlete will, after great exertion, walk to cool down and then rest, not engage in another high-energy activity.

Figure 15.3 At higher outside temperatures (especially with high humidity and exertion) the dog's body temperature increases, which the dog tries to prevent by panting. In such a situation, unless steps are taken to modify the dog's heat, it can develop heat stroke quickly.

Figure 15.4 Intensive playing (e.g., throwing a ball) with the dog after the effort of tracking is not a good way to finish work or training. An easy walk would be far better.

Importance of Heat Regulation

The metabolism of the dog, even in rest, creates heat. With physical stress, like tracking, the production of heat increases. To avoid a damaging increase of body temperature, organisms shed superfluous heat all the time. Humans lose heat through perspiration (as do horses). The dog cannot perspire, except by the glands in their paw pads, but it can shed heat via the pharynx and trachea by fast and shallow respiration (panting). That panting looks exhausting, but it isn't so bad. Allow the dog to choose his position (sitting, standing, or lying down) to ensure he is comfortable as his body works to restore a proper body temperature.

Heat regulation takes place in the brainstem. Based on blood temperature and the stimulation of temperature senses in the skin, the heat control center in the brain regulates by creating or giving off heat. In hot conditions, the animal can't easily shed heat to the environment, so the dog has more trouble regulating itself. (In cold weather, increasing heat production is simpler through muscle movements like shivering, or by running around or other movements.)

At environmental temperatures over 28°C (especially in high humidity), the dog's body temperature increases, which will be moderated by panting as much as possible. If the environmental temperature increases, the body temperature of the dog also increases, in spite of his attempts to lose the superfluous heat in another way (e.g., by lying down on cold pavement).

Remedies for an overheating dog consist of, first, doing things to decrease the body temperature, such as bringing the dog into the shade or into a cool room (e.g., cellar, basement, air conditioned space), moistening the dog's limbs with cold water, placing ice packs around the head and neck, or careful sprinkling his body with cold water.

If you do not discover in time that the dog's heat control is threatening to break down, the dog may develop heat stroke,

Figure 15.5 If a dog shows signs of overheating, take steps immediately to lower its body temperature.

which can cause permanent damage. A body temperature of 40°C is at a critical level. Because of dilation of peripheral capillaries, the total blood vessel volume increases excessively and circulation fails. The pulse becomes irregular and weak, and the dog may exhibit vomiting and diarrhea. The dog will become exhausted and may lose consciousness.

At a body temperature of 41.5°C, the dog is in serious trouble. Cerebral and spinal cord functions become disordered, the dog may have problems moving, his heartbeat increases, and the dog will breathe quickly and deeply. Unlike panting, this fast, deep breathing is very hard on him.

Body temperatures of 42°C–43°C, even for a short time, are fatal. Animals that survive temperatures of 41°C can suffer permanent brain damage and cardiac arrhythmia. Such dogs are weak in the limbs (particularly the hindquarters). They look like they will faint, and often we see the eyes of the dog rolling up. Even if he survives the high body temperature, the dog has to be withdrawn from sports or operational service.

Pre-Hydration Strategies

In their 2020 study, Niedermeyer et al. evaluated four pre-exercise hydration strategies (oral water, chicken-flavored water, chicken-flavored oral electrolyte solution, and subcutaneous electrolyte solution) in working dogs conducting rigorous tracking operations in hot, arid conditions.[2] Seven border patrol search and rescue dogs in Texas were randomly assigned one of the hydration strategies for four days. After receiving the pre-hydration treatment, the dogs then ran two 1-mile tracks. All dogs were offered water while tracking.

Body weight, blood, and urine were collected at the beginning of the study day and at the end of each track. Core body temperatures were recorded using internal temperature sensing capsules. The impact of hydration strategy on change in weight, peak temperature, and serum chemical, hematological, and urinary parameters were analyzed.

Compared to the other three hydration strategies, dogs receiving chicken-flavored water had higher blood creatine kinase values at the end of the second track. Otherwise, the hydration strategies had minimal effects on blood or urine parameters.

Total fluid intake was lower with water only compared to the other three hydration strategies. Dogs taking water only developed elevated core body temperatures (median 41°C; 106°F) without signs of heat exhaustion or heat stroke. Alternate hydration strategies increased total fluid intake compared to water alone; however, chicken-flavored water resulted in increased markers of muscle injury, suggesting electrolyte-enriched strategies may have an advantage as a hydration strategy. Additionally, electrolyte-enriched fluids before exercise may help these dogs maintain lower peak temperatures.

OTHER PRECAUTIONS

Knowledge of the basic principles of heat regulation in dogs enables us to decide in every situation whether the conditions are acceptable. But the factors that determine the dog's resistance to high environmental temperatures are variable. Following are some of the factors to consider when dogs are exposed to high environmental temperatures:

- In hot conditions, dogs have more problems shedding excess heat than humans, so their body temperature increases faster than ours. Like wolves, the ancestor of the dog, they are more adapted to cold temperatures. That's why we cannot use our comfort level as a gauge for the dog's ability to endure heat: room temperature is often too warm for even an inactive dog.
- Shedding heat by panting is less effective for bigger, heavier dogs.
- Dogs with thicker subcutaneous fat tissue are more prone to overheating.
- Short-skulled breeds (e.g., Bulldogs and Boxers) are particularly sensitive to heat. In such dogs, the heat regulating surface in the respiratory system is small relative to other breeds.
- Sudden heat waves in the early spring will be more difficult for dogs to endure than the heat later in the summer when they are more acclimatized.
- Sudden shifts in weather and temperature are the most difficult to deal with.
- After eating, a body's metabolism (and therefore heat production) increases, which further stresses an organism in a hot environment. That's why in hot environments it's recommended that you divide your dog's food into two to four portions a day, providing the main portions early in the morning and/or later in the evening.
- Active animals produce more heat than resting animals. The same is true for temperamental, passionate, and nervous dogs.
- Dogs can pick up environmental radiant heat not only as direct solar rays, but also as radiation from the warm ground surface, as when tracking on a sunny day.
- There's a lot of evidence that thicker and/or longer coats not only protect animals in winter, but also against sun heat. It is not coincidental that sheep have excellent resistance to high temperatures. On this basis and other information, one might expect thick-coated and long-coated dog breeds to be better protected against heat radiation than short-haired breeds (e.g., Malinois and Doberman).
- Different dog breeds, based on their build, have different heat resistance. Boxers have at least three unfavorable factors: size, short

skull, and short-hair. Dobermans and Malinois have at least four unfavorable conditions: size, short-hair, spirit (drive, nervousness), and because of that, more energy consumption (hunger).

- It is often believed that well-trained dogs with a good performance record have the best resistance against heat. Such a belief is absolutely unfounded.

How Long?

In our seminars, people often ask how long a track is perceptible to dogs. Table 15.2 captures the data we've collected with numerous excellent tracking dogs. The oldest tracks of 36 hours were measured during very special weather conditions in the spring during exams of the former East German police dogs of the DDR Police Dog School in Naustadt in Saxony, which we witnessed in the late 1980s in the vicinity of Dresden. Under other favorable circumstances, the maximum times at which old tracks were worked out by the dogs vary between 18 and 24 hours. The 6-day-old track discussed in Chapter 7 was a very special exception.

We should add that the perception times recorded in Table 15.2 depend heavily on the condition of the ground surface (just mowed, short or long grass, freshly plowed or old field, manure or fertilizer present, age of the concrete, bricks or asphalt, etc.), the amount of rain and sunshine, the season, the time of the day the track was laid (morning, afternoon, evening, night) and the time of the day the dog worked out the track, whether the dog is working his own handler's track or a stranger's tracks, and the presence of cross-tracks.

Table 15.2. Perceptibility Under Various Conditions

	WEATHER	WIND	BEAUFORT NUMBER	TEMPERATURE °C	°F	HUMIDITY	PERCEPTION (hrs)
GRASS	Cloudy	Calm	0–1	17	63	Moist	18–36
	Bright	Gentle breeze	3	22	72	Normal	12–24
	Rain	Near gale	7	10	50	Moist	4–6
	Snow	Calm	0–1	–4	25	Moist	6–8
	Snow	Near gale	7	–8	17	Moist	2–4
FIELD	Bright	Calm	0–1	20	68	Moist	18–24
	Bright	Gentle breeze	3	22	72	Normal	10–16
	Cloudy	Near gale	7	17	63	Normal	6–8
	Rain	Moderate breeze	4	25	77	Moist	3–5
	Bright	Light air	1	–5	23	Normal	10–12
	Snow	fresh breeze	5	–8	17	Moist	4–6
SAND	Cloudy	Gentle breeze	3	21	70	Normal	6–8
	Bright	Gentle breeze	3	24	75	Dry	2–5
	Rain	Gale	8	10	50	Moist	1–2
	Cloudy	Moderate breeze	4	–10	14	Normal	6–12
	Snow	Near gale	7	–5	23	Moist	3–4
WOOD	Cloudy	Calm	0–1	17	63	Moist	18–24
	Bright	Gentle breeze	3	20	68	Normal	10–16
	Rain	Moderate breeze	4	15	59	Moist	8–12
	Snow	Light air	1	–4	25	Moist	6–8
CONCRETE	Cloudy	Calm	1	20	68	Normal	6–8
	Bright	Near gale	7	25	77	Dry	2–4
	Rain	Fresh breeze	5	11	52	Moist	1–2
	Snow	Light breeze	2	–5	23	Moist	4–6

(Continued)

Table 15.2. (Continued)

	WEATHER	WIND	BEAUFORT NUMBER	TEMPERATURE		HUMIDITY	PERCEPTION (hrs)
				°C	°F		
ASPHALT	Cloudy	Light air	1	15	59	Moist	4–6
	Rain	Light breeze	2	20	68	Moist	3–5
	Bright	Gentle breeze	3	20	68	Normal	2–4
	Bright	Light air	1	25	77	Dry	1–2
	Snow	Near gale	7	–6	21	Moist	3–4

The average perceptibility of human tracks by experienced tracking dogs. Wind-force, temperature and humidity measured at about 6 feet (1.75 m).

Conclusion

Although there are limits to their capabilities, and it is important for handlers to understand such limitations so their expectations are reasonable, dogs can smell more than we often realize and with focused training can often surpass our expectations.

To illustrate this, recall how dogs are not naturally sensitive to the odors of flowers. However, with the right training, these odors become interesting for dogs and they can attain exceptional achievements in this area, as drug detector dogs searching for marihuana and hashish (both odors of plants) daily demonstrate. Furthermore, we would like to remind you of the differences in prickle thresholds: Odors that are uninteresting to normal dogs (e.g., chemical odors, like amphetamines and XTC), become very interesting odors for drug detector dogs through focused training.

The same is true of our tracking dogs, although only dogs with a natural enthusiasm and interest for the odors of the track are able to become, and stay, track-sure. Successful tracking dogs must be trained clean-scent from the very beginning. Along with the passion and full attention of the dog, success also requires precision, attention, patience, and care from the handler. A clean-scent training method may take more time than other methods, but the achievements in tracking for sports and operational service dogs will increase enormously as a result.

Figure 16.1 Training clean-scent tracking may take more time than regular training, but the performance of your dog will be worth it.

Notes

INTRODUCTION
1. Organization of Scientific Area Committees for Forensic Science, Dogs and Sensors Subcommittee, "Crime Scene / Death Investigation – Dogs and Sensors Terms and Definitions," ASB Technical Report 025, 1st edition, (Colorado Springs, CO: AAFS Standards Board, 2017).

CHAPTER 1
1. R. J. Walker, *The Ichneutae of Sophocles* (London: Burns and Oates Ltd., 1919).
   F. R. Walton, "A Problem in the Ichneutae of Sophocles," *Harvard Studies in Classical Philology* 46 (1935): 167–189.
2. J. Bostock and H. T. Riley, *Pliny the Elder, The Natural History* (1855). www.perseus.tufts.edu/hopper/text?doc=Plin.+Nat.+toc.
3. H. Mynsinger, *Puoch von den valken, habichten, sperbern, pfaeriden, und hunden*, in M. von Stephanitz, *Der deutsche Schäferhund in Wort und Bild* (Jena: Anton Kampfe, 1473).
4. L. Huyghebaert, *Onze Belgische rashonden* (Antwerp: Cultura, 1925).
5. H. G. A. Gross, *Handbuch für Untersuchungsrichter, Polizeibeamte, Gendarmen, usw.* (*Handbook for Examining Magistrates, Police Officials, Military Policemen, etc.*) (Graz: Leuschner & Lubensky's Universitäts-Buchhandlung, 1893).
6. H. G. A. Gross, *"Gehilfe des Gendarmen" ("A Police Assistant"), Jahrbuch für die k.k. Gendarmerie* (Wien: Selbstverlag des Herausgebers, 1896).
7. J. Hansmann, *"Unter welchen Gesichtspunkten erfolgt die praktische Verwendung des Polizeifährtenhundes?" Zeitschrift für Hundeforschung* I (1931): 14–30.
8. F. Clater, *Die Abrichtung und Dressur des Hundes, insbesondere des Luxus-, Gebrauchs-, Kriegs-, Polizei- und Sanitäts-Hundes.* (*The Training of the Dog, Especially the Luxury, Utility, War, Police and SAR Dog*) 2nd edition (Leipzip: Ernst'sche Verlagsbuchhandlung, 1914).
9. G. J. Romanes, "Experiments on the Sense of Smell in Dogs," *Nature* 36 (1887): 273–274.
10. F. Schmidt, *Verbrecherspur und Polizeihund* (*Criminal Trails and Police Dogs*) (Augsburg: Selbstverlag SV, 1910).

11. F. Schmidt, *Polizeihund-Erfolge und Neue Winke für Polizeihund-Führer, -Liebhaber und Behörden (Police Dog Achievements and New Tips for the Police Dog Handler, -Enthusiasts and Authorities)* (Augsburg: Selbstverlag SV, 1911).
12. G. J. Romanes, "Experiments."
13. Th. Zell, *Der Polizeihund als Gehilfe der Strafrechtsorgane* (Berlin: Verlag Guttentag, 1909).
14. R. Blunk, *Die Ausbildung des Hundes zur Spurenreinheit* (Rostock: Hinstorff, 1926).
15. E. Brough, *The Bloodhound and Its Use in Tracking Criminals* (London: Illustrated Kennel News, 1905).
16. K. Most, *Leitfaden für die Abrichtung des Diensthundes auf Wissenschaftlicher Grundlage (Guide for Training the Service Dog on a Scientific Basis)* (Berlin: Kameradschaft Verlagsgesellschaft, 1920).
17. J. Hansmann, "Unter welchen Gesichtspunkten."
18. P. Böttger, "Hunde im Dienste der Kriminalpolizei," *Zeitschrift für Hundeforschung* V (1937): 1–32.
19. R. Blunk, *Die Ausbildung.*
20. R. Menzel and R. Menzel, *Die Verwertung der Riechfähigkeit des Hundes im Dienste der Menschheit* (Berlin: Kameradschaft-Verlag, 1930).
21. K. Most and G. H. Brückner, "Über Voraussetzungen und den derzeitigen Stand der Nasenleistungen von Hunden," *Zeitschrift für Hundeforschung* 5 (1936): 9–30.
22. R. Belleville, "Neue Versuche auf dem Gebiet der Fährtenarbeit und des Identifizierens von Gegenständen auf der Fährte," *Zeitschrift für Hundeforschung* XIII (1938): 17–28.
23. K. Most, "Neue Versuche über Spürfähigkeit," *Zeitschrift Der Hund* 18 (1926): 31–35.
    J. Hansmann, "Unter welchen Gesichtspunkten."
24. K. Most and G. H. Brückner, "Über Voraussetzungen."
25. R. J. Clifford, "Some Notes and Theories on Scent, Its Formation, Properties and Usage as Derived from Observations on and Experience with Tracker and Patrol Dogs," *J. R. Army Veteran Corps* 29 (1958): 145.
26. W. G. Syrotuck, *Scent and the Scenting Dog* (Westmoreland, NY: Arner Publications, 1972).
27. F. J. J. Buytendijk, *De psychologie van den hond* (Amsterdam: Kosmos, 1932).
28. R. Belleville, "Neue Versuche auf dem Gebiet der Fährtenarbeit und des Identifizierens von Gegenständen auf der Fährte," *Zeitschrift für Hundeforschung* XIII (1938): 17–28.
29. R. Menzel and R. Menzel, *Die Verwertung.*
30. R. Menzel and R. Menzel, *Die Verwertung.*
31. B. Schmid, "Umfang und Grenzen der Nasenleistung von Hunden," *Forschung Fortschritte* 13 (1937): 26–27.

CHAPTER 2

1. L. K. Cole, "Anatomy and Physiology of the Canine Ear," *Veterinary Dermatology* 20 (2009): 412–421. https://doi.org/10.1111/j.1365-3164.2009.00849.x.
   D. Michel, *Dogs and Hearing: Why Can They Hear Things We Can't?* Audicus (2015). https://www.audicus.com/dogs-and-hearing/.

2. A. Barber et al., "A Comparison of Hearing and Auditory Functioning Between Dogs and Humans," *Comparative Cognition and Behavior Reviews* 15 (2020): 1–36. researchgate.net/publication/343021593 doi: 10.3819/CCBR.2020.150005E

3. H. Stephan, *"Die Anwendung der Schnell'schen Formel h=ks.p auf Hirn- Körpergewichtsbeziehungen bei verschiedene Hunderassen,"* *Zoologischer Anzeiger* 153 (1954): 15–27.

4. R. Menzel and R. Menzel, *Pariahunde* (Wittenberg Lutherstadt: A. Ziemsen Verlag, 1960).

5. S-E. Byosiere et al., "What Do Dogs (*Canis familiaris*) See? A Review of Vision in Dogs and Implications for Cognition Research," *Psychonomic Bulletin & Review* 25 (2018): 1798–1813.

6. P. E. Miller and C. J. Murphy, "Vision in Dogs," *Journal of the American Veterinary Medical Association* 207 (1995):1623–1634.

7. I. Gazit et al, "Formation of an Olfactory Search Image for Explosives Odours in Sniffer Dogs," *Ethology* 111 (2005): 669–680.

8. A. Kokocińska-Kusiak et al., "Canine Olfaction: Physiology, Behavior, and Possibilities for Practical Applications," *Animals* 11 (2021): 2463. https://doi.org/10.3390/ani11082463.

9. H. Stephan, "Die Anwendung."

10. I. Salazar et al., "Chapter 4: Anatomy of the Olfactory Mucosa," in *Handbook of Clinical Neurology* 164 (2019): 47–65. https://doi.org/10.1016/B978-0-444-63855-7.00004-6.

11. P. G. Hepper and D. L. Wells, "Perinatal Olfactory Learning in the Domestic Dog," *Chemical Senses* 31 (2005): 207–212.

12. J. K. Olofsson et al., "A Cortical Pathway to Olfactory Naming: Evidence from Primary Progressive Aphasia," *Brain: A Journal of Neurology* 136 (2013): 1245–1259. https://doi.org/10.1093/brain/awt019.

13. J. v. Uexküll and G. Kriszat, *"Streifzüge durch die Umwelten von Tieren und Menschen,"* *Verständliche Wissenschaft* XXI (Berlin, 1934).

14. F. J. J. Buytendijk, *De Psychologie van den Hond* (Amsterdam: Kosmos, 1932).

15. P. Vroon, *Zonder geur geen Emoties* (Amsterdam: De Volkskrant, 1989).

16. O. Sacks, *The Man Who Mistook His Wife for a Hat, and Other Clinical Tales* (New York: Summit Books, 1985).

17. R. W. Moncrieff, *The Chemical Senses* (London: Leonard Hill, 1967).
    W. Neuhaus, *"Die Unterscheidung von Duftquantitäten bei Mensch und Hund nach Versuchen mit Buttersäure,"* *Zeitschrift für vergleichende Physiologie* 37 (1955): 234–252.

18. Y. Yeshurun and N. Sobel, "An Odor Is Not Worth a Thousand Words: From Multidimensional Odors to Unidimensional Odor Objects," *Annual Review of Psychology* 61 (2020): 219–241.

19. T. Lord and M. Kasprzak, "Identification of Self through Olfaction," *Perceptual and Motor Skills* 69 (1989): 219–224.

20. R. H. Porter et al., "Maternal Recognition of Neonates through Olfactory Cues," *Physiology & Behavior* 30 (1983): 151–154.

21. B. Schaal et al., "Olfactory Stimulations in Mother–Child Relations," *Reproduction, Nutrition, Development* 20 (1980): 843–858.

22. K. R. Hovis et al., "Activity Regulates Functional Connectivity from the Vomeronasal Organ to the Accessory Olfactory Bulb," *Journal of Neuroscience* 32 (2012): 7907–7916.

23. J. Porter et al., "Mechanisms of Scent-Tracking in Humans," *Natural Neuroscience* 10 (2007): 27–29.
24. L. Sela and N. Sobel, "Human Olfaction: A Constant State of Change-Blindness," *Experimental Brain Research* 205 (2010): 13–29.
25. J. Bodingbauer, *Das Wunder der Hundenase* (Wien: Unsere Hunde, 1977).

CHAPTER 3
1. A. Schoon and R. Haak, *K9 Suspect Discrimination: Training and Practicing Scent Identification Line-Ups* (Calgary, AB: Detselig Enterprises Ltd., now Brush Education Inc., 2002).
2. J. Bodingbauer, *Das Wunder der Hundenase* (Wien: Unsere Hunde, 1977).
3. M. D. Pearsall and H. Verbruggen, *Scent* (Colorado: Alpine Publishing, Inc., 1982).
4. K. Wagner, *Rezente Hunderassen: Eine osteologische Untersuchung* (Oslo: J. Dybwad, 1930).
5. M. Nelissen, *Introductie tot de gedragsbiologie* (Garant, Leuven/Apeldoorn, 1996).
6. T. Jezierski et al., *Canine Olfaction Science and Law: Advances in Forensic Science, Medicine, Conservation, and Environmental Remediation* (CRC Press, 2016).
7. L. Briand et al., "Evidence of an Odorant-Binding Protein in the Human Olfactory Mucus: Location, Structural Characterization, and Odorant-Binding Properties," *Biochemistry* 41 (2002): 7241–52. doi: 10.1021/bi015916c.
8. C. M. Blatt et al., "Thermal Panting in Dogs: The Lateral Nasal Gland, A Source of Water for Evaporative Cooling," *Science* (1972): 804–5.
9. J. Bodingbauer, *Das Wunder der Hundenase.*
10. A. Horowitz, *Being a Dog: Following the Dog into a World of Smell* (New York: Scribner, 2017, p. 8–9).
11. J. Kaldenbach, *K9 Scent Detection, My Favorite Judge Lives in a Kennel* (Calgary, AB: Detselig Enterprises Ltd., now Brush Education Inc., 1998).
12. W. Neuhaus, "*Die Unterscheidungsfähigkeit des Hundes für Duftgemische,*" *Zeitschrift für vergleichende Physiologie* 39 (1956): 25–43.
13. A. Thesen et al., "Behaviour of Dogs During Olfactory Tracking," *Journal of Experimental Biology* 180 (1993): 247–251.
14. P. G. Hepper and D. L. Wells, "How Many Footsteps Do Dogs Need to Determine the Direction of an Odour Trail?" *Chemical Senses* 30 (2005): 291–298.
15. A. Thesen et al., "Behaviour."
16. W. Neuhaus, "*Über die Riechschärfe des Hundes für Fettsäuren,*" *Zeitschrift für vergleichende Physiologie* 35 (1953): 527–552.
17. N. Sobel et al., "The World Smells Different to Each Nostril," *Nature* 402 (2000): 35.
18. K. C. Catania, "Stereo and Serial Sniffing Guide Navigation to an Odour Source in a Mammal," *Nature Communications* 4 (2013): 1441.
M. E. Staymates et al., "Biomimetic Sniffing Improves the Detection Performance of a 3D Printed Nose of a Dog and a Commercial Trace Vapor Detector," *Scientific Reports* 6, 36876 (2016).

CHAPTER 4

1. G. E. Schwartz, et al., "EEG Responses to Low-Level Chemicals in Normals and Cacosmics," *Toxicology and Industrial Health* 10 (1995): 633–643.
2. A. Schoon, *The Performance of Dogs in Identifying Humans by Scent*, Dissertation (The Netherlands: University of Leiden, 1997).
3. W. Neuhaus, *"Die Bedeutung des Schnüffelns für das Riechen des Hundes,"* *Zeitung für Säugetierkunde* 46 (1981): 301–310.
4. K. Zuschneid, *Die Riechleistung des Hundes*, Dissertation (Berlin: Freie University, 1973).
5. L. Issel-Tarver and J. Rine, "Organization and Expression of Canine Olfactory Receptor Genes," Proceedings of the National Academy of Sciences of the USA, 93 (1996): 10897–10902.
6. P. Pelosi, "Odorant-Binding Proteins," *Critical Reviews in Biochemistry and Molecular Biology* 29 (1994): 199–228.
7. S. L. Sullivan, et al., "Spatial Patterning and Information Coding in the Olfactory System," *Current Opinion in Genetics and Development* 5 (1995): 516–523.
8. P. Mombaerts, "Genes and Ligands for Odorant, Vomeronasal and Taste Receptors," *Nature Reviews Neuroscience* 5 (2004): 263–278.
9. K. Mori and Y. Yoshihara, "Molecular Recognition and Olfactory Processing in the Mammalian Olfactory System," *Progress in Neurobiology* 45: (1995): 585–619.
10. R. Vassar, et al., "Topographic Organization of Sensory Projections to the Olfactory Bulb," *Cell* 76 (1995): 981–991.
11. H. Hatt, *"Von der Nase bis ins Gehirn: Düfte nehmen Gestalt an." Zellphysiologie Neurorubin* (2003): 17.
12. D. M. Stoddart, *The Scented Ape* (Cambridge: Cambridge University Press, 1990).
13. T. S. Lorig, "EEG and ERP Studies of Low-Level Odor Exposure in Normal Subjects," *Toxicology and Industrial Health* 10 (1995): 579–586.
14. T. Komori, et al., "Potential Antidepressant Effects of Lemon Odor in Rats," *European Neuropsychopharmacology* 5 (1995): 477–480.
15. D. M. Stoddart, *The Scented Ape.*
16. A. Schoon, *The Performance of Dogs.*
17. S. Gadbois and C. Reeve, "Canine Olfaction: Scent, Sign, and Situation," in A. Horowitz (ed.), *Domestic Dog Cognition and Behavior* (Berlin: Springer-Verlag, 2014).
18. C. D. Arons and W. J. Shoemaker, "The Distribution of Catecholamines and Beta-Endorphin in the Brains of Three Behaviorally Distinct Breeds of Dogs and Their F1 Hybrids," *Brain Research* 594 (1992): 31–39.
19. S. Gadbois and C. Reeve, "Canine Olfaction."
20. B. Schaal, et al., "Olfactory Preferences in Newborn Lambs: Possible Influence of Prenatal Experience," *Behaviour* 132 (1995): 351–365.
    B. Schaal, et al., "Responsiveness to the Odour of Amniotic Fluid in the Human Neonate," *Biology of the Neonate* 67 (1995): 397–406.
21. P. G. Hepper, "Long-Term Retention of Kinship Recognition Established During Infancy in the Domestic Dog," *Behavioural Processes* 33 (1994): 14.
22. R. E. Lubow, et al., "Information Processing of Olfactory Stimuli by the Dog: I. The Acquisition and Retention of Four Odor-Pair Discriminations," *Bulletin of the Psychonomic Society* 1 (1973): 143–145.

23. J. D. Pierce, et al., "Cross-Adaptation of Sweaty-Smelling 3-Methyl-2-Hexonoic Acid by a Structurally Similar, Pleasant Smelling Odorant," *Chemical Senses* 20 (1995): 401–411.

24. J. Corwin, et al., "Workplace, Age and Sex as Mediators of Olfactory Function: Data from the National Geographic Smell Survey," *Journals of Gerontology Series B –Psychological Sciences and Social Sciences* 50 (1995): P179–P186.

25. R. Gross-Isseroff and D. Lancet, "Concentration Dependent Changes of Perceived Odor Quality," *Chemical Senses* 13 (1988): 191–204.

26. M. Laska and R. Hudson, "Discriminating Parts from a Whole: Determinants of Odor Mixture Perception in Squirrel Monkeys, *Saimiri sciureus*," *Journal of Comparative Physiology A – Sensory Neural and Behavioral Physiology* 173 (1993): 249–256.

27. D. G. Laing, et al., "Odor Masking in the Rat," *Physiology & Behavior* 45 (1989): 689–694.

28. U. Staubli, et al., "Olfaction and the 'Data' Memory System in Rats," *Behavioral Neuroscience* 101 (1987): 757–765.

29. J. Najbauer and M. Leon, "Olfactory Experience Modulates Apoptosis in the Developing Olfactory Bulb," *Brain Research* 674 (1995): 245–251.

30. R. J. Pietras and D. G. Moulton, "Hormonal Influences on Odor Detection in Rats: Changes Associated with the Estrous Cycle, Pseudopregnancy, Ovariectomy, and Administration of Testosterone," *Physiology & Behavior* 12 (1974): 475–491.

31. W. J. Evans, et al., "Olfactory Event-Related Potentials in Normal Human Objects: Effects of Age and Gender," *Electroencephalography and Clinical Neurophysiology* 95 (1995): 293–301.

32. D. A. Marshall, et al., "Odor Detection Curves for *n*-Pentanoic Acid in Dogs and Humans," *Chemical Senses* 6 (1981): 445–453.

33. J. C. Stevens, et al., "Variability of Olfactory Thresholds," *Chemical Senses* 13 (1988): 643–653.

34. N. L. Segal, et al., "A Twin Study of Odor Identification and Olfactory Sensitivity," *Acta Geneticae Medicae Gemellologiae* 41 (1992): 113–121.

35. E. K. Altom, et al., "Effect of Dietary Fat Source and Exercise on Odorant-Detecting Ability of Canine Athletes," *Research in Veterinary Science* 75 (2003): 149–55.

36. E. K. Jenkins, et al., "When the Nose Doesn't Know: Canine Olfactory Function Associated with Health, Management, and Potential Links to Microbiota," *Frontiers in Veterinary Science* 5 (2018).

37. L. J. Myers, et al., "Dysfunction of Sense of Smell Caused by Canine Parainfluenza Infection in Dogs," *American Journal of Veterinary Research* 49 (1988): 188–190.

38. J. Corwin, "Olfactory Identification in Hemodialysis: Acute and Chronic Effects on Discrimination and Response Bias," *Neuropsychologia* 27 (1990): 513–522.

39. P. I. Ezeh, et al., "Effects of Steroids on the Olfactory Function of the Dog," *Physiology and Behavior* 51 (1992): 1183–1187.

40. M. S. Lewitt, et al. "Sensory Perception and Hypothyriodism," *Chemical Senses* 14 (1989): 537–546.

41. J. A. Ship and J. M. Weiffenbach, "Age, Gender, Medical Treatment, and Medication Effects on Smell Identification," *Journal of Gerontology: Medical Sciences* 48 (1993): M26–M32.

42. E. K. Jenkins, et al., "When the Nose."
43. L. J. Myers, "Dysosmia of the Dog in Clinical Veterinary Medicine," *Progress in Veterinary Neurology* 1 (1990): 171–9.
44. E. J. M. McNeill and S. Carrie, "Olfactory Dysfunction – Assessment and Management," *Journal of ENT Masterclass* 2 (2009): 68–73.
45. A. Schoon and R. Haak, *K9 Suspect Discrimination: Training and Practicing Scent Identification Line-Ups* (Calgary, AB: Detselig Enterprises Ltd., now Brush Education Inc., 2002).

CHAPTER 5

1. K. Most and G. H. Brückner, "*Über Voraussetzungen und den derzeitigen Stand der Nasenleistungen von Hunden,*" Zeitschrift für Hundeforschung 5 (1936): 9–30.
2. K. Most, *Leitfaden für die Abrichtung des Diensthundes auf Wissenschaftlicher Grundlage* (Berlin: Kameradschaft Verlagsgesellschaft, 1920).
3. A. S. Romer, *The Vertebrate Body* (Philadelphia: W.B. Saunders Company, 1962).
4. E. J. King, et al., "Studies on Olfactory Discrimination in Dogs: (3) Ability to Detect Human Odour Trace," *Animal Behaviour* 12 (1964): 311–315.
5. R. S. Ramotowski, "Composition of Latent Fingerprint Residue," in *Advances in Fingerprint Technology*, Ed. H. C. Lee and R. E. Gaensslen (Boca Raton: CRC Press, 2001).
6. A. I. Spielman, et al., "Proteinacceous Precusors of Human Axillary Odor: Isolation of Two Novel Odor-Binding Proteins," *Experientia* 51 (1995): 40–47.
7. D. M. Stoddart, *The Ecology of Vertebrate Olfaction* (London: Chapman and Hall, 1980).
8. R. S. Ramotowski, "Composition."
9. H. C. Korting, et al., "Microbial Flora and Odor of the Healthy Human Skin," *Hautarzt* 39 (1988): 564–568.
10. N. Nicolaides, "Skin Lipids: Their Biochemical Uniqueness," *Science* 186 (1974): 19–26.
    N. Nicolaides and J. M. B. Apon, "The Saturated Methyl Branched Fatty Acids of Adult Human Skin Surface Lipid," *Biomedical Mass Spectrometry* 4 (1977): 337–347.
11. L. Norlen, et al., "Inter- and Intra-Individual Differences in Human Stratum Corneum Lipid Content Related to Physical Parameters of Skin Barrier Function In Vivo," *Journal of Investigative Dermatology* 112 (1999): 72–77.
    L. Bonifort, et al., "Skin Surface Lipids. Identification and Determination by Thin-Layer Chromatography and Gas-Liquid Chromatography," *Clinica Chimica Acta* (1973): 223–231.
    S. C. Green, et al., "Variation in Sebum Fatty Acid Composition Among Adult Humans," *Journal of Investigative Dermatology* 83 (1984): 114–117.
    M. E. Stewart, et al., "Possible Genetic Control of the Proportions of Branched-Chain Fatty Acids in Human Sebaceous Wax Esters," *Journal of Investigative Dermatology* 86 (1986): 706–708.
12. L. Löhner, "*Über menschliche Individual- und Regionalgerüche,*" Archiv gesellschaft für Physiologie 202 (1924): 25–45.

13. W. Neuhaus, *"Über die Riechschärfe des Hundes für Fettsäuren,"* *Zeitschrift für vergleichende Physiologie* 35 (1953): 527–552.
14. I. L. Brisbin, Jr. and S. N. Austed, "Testing the Individual Odour Theory of Canine Olfaction," *Animal Behavior* 42 (1991): 63–69.
15. I. L. Brisbin, Jr. and S. N. Austed, "The Use of Trained Dogs to Discriminate Human Scent," *Animal Behavior* 46 (1993): 191–192
16. I. L. Brisbin, Jr. and S. N. Austed, "Testing."
17. A. Schoon and J. C. de Bruin, "The Ability of Dogs to Recognize and Cross-Match Human Odours," *Forensic Science International* 69 (1994): 111–118.
18. D. M. Stoddart, *The Scented Ape* (Cambridge: Cambridge University Press, 1990).
19. Z. T. Halpin, "Individual Odors among Mammals: Origin and Functions," *Advances in the Study of Behavior* 16 (1986): 39–70.
20. R. E. Brown, "What Is the Role of the Immune System in Determining Individually Distinct Body Odours?" *International Journal of Immunopharmacology* 17 (1985): 655–661.
21. E. A. Boyse, "HLA and the Chemical Senses," *Human Immunology* 15 (1986): 391–395.
24. R. S. Ramotowski, "Composition."
25. R. S. Ramotowski, "Composition."
26. R. M. Wilcox, and R. E. Johnston, "Scent Counter-Marks: Specialised Mechanisms of Perception and Response to Individual Odors in Golden Hamsters *(Mesocricetus auratus)*" *Journal of Comparative Psychology* 109 (1995): 349–356.
27. R. E. Johnston, et al., "Scent Counter-Marking in Meadow Voles: Females Prefer the Top-Scent Male," *Ethology* 103 (1997): 443–453.
28. H. Kalmus, "The Discrimination by the Nose of the Dog of Individual Human Odours and in Particular of the Odours of Twins," *British Journal of Animal Behavior* 5 (1955): 25–31.
29. L. Löhner, *"Über menschliche."*
30. M. Rogowski, "Possibility of Removing the Individual Scent with the Aid of Clothes," Paper presented at conference: Osmology: Overestimated or Neglected Area of Forensic Science? *Problemy Kryminalistyki* 230 (2000): 56–58.

CHAPTER 6

1. W. Neuhaus, *"Über die Riechschärfe des Hundes für Fettsäuren,"* *Zeitschrift für vergleichende Physiologie* 35 (1953): 527–552.
2. W. Neuhaus, *"Die Unterscheidungsfähigkeit des Hundes für Duftgemische,"* *Zeitschrift für vergleichende Physiologie* 39 (1956): 25–43.
3. L. Löhner, *"Über menschliche Individual- und Regionalgerüche,"* *Archiv gesellschaft für Physiology* 202 (1924): 25–45.
4. W. Neuhaus, *"Die 'Fährtenreinheit' des Hundes,"* *Die Umschau* 6 (1958): 161–163.
5. J. Hansmann, *"Unter welchen Gesichtspunkten erfolgt die praktische Verwendung des Polizeifährtenhundes?"* *Zeitschrift für Hundeforschung* I (1931): 14–30.
6. F. Kanda, et al., "Elucidation of Chemical Compounds Responsible for Foot Malodour," *British Journal of Dermatology* 122 (1990), 771–6.

7. W. Neuhaus, *"Über die Riechschärfe."*
   W. Neuhaus, *"Die Unterscheidung von Duftquantitäten bei Mensch und Hund nach Versuchen mit Buttersäure,"* *Zeitschrift für vergleichende Physiologie* 37 (1955): 234–252.
8. W. Neuhaus, *"Die 'Fährtenreinheit.'"*

CHAPTER 7
1. R. Menzel and R. Menzel, *Die Verwertung der Riechfähigkeit des Hundes im Dienste der Menschheit* (Berlin: Kameradschaft Verlag, 1930).
2. J. Jinn, et al., "How Ambient Environment Influences Olfactory Orientation in Search and Rescue Dogs," *Chemical Senses* 45 (2020): 625–634.
3. L. Haberhauffe, *Ungewöhnliches Fährtenalter*, Personal message, 2003.
4. G. M. Niedermeyer, et al., "A Randomized Cross-Over Field Study of Pre-Hydration Strategies in Dogs Tracking in Hot Environments," *Frontiers in Veterinary Science* 7 (2020): 292.

CHAPTER 11
1. W. Neuhaus, *"Die Unterscheidungsfähigkeit des Hundes für Duftgemische,"* *Zeitschrift für vergleichende Physiologie* 39 (1956): 25–43.
2. H. G. Niemand, *"Ist der Individualgeruch für den Hund richtunggebend zum Erkennen seines Herrn?"* *Zeitschrift für Hundeforschung* XII (1938).
3. K. Most, and G. H. Brückner, *"Über Voraussetzungen und den derzeitigen Stand der Nasenleistungen von Hunden,"* *Zeitschrift für Hundeforschung* 5 (1936): 9–30.
4. A. Thesen, et al., *"*Behaviour of Dogs During Olfactory Tracking," *Journal of Experimental Biology* 180 (1993): 247–251.
5. J. Bräuer and D. Blasi, "Dogs Display Owner-Specific Expectations Based on Olfaction," *Scientific Reports* 11 (2021): 3291.
6. K. Krall, *Denkende Tiere, Beiträge zur Tierseelenkunde auf Grund eigener Versuche, der Kluge Hans und meine Pferde Muhamed und Zarif* (Leipzig: Friedrich Engelman, 1912).
7. O. Pfungst, *Clever Hans: The Horse of Mr. Von Osten* (New York: Holt, Rinehart & Winston, 1911).
8. K. Soproni, et al., "Comprehension of Human Communicative Signs in Pet Dogs (*Canis familiaris*)," *Journal of Comparative Psychology* 115 (2001): 122–126.
9. K. Soproni, et al., "Dogs' (*Canis familiaris*) Responsiveness to Human Pointing Gestures," *Journal of Comparative Psychology* 116 (2002): 27–34.
10. M. T. DeChant, et al., "Effect of Handler Knowledge of the Detection Task on Canine Search Behavior and Performance," *Frontiers in Veterinary Science* 7 (2020): 250.
11. D. Katz, *Animals and Men: Studies in Comparative Psychology* (London: Harmondsworth Penguin, 1953).

CHAPTER 14
1. T. Uchida, *Proceedings: XIV International Congress of Zoology* (1953): 292.
2. J. Honhon, *L'Olfaction chez le Chien. Son Rôle dans le Pistage et la Localisation d'une Source Odorante*, Dissertation, Paris, 1967.

CHAPTER 15
1. G. Radke, Police Dog Service Training Centre, Innisfail, Alberta, Canada, Personal communication, November 6, 1998.
2. G. M. Niedermeyer, et al., "A Randomized Cross-Over Field Study of Pre-Hydration Strategies in Dogs Tracking in Hot Environments," *Frontiers in Veterinary Science* 7 (2020): 292.

Photo Credits

Joseph Bodingbauer: 3.6. Ruud Haak/ Korps Landelijke Politie Diensten: 11.2, 12.7, 12.8, 13.8, 14.5. Will Harford (freerangestock. com): 2.10. *Hondensport & Sporthonden* (Topaaz): 6.5. Marco Leeflang: 11.11. Micke Månsson: 7.14. *Onze Hond* (archive): 1.1, 1.2, 1.3 (Roger De Caluwé), 1.6, 1.16, 2.4, 2.7, 2.8, 2.11, 3.1, 3.10 (A. Thesen et al.), 4.3 (K. Zuschneid), 4.10, 5.4, 5.6, 6.3, 6.4, 6.6, 6.7, 8.2, 8.3, 8.4, 8.5, 8.6, 8.8, 8.10, 11.7, 15.3, 15.5. Hans Scheffers: 8.9. Friedo Schmidt (*Verbrecherspur und Polizeihund*): 1.4. Max von Stephanitz (*Der deutsche Schäferhund in Wort und Bild*): 1.13, 1.14. U.S. Department of Defence (Cpl. Tyler Giguere): 4.2. Wikimedia Commons: 2.5 (Arcadiuš, https://commons.wikimedia.org/ wiki/File:203-365_Zinneke_Pis,_Bruxelles.jpg), 3.3 (Waugsberg, https://commons.wikimedia.org/w/index.php?curid=4567105).

Bibliography

Adams, G. J., and Johnson, K. G. (1994). "Sleep, Work and the Effects of Shift Work in Drug Detector Dogs." *Applied Animal Behaviour Science* 41: 115–126.

Allison, A. C. (1953). "The Morphology of the Olfactory System in the Vertebrates." *Biological Reviews* 28 (2): 195–244. https://doi.org/10.1111/j.1469-185X.1953. tb01376.x.

Altom, E. K., Davenport, G. M., Myers, L. J., and Cummins, K. A. (2003). "Effect of Dietary Fat Source and Exercise on Odorant-Detecting Ability of Canine Athletes." *Research in Veterinary Science* 75: 149–55. doi:10.1016/S0034-5288(03)00071-7.

Arons, C. D., and Shoemaker, W. J. (1992). "The Distribution of Catecholamines and Beta-endorphin in the Brains of Three Behaviorally Distinct Breeds of Dogs and Their F1 Hybrids." *Brain Research* 594: 31–39.

Ashton, E. H., and Eayrs, J. T. (1970). "Detection of Hidden Objects by Dogs." *Symposium on Taste and Smell in Vertebrates*, 251–263.

Barber, A., Wilkinson, A., Montealegre-Z, F., Ratcliffe, V., Guo, K., and Mills, D. (2020). *A Comparison of Hearing and Auditory Functioning Between Dogs and Humans.* doi: 10.3819/CCBR.2020.150005E.

Barrios, A. W., Sánchez-Quinteiro, P., and Salazar I. (2014). "Dog and Mouse: Toward a Balanced View of the Mammalian Olfactory System." *Frontiers in Neuroanatomy* 8: 106. doi: 10.3389/fnana.2014.00106.

Belleville, R. (1938). *"Neue Versuche auf dem Gebiet der Fährtenarbeit und des Identifizierens von Gegenständen auf der Fährte."* *Zeitschrift für Hundeforschung* XIII: 17–28.

Blatt, C. M., Taylor, C. R., and Habal, M. B. (1972). "Thermal Panting in Dogs: The Lateral Nasal Gland, A Source of Water for Evaporative Cooling." *Science* 177 (4051): 804–5.

Blunk, R. (1926). *Die Ausbildung des Hundes zur Spurenreinheit.* Rostock: Hinstorff.

Bodingbauer, J. (1977). *Das Wunder der Hundenase.* Wien: Unsere Hunde.

Boekh, J. (1972). *"Die chemische Sinne Geruch und Geschmack,"* in *Somatische Sensibilität, Geruch und Geschmack, Sinnesphysiologie 1, Physiologie des Menschen* 11, Wien.

Bonifort, L., Passi, S., Caprilli, F., and Nazarro-Porro, M. (1973). "Skin Surface Lipids. Identification and Determination by Thin-Layer Chromatography and Gas-Liquid Chromatography." *Clinica Chimica Acta* 47: 223–231.

Bostock, J., and Riley, H. T. (1855). *Pliny the Elder, The Natural History.* http://www. perseus.tufts.edu/hopper/text?doc=Plin.+Nat.+toc.

Böttger, P. (1930). *Der Hund als Freund und Helfer des Menschen.* Presentation, Whitsun Conference, Linz, Austria.

Böttger, P. (1937). *"Hunde im Dienste der Kriminalpolizei." Zeitschrift für Hundeforschung* V: 1– 32.

Boyse, E. A. (1986). "HLA and the Chemical Senses." *Human Immunology* 15: 391–395.

Bräuer, J., and Blasi, D. (2021). "Dogs Display Owner-Specific Expectations Based on Olfaction." *Scientific Reports* 11: 3291. https://doi.org/10.1038/s41598-021-82952-4.

Briand, L., Eloit, C., Nespoulous, C., Bézirard, V., Huet, J. C., Henry, C., Blon, F., Trotier, D., and Pernollet, J. C. (2002). "Evidence of an Odorant-Binding Protein in the Human Olfactory Mucus: Location, Structural Characterization, and Odorant-Binding Properties." *Biochemistry* 41 (23): 7241–52. doi: 10.1021/bi015916c.

Briewasser, I. (1989). *"Fährtenarbeit, die Grenze der Belastbarkeit." Magazine Unsere Hunde*, January.

Brisbin, Jr., I. L., and Austed, S. N. (1991). "Testing the Individual Odour Theory of Canine Olfaction." *Animal Behavior* 42: 63–69.

Brisbin, Jr., I. L., and Austed, S. N. (1993). "The Use of Trained Dogs to Discriminate Human Scent." *Animal Behavior* 46: 191–192.

Brough, E. (1905). "The Bloodhound and Its Use in Tracking Criminals." *Illustrated Kennel News*, London.

Brown, R. E. (1995). "What Is the Role of the Immune System in Determining Individually Distinct Body Odours?" *International Journal of Immunopharmacology* 17 (8): 655–661.

Brückner, G. H. (1944). *"Der Hund im Kriege: Erfahrungen über Abrichtung und Einsatz." Zeitschrift für Hundeforschung* XVIII.

Buytendijk, F. J. J. (1932). *De psychologie van den hond.* Amsterdam: Kosmos.

Byosiere, S-E., Chouinard, P. A., Howell, T. J., and Bennett, P. C. (2018). "What Do Dogs *(Canis familiaris)* See? A Review of Vision in Dogs and Implications for Cognition Research." *Psychonomic Bulletin & Review* 25: 1798–1813.

Catania, K. C. (2013). "Stereo and Serial Sniffing Guide Navigation to an Odour Source in a Mammal." *Nature Communications* 4: 1441.

Clater, F. (1914). *Die Abrichtung und Dressur des Hundes, insbesondere des Luxus-, Gebrauchs-, Kriegs-, Polizei- und Sanitäts-Hunde,* 2nd edition. Leipzig: Ernst'sche Verlagsbuchhandlung.

Clifford, R. J. (1958). "Some Notes and Theories on Scent, Its Formation, Properties and Usage as Derived from Observations on and Experience with Tracker and Patrol Dogs." *J. R. Army Veteran Corps* 29: 145.

Cole, L. K. (2009). "Anatomy and Physiology of the Canine Ear." *Veterinary Dermatology* 20 (5–6): 412–421. https://doi.org/10.1111/j.1365-3164.2009.00849.x.

Corwin, J. (1990). "Olfactory Identification in Hemodialysis: Acute and Chronic Effects on Discrimination and Response Bias." *Neuropsychologia* 27: 513–522.

Corwin, J., Loury, M., and Gilbert, A. N. (1995). "Workplace, Age and Sex as Mediators of Olfactory Function: Data from the National Geographic Smell Survey." *Journals of Gerontology Series B-Psychological Sciences and Social Sciences* 50 (4): 179–186.

Craven, B. A., Neuberger, T., Paterson, E. G., Webb, A. G., Josephson, E. M., Morrison, E. E., and Settles, G. S. (2007). "Reconstruction and Morphometric Analysis of the Nasal Airway of the Dog *(Canis familiaris)* and Implications Regarding Olfactory Airflow." *Anatomical Record* (Hoboken) 290 (11): 1325–40. https://doi.org/10.1002/ar.20592.

Craven, B. A., Paterson, E .G., and Settles, G. S. (2010). "The Fluid Dynamics of Canine Olfaction: Unique Nasal Airflow Patterns as an Explanation of Macrosmia." *Journal of the Royal Society Interface* 7: 933–943. https://doi.org/10.1098/rsif.2009.0490.

DeChant, M. T., Ford, C., and Hall, N. J. (2020). "Effect of Handler Knowledge of the Detection Task on Canine Search Behavior and Performance." *Frontiers in Veterinary Science* 7: 250. doi: 10.3389/fvets.2020.00250.

DeChant, M. T., and Hall, N. J. (2021). "Training with Varying Odor Concentrations: Implications for Odor Detection Thresholds in Canines." *Animal Cognition* 24: 889–896. https://doi.org/10.1007/s10071-021-01484-6.

Evans, W. J., Cui, L. Y., and Starr, A. (1995). "Olfactory Event-Related Potentials in Normal Human Objects: Effects of Age and Gender." *Electroencephalography and Clinical Neurophysiology* 95 (4): 293–301.

Ezeh, P. I., Myers, L. J., Hanrahan, L. A., Kemppainen, R. J., and Cummins, K. A. (1992). "Effects of Steroids on the Olfactory Function of the Dog." *Physiology & Behavior* 51 (6): 1183–1187.

Gadbois, S., and Reeve, C. (2014). "Canine Olfaction: Scent, Sign, and Situation," in A. Horowitz (ed.), *Domestic Dog Cognition and Behavior*. Berlin: Springer-Verlag. doi: 10.1007/978-3-642-53994-7_1.

Gazit, I., Goldblatt, A., and Terkel, J. (2005). "Formation of an Olfactory Search Image for Explosives Odours in Sniffer Dogs." *Ethology* 111 (7): 669–680.

Gerritsen, R. (1986). *"Reddingshonden in opleiding." Magazine Onze* Hond, 1–10.

Gerritsen, R., and Haak, R. (2014). *K9 Search and Rescue: A Manual for Training the Natural Way*. Edmonton, AB: Brush Education Inc.

Gerritsen, R., and Haak, R. (2021). *K9 Schutzhund Training: A Manual for IGP Training through Positive Reinforcement*. Edmonton, AB: Brush Education Inc.

Goss, K.-U. (2021). "Mantrailing as Evidence in Court?" *Forensic Science International: Reports* 3 (July). https://doi.org/10.1016/j.fsir.2021.100204.

Goss, K.-U., and Schoon, A. (2021). "Concerns Regarding Individual Human Scent as a Forensic Identifier Using Mantrailing." *Forensic Science International*, 318. http://dx.doi.org/10.1016/j.forsciint.2020.110606.

Green, S. C., Stewart, M. E., and Downing, D. T. (1984). "Variation in Sebum Fatty Acid Composition Among Adult Humans." *Journal of Investigative Dermatology* 83: 114–117.

Gross, H. G. A. (1893). *Handbuch für Untersuchungsrichter, Polizeibeamte, Gendarmen, usw.* Graz: Leuschner & Lubensky's Universitäts-Buchhandlung.

Gross, H. G. A. (1896). *"Gehilfe des Gendarmen." Jahrbuch für die k.k. Gendarmerie*. Wien: Selbstverlag des Herausgebers.

Gross-Isseroff, R., and Lancet, D. (1988). "Concentration Dependent Changes of Perceived Odor Quality." *Chemical Senses* 13 (2): 191–204.

Haak, R. (1986). *Het speuren van honden in theorie en praktijk*. Best: Zuidboek.

Haak, R. (1988). *Honden en hun gedrag*. Lisse: Zuid Boekprodukties b.v.

Haberhauffe, L. (2003). *Ungewöhnliches Fährtenalter*. Personal message.

Haberhauffe, L., and Albrecht, G. (1982). *Schutz- und Diensthunde*. Melsungen: Verlag J. Neumann-Neudamm.

Hager, G. (1986). *Zur Geruchsempfindung bei Mensch und Hund*. Wien: Unsere Hunde.

Halpin, Z. T. (1986). "Individual Odors among Mammals: Origin and Functions." *Advances in the Study of Behavior* 16: 39–70.

Hansmann, J. (1930). *"Die praktische Bedeutung der Fährtenreinheit für den Polizeifährtenhund."* Presentation, Whitsun Conference, Linz, Austria.

Hansmann, J. (1931). *"Unter welchen Gesichtspunkten erfolgt die praktische Verwendung des Polizeifährtenhundes?"* Zeitschrift für Hundeforschung I: 14–30.

Hatt, H. (2003). *"Von der Nase bis ins Gehirn: Düfte nehmen Gestalt an." Zellphysiologie Neurorubin*, 13–17.

Hauck, E. (1930). *"Sachliche und seelische Voraussetzungen von Seiten des Hundeführers."* Presentation, Whitsun Conference, Linz, Austria.

Hepper, P. G. (1988). "The Discrimination of Human Odour by the Dog." *Perception* 17 (4): 549–554.

Hepper, P. G. (1994). "Long-Term Retention of Kinship Recognition Established During Infancy in the Domestic Dog." *Behavioural Processes* 33: 14.

Hepper, P. G., and Wells, D. L. (2005). "How Many Footsteps Do Dogs Need to Determine the Direction of an Odour Trail?" *Chemical Senses* 30: 291–298.

Hepper, P. G., and Wells, D. L. (2005). "Perinatal Olfactory Learning in the Domestic Dog." *Chemical Senses* 31: 207–212.

Honhon, J. (1967). *L'olfaction chez le Chien. Son rôle dans le pistage et la localisation d'une source odorante.* Dissertation, Paris.

Horowitz, A. (2017). *Being a Dog: Following the Dog into a World of Smell.* New York: Scribner.

Hovis, K. R., Ramnath, R., Dahlen, J. E., Romanova, A. L., LaRocca, G., Bier, M. E., and Urban, N. N. (2012). "Activity Regulates Functional Connectivity from the Vomeronasal Organ to the Accessory Olfactory Bulb." *Journal of Neuroscience* 32 (23): 7907–7916.

Huyghebaert, L. (1925). *Onze Belgische rashonden.* Antwerp: Cultura.

Issel-Tarver, L., and Rine, J. (1996). "Organization and Expression of Canine Olfactory Receptor Genes." *Proceedings of the National Academy of Sciences of the USA* 93 (20): 10897–10902.

Jenkins, E. K., DeChant, M. T., and Perry, E. B. (2018). "When the Nose Doesn't Know: Canine Olfactory Function Associated with Health, Management, and Potential Links to Microbiota." *Frontiers in Veterinary Science* 5 (56). doi: 10.3389/fvets.2018.00056.

Jezierski, T., Ensminger, J., and Papet, L. E. (2016). *Canine Olfaction Science and Law: Advances in Forensic Science, Medicine, Conservation, and Environmental Remediation.* Boca Raton: CRC Press.

Jinn, J., Connor, E. G., and Jacobs, L. F. (2020). "How Ambient Environment Influences Olfactory Orientation in Search and Rescue Dogs." *Chemical Senses* 45 (8): 625–634.

Johnston, R. E., Soroking, E. S., and Ferkin, M. H. (1997). "Scent Counter-Marking in Meadow Voles: Females Prefer the Top-Scent Male." *Ethology* 103 (6): 443–453.

Kaldenbach, J., (1998). *K9 Scent Detection: My Favorite Judge Lives in a Kennel.* Calgary, AB: Detselig Enterprises Ltd.

Kalmus, H. (1955). "The Discrimination by the Nose of the Dog of Individual Human Odours and in Particular of the Odours of Twins." *British Journal of Animal Behavior* 5: 25–31.

Kanda, F., Yagi, E., Fukuda, M., Nakajima, K., Ohta, T., and Nakata, O. (1990). "Elucidation of Chemical Compounds Responsible for Foot Malodour." *British Journal of Dermatology* 122 (6): 771–6.

Katz, D. (1953). *Animals and Men: Studies in Comparative Psychology.* London: Harmondsworth Penguin.

King, E. J., Becker, F. R., and Markee, J. E. (1964). "Studies on Olfactory Discrimination in Dogs: (3) Ability to Detect Human Odour Trace." *Animal Behaviour* 12: 311–315.

Kokocińska-Kusiak, A., Woszczyło, M., Zybala, M., Maciocha, J., Barłowska, K., and Dzięcioł, M. (2021). "Canine Olfaction: Physiology, Behavior, and Possibilities for Practical Applications." *Animals* 11: 2463. https://doi.org/10.3390/ani11082463.

Komori, T., Fujiwara, R., Tanida, M., and Nomura, J. (1995). "Potential Antidepressant Effects of Lemon Odor in Rats." *European Neuropsychopharmacology* 5(4): 477–480.

Korting, H. C., Lukac, A., and Braun-Falco, O. (1988). "Microbial Flora and Odor of the Healthy Human Skin." *Hautarzt* 39 (9): 564–568.

Krall, K. (1912). *Denkende Tiere, Beitrage zur Tierseelenkunde auf Grund eigener Versuche, der Kluge Hans und meine Pferde Muhamed und Zarif.* Leipzig: Friedrich Engelman.

Laing, D. G., Panhuber, H., and Slotnick, B. M. (1989). "Odor Masking in the Rat." *Physiology & Behavior* 45: 689–694.

Lancet, D. (1986). "Vertebrate Olfactory Reception." *Annual Review of the Neurosciences* 9: 329–355.

Laska, M., and Hudson, R. (1993). "Discriminating Parts from a Whole: Determinants of Odor Mixture Perception in Squirrel Monkeys, *Saimiri sciureus.*" *Journal of Comparative Physiology A – Sensory Neural and Behavioral Physiology* 173 (2): 249–256.

Lauruschkus, G. (1942). *"Über Riechfeldgröße und Riechfeldkoeffizient bei einigen Hunderassen und der Katze."* *Archiv für Tierheilkunde* 77: 473–497.

Lawson, M. J., Craven, B. A., Paterson, E. G., and Settles, G. S. (2012). "A Computational Study of Odorant Transport and Deposition in the Canine Nasal Cavity: Implications for Olfaction." *Chemical Senses* 37 (6): 553–566. https://doi. org/10.1093/chemse/bjs039.

Lee Sela, L., and Sobel, N. (2010). "Human Olfaction: A Constant State of Change-Blindness." *Experimental Brain Research* 205 (1): 13–29.

Lewitt, M. S., Laing, D. G., Panhuber, H., Corbett, A., and Carter, J. N. (1989). "Sensory Perception and Hypothyriodism. *Chemical Senses* 14 (4): 537–546.

Löhner, L. (1924). *"Über menschliche Individual- und Regionalgerüche."* *Archiv gesellschaft für Physiologie* 202: 25–45.

Lord T., and Kasprzak, M. (1989). "Identification of Self through Olfaction." *Perception and Motor Skills* 69: 219–224.

Lorig, T. S. (1995). "EEG and ERP Studies of Low-Level Odor Exposure in Normal Subjects." *Toxicology and Industrial Health* 10 (4–5): 579–586.

Lubow, R. E., Kahn, M., and Frommer, R. (1973). "Information Processing of Olfactory Stimuli by the Dog: I. The Acquisition and Retention of Four Odor-Pair Discriminations." *Bulletin of the Psychonomic Society* 1 (2): 143–145.

MacLean, P. D. (1990). *The Triune Brain in Evolution: Role in Paleocerebral Functions.* New York: Plenum Press.

Marples, E. (1969). "Life on the Human Skin." *Scientific American*, January.

Marshall, D. A., Blumer, L., and Moulton, D. G. (1981). "Odor Detection Curves for *n*-Pentanoic Acid in Dogs and Humans." *Chemical Senses* 6: 445–453.

Matthes, E. (1934). *"Geruchsorgan"* in L. Bolk, E. Göppert, E. Kallius, and W. Lubosch, *Handbuch der vergleichende Anatomie der Wirbeltiere, Volume II-2.* Berlin: Urban und Schwarzenberg, 879–948.

McNeill, E. J. M., and Carrie, S. (2009). "Olfactory Dysfunction – Assessment and Management." *J ENT Masterclass* 2: 68–73.

Menzel, R. (1930). *"Geschichtliche Einführung in das Fragenbereich der Hundenase."* Presentation, Whitsun Conference, Linz, Austria.

Menzel, R., and Menzel, R. (1930). *Die Verwertung der Riechfähigkeit des Hundes im Dienste der Menschheit.* Berlin: Kameradschaft Verlag.

Menzel, R., and Menzel, R. (1960). *Pariahunde.* Wittenberg Lutherstadt: A. Ziemsen Verlag.

Michel, D. (2015). *Dogs and Hearing: Why Can They Hear Things We Can't?* Audicus. https://www.audicus.com/dogs-and-hearing/.

Miller, P. E., and Murphy, C. J. (1995). "Vision in Dogs." *Journal of the American Veterinary Medical Association* 207: 1623–1634.

Mombaerts, P. (2004). "Genes and Ligands for Odorant, Vomeronasal and Taste Receptors." *Nature Reviews Neuroscience* 5: 263–278.

Moncrieff, R. W. (1967). *The Chemical Senses*. London: Leonard Hill.

Mori, K., and Yoshihara, Y. (1995). "Molecular Recognition and Olfactory Processing in the Mammalian Olfactory System." *Progress in Neurobiology* 45: 585–619.

Most, K. (1920). *Leitfaden für die Abrichtung des Diensthundes auf Wissenschaftlicher Grundlage.* Berlin: Kameradschaft Verlagsgesellschaft.

Most, K. (1926). *"Neue Versuche über Spürfähigkeit." Zeitschrift Der Hund* 18: 31–35.

Most, K. (1930). *"Über die Voraussetzungen für die Verwertung der Hundenase im Polizei und Heeresdienst."* Presentation, Whitsun Conference, Linz, Austria.

Most, K., and Brückner, G. H. (1936). *"Über Voraussetzungen und den derzeitigen Stand der Nasenleistungen von Hunden." Zeitschrift für Hundeforschung* 5: 9–30.

Moulton, D. G. (1977). "Minimum Odorant Concentrations Detectable by the Dog and Their Implications for Olfactory Receptor Sensitivity" in D. Müller-Schwartz et al., *Chemical Signals in Vertebrates*, 455–464. New York: Plenum Press.

Müller, A. (1955). *"Quantitative Untersuchungen am Riechepithel des Hundes." Zeitschrift für Zellforschung* 41: 335–350.

Myers, L. J. (1990). "Dysosmia of the Dog in Clinical Veterinary Medicine." *Progress in Veterinary Neurology* 1: 171–9.

Myers, L. J., Nusbaum, K. E., Swango, L. J., Hanrahan, L. N., and Sartin, E. (1988). "Dysfunction of Sense of Smell Caused by Canine Parainfluenza Infection in Dogs." *American Journal of Veterinary Research* 49 (2): 188–190.

Mynsinger, H. (1473). *"Puoch von den valken, habichten, sperbern, pfaeriden, und hunden"* in M. von Stephanitz, *Der deutsche Schäferhund in Wort und Bild*. Jena: Anton Kampfe.

Najbauer, J., and Leon, M. (1995). "Olfactory Experience Modulates Apoptosis in the Developing Olfactory Bulb." *Brain Research* 674 (2): 245–251.

National Weather Service. (2021). *Beaufort Wind Scale.* https://www.weather.gov/mfl/beaufort.

Nelissen, M. (1996). *Introductie tot de gedragsbiologie.* Leuven/Apeldoorn: Garant.

Neuhaus, W. (1953). *"Über die Riechschärfe des Hundes für Fettsäuren." Zeitschrift für vergleichende Physiologie* 35: 527–552.

Neuhaus, W. (1955). *"Die Unterscheidung von Duftquantitäten bei Mensch und Hund nach Versuchen mit Buttersäure." Zeitschrift für vergleichende Physiologie* 37: 234–252.

Neuhaus, W. (1956). *"Die Unterscheidungsfähigkeit des Hundes für Duftgemische." Zeitschrift für vergleichende Physiologie* 39: 25–43.

Neuhaus, W. (1958). *"Die 'Fährtenreinheit' des Hundes." Die Umschau* 6, 161–163.

Neuhaus, W. (1981). *"Die Bedeutung des Schnüffelns für das Riechen des Hundes." Zeitung für Säugetierkunde* 46: 301–310.

New York Academy of Sciences. (1965). "Marvels of Mini-Weather." *The Sciences* 5: 1–4. https://doi.org/10.1002/j.2326-1951.1965.tb00178.x.

Nickel, R., Schummer, A., and Seiferle, E. (1984). *Lehrbuch der Anatomie der Haustiere. Band IV. Nervensystem, Sinnesorgane, Endokrine Drüsen.* Berlin: Paul Parey.

Nicolaides, N. (1974). "Skin Lipids: Their Biochemical Uniqueness." *Science* 186: 19–26.

Nicolaides, N., and Apon, J. M. B. (1977). "The Saturated Methyl Branched Fatty Acids of Adult Human Skin Surface Lipid." *Biomedical Mass Spectrometry* 4 (6): 337–347.

Niedermeyer, G. M., Hare, E., Brunker, L. K., Berk, R. A., Kelsey, K. M., Darling, T. A., Nord, J. L., Schmidt, K. K., and Otto, C. M. (2020). "A Randomized Cross-Over Field Study of Pre-Hydration Strategies in Dogs Tracking in Hot Environments." *Frontiers in Veterinary Science* 7: 292. doi: 10.3389/fvets.2020.00292.

Niemand, H. G. (1938). *"Ist der Individualgeruch für den Hund richtunggebend zum Erkennen seines Herrn?" Zeitschrift für Hundeforschung* XII (2).

Norlen, L., Nicander, I., Lundh-Rozell, B., Ollmar, S., and Forslind, B. (1999). "Inter- and Intra-Individual Differences in Human Stratum Corneum Lipid Content Related to Physical Parameters of Skin Barrier Function In Vivo." *Journal of Investigative Dermatology* 112 (1): 72–77.

Olofsson, J. K., Rogalski, E., Harrison, T., Mesulam, M. M., and Gottfried, J. A. (2013). "A Cortical Pathway to Olfactory Naming: Evidence from Primary Progressive Aphasia." *Brain: A Journal of Neurology* 136 (4): 1245–1259. https://doi.org/10.1093/brain/awt019.

Organization of Scientific Area Committees for Forensic Science, Dogs and Sensors Subcommittee (2017). "Crime Scene / Death Investigation – Dogs and Sensors Terms and Definitions," ASB Technical Report 025, 1st edition. Colorado Springs, CO: AAFS Standards Board.

Panksepp, J. (1998). *Affective Neuroscience. The Foundations of Human and Animal Emotions.* New York: Oxford University Press.

Panksepp, J., and Biven, L. (2012). *The Archaeology of Mind: Neuroevolutionary Origins of Human Emotions.* New York: W. W. Norton.

Pearsall M. D., and Verbruggen, H. (1982). *Scent.* Colorado: Alpine Publ., Inc.

Pelosi, P. (1994). "Odorant-Binding Proteins." *Critical Reviews in Biochemistry and Molecular Biology* 29 (3): 199–228.

Pfungst, O. (1911). *Clever Hans: The Horse of Mr. Von Osten.* New York: Holt, Rinehart & Winston.

Pierce, J. D., Zeng, X. N., Aronov, E. V., Preti, G., and Wysocki, C. J. (1995). "Cross-Adaptation of Sweaty-Smelling 3-methyl-2-hexonoic Acid by a Structurally Similar, Pleasant Smelling Odorant." *Chemical Senses* 20 (4): 401–411.

Pietras, R. J., and Moulton, D. G. (1974). "Hormonal Influences on Odor Detection in Rats: Changes Associated with the Estrous Cycle, Pseudopregnancy, Ovariectomy, and Administration of Testosterone." *Physiology & Behavior* 12 (3): 475–491.

Porter, J., Craven, B., Khan, R. M., Chang, S. J., Kang, I., Judkewitz, B., Volpe, J., Settles, G., and Sobel, N. (2007). "Mechanisms of Scent-Tracking in Humans." *Natural Neuroscience* 10 (1): 27–29.

Porter, R. H., Cernoch, J. M., and McLaughlin, F. J. (1983). "Maternal Recognition of Neonates through Olfactory Cues." *Physiology & Behavior* 30: 151–154.

Preciuso, L. (1927). *"Die Oberfläche der Regio olfactoria bei den Haustieren." Il Nuovo Ercolani* 32 (8/9).

Radke, G. (1998). Personal communication, RCMP Police Dog Service Training Centre, Innisfail, AB, Nov. 6.

Ramotowski, R. S. (2001). "Composition of Latent Fingerprint Residue" in H. C. Lee and R. E. Gaensslen, (eds.), *Advances in Fingerprint Technology.* Boca Raton: CRC Press.

Ringers, C., Olstad, E. W., and Jurisch-Yaksi, N. (2019). "The Role of Motile Cilia in the Development and Physiology of the Nervous System." *Philosophical Transactions of the Royal Society B* 375: 20190156. http://dx.doi.org/10.1098/rstb.2019.0156.

Rogowski, M. (2000). "Possibility of Removing the Individual Scent with the Aid of Clothes." Paper presented at Osmology: Overestimated or Neglected Area of Forensic Science? *Problemy Kryminalistyki* 230: 56–58.

Romanes, G. J. (1887). "Experiments on the Sense of Smell in Dogs." *Nature* 36: 273–274.

Romer, A. S. (1962). *The Vertebrate Body.* Philadelphia: W. B. Saunders Company.

Sacks, O. (1985). *The Man Who Mistook His Wife for a Hat, and Other Clinical Tales*. New York: Summit Books.

Salazar, I., Barber, P. C., and Cifuentes J. M. (1992). "Anatomical and Immunohistological Demonstration of the Primary Neural Connections of the Vomeronasal Organ in the Dog." *The Anatomical Record* 233: 309–313.

Salazar, I., Sanchez-Quinteiro, P., Barrios, A. W., Amad, M. L., and Vega, J. A. (2019). "Chapter 4 – Anatomy of the Olfactory Mucosa" in *Handbook of Clinical Neurology* 164: 47–65. https://doi.org/10.1016/B978-0-444-63855-7.00004-6.

Schaal, B., Marlier, L., and Soussignan, R. (1995). "Responsiveness to the Odour of Amniotic Fluid in the Human Neonate." *Biology of the Neonate* 67 (6): 397–406.

Schaal, B., Montagner, H., Hertling, E., Bolzoni, D., Moyse, A., and Quichon, R. (1980). "Olfactory Stimulations in Mother–Child Relations." *Reproduction, Nutrition, Development* 20: 843–858.

Schaal, B., Orgeur, P., and Arnould, C. (1995). "Olfactory Preferences in Newborn Lambs: Possible Influence of Prenatal Experience." *Behaviour* 132 (5–6): 351–365.

Scheunert, A., and Trautmann, A. (1976). *Lehrbuch der Veterinärphysiologie*. Berlin: Verlag Paul Parey.

Schmid, B. (1937). *"Umfang und Grenzen der Nasenleistung von Hunden." Forschung und Fortschritte* 13: 26–27.

Schmidt, F. (1910). *Verbrecherspur und Polizeihund*. Augsburg: Selbstverlag SV.

Schmidt, F. (1911). *Polizeihund-Erfolge und Neue Winke*. Augsburg: Selbstverlag SV.

Schoon, A. (1997). *The Performance of Dogs in Identifying Humans by Scent*. Dissertation, University of Leiden, The Netherlands.

Schoon, A., and de Bruin, J. C. (1994). "The Ability of Dogs to Recognize and Cross-Match Human Odours." *Forensic Science International* 69: 111–118.

Schoon, A., and Haak, R. (2002). *K9 Suspect Discrimination: Training and Practicing Scent Identification Line-Ups*. Calgary, AB: Detselig Enterprises Ltd., now Brush Education Inc.

Schwartz, G. E., Bell, I. R., Dikman, Z. V., Fernandez, M., Kline, J. P., and Peterson, J. M. (1995). "EEG Responses to Low-Level Chemicals in Normals and Cacosmics." *Toxicology and Industrial Health* 10 (4–5): 633–643.

Segal, N. L., Brown, K. W., and Topolski, T. D. (1992). "A Twin Study of Odor Identification and Olfactory Sensitivity." *Acta Geneticae Medicae Gemellologiae* 41: 113–121.

Ship, J. A., and Weiffenbach, J. M. (1993). "Age, Gender, Medical Treatment, and Medication Effects on Smell Identification." *Journal of Gerontology: Medical Sciences* 48 (1): M26–M32.

Siber, M. (1899). *Die Hunde Afrikas*. St. Gallen.

Silbernagl, S., and Despopoulos, A. (1981). *Sesam Atlas van de Fysiologie*. Baarn: Bosch & Keuning.

Sobel, N., Khan, R., Sullivan, E., and Gabrieli, J. D. E. (2000). "The World Smells Different to Each Nostril." *Nature* 402: 35.

Sobel, N., Prabhakaran, V., Desmond, J. E., Glover, G. H., Goode, R. L., Sullivan, E. V., and Gabrieli, J. D. (1998). "Sniffing and Smelling Separate Subsystems in the Human Olfactory Cortex." *Nature* 19: 282–286.

Sobel, N., Prabhakaran, V., Zhao, Z., Desmond, J. E., Glover, G. H., Sullivan, E. V., and Gabrieli, J. D. (2000). "Time-Course of Odorant-Induced Activation in the Primary Olfactory Cortex of the Human." *Journal of Neurophysiology* 83: 537–551.

Soproni, K., Miklósi, A., Topál, J., and Csányi, V. (2001). "Comprehension of Human Communicative Signs in Pet Dogs *(Canis familiaris)*." *Journal of Comparative Psychology* 115 (2): 122–126.

Soproni, K., Miklósi, A., Topál, J., and Csányi, V. (2002). "Dogs' *(Canis familiaris)* Responsiveness to Human Pointing Gestures." *Journal of Comparative Psychology* 116 (1): 27–34.

Spielman, A. I., Zeng, X. N., Leyden, J. J., and Preti, G. (1995). "Proteinaceous Precusors of Human Axillary Odor: Isolation of Two Novel Odor-Binding Proteins." *Experientia* 51: 40–47.

Staubli, U., Fraser, D., Faraday, R., and Lynch, G. (1987). "Olfaction and the 'Data' Memory System in Rats." *Behavioral Neuroscience* 101: 757–765.

Staymates, M., MacCrehan, W., Staymates, J., and Kunz, R. R. (2016). "Biomimetic Sniffing Improves the Detection Performance of a 3D Printed Nose of a Dog and a Commercial Trace Vapor Detector." *Scientific Reports* 6: 36876.

Steen, J. B., Mohus, I., Kvesetberg, K., and Walløe L. (1996). "Olfaction in Bird Dogs During Hunting." *Acta Physiologica Scandanavia* 157: 115–119.

Stephan, H. (1954). *"Die Anwendung der Schnell'schen Formel h=k¹.p auf Hirn-Körpergewichtsbeziehungen bei verschiedene Hunderassen."* *Zoologischer Anzeiger* 153: 15–27.

Stephanitz, M. v. (1923). *Der deutsche Schäferhund in Wort und Bild.* Jena: Anton Kampfe.

Stevens, J. C., Cain, W. S., and Burke, R. J. (1988). "Variability of Olfactory Thresholds." *Chemical Senses* 13 (4): 643–653.

Stewart, M. E., McDonnell, M. W., and Downing, D. T. (1986). "Possible Genetic Control of the Proportions of Branched-Chain Fatty Acids in Human Sebaceous Wax Esters." *Journal of Investigative Dermatology* 86: 706–708.

Stewart, M. E., Steele, W. A., and Downing, D. T. (1989). "Changes in the Relative Amounts of Endogenous and Exogenous Fatty Acids in the Sebaceous Lipids During Early Adolescence." *Journal of Investigative Dermatology* 92: 371–378.

Stoddart, D. M. (1980). *The Ecology of Vertebrate Olfaction.* London: Chapman and Hall.

Stoddart, D. M. (1990). *The Scented Ape.* Cambridge: Cambridge University Press.

Stuchly, E. (1989). *Die Erfolgreiche Fährtenarbeit.* Schlins: Eigenverlag.

Sullivan, S. L., Ressler, K. J., and Buck, L. B. (1995). "Spatial Patterning and Information Coding in the Olfactory System." *Current Opinion in Genetics and Development* 5: 516–523.

Syrotuck, W. G. (1972). *Scent and the Scenting Dog.* Westmoreland, NY: Arner Publications.

Szynak, J. (1985). "Identification of Odours." *International Criminal Police Review* (March): 58–63.

Thesen, A., Steen, J. B., and Døving, K. B. (1993). "Behaviour of Dogs During Olfactory Tracking." *Journal of Experimental Biology* 180: 247–251.

Toner, B. S., and Miller, Jr., D. I. (1993). "Olfactory Discrimination of Individual Human Odors Using Experienced Tracking Police Work Dogs." *Animal Behavior* 10 (4).

Uchida, T. (1953). Proceedings. XIV International Congress of Zoology, 292.

Uexküll, J. v., and Kriszat, G. (1934). *"Streifzüge durch die Umwelten von Tieren und Menschen."* *Verständliche Wissenschaft* XXI.

Vroon, P. (1989). *Zonder geur geen emoties.* Amsterdam: De Volkskrant.

Wagner, K. (1930). *Rezente Hunderassen. Eine osteologische Untersuchung.* Oslo: J. Dybwad.

Walker, R. J. (1919). *The Ichneutae of Sophocles.* London: Burns and Oates Ltd.

Walton, F. R. (1935). "A Problem in the Ichneutae of Sophocles." *Harvard Studies in Classical Philology* 46: 167–189.

Wedekind, C., and Penn, D. (2000). "MHC Genes, Body Odours, and Odour Preferences." *Nephrology Dialysis Transplantation* 15 (9): 1269–1271.

Wedekind, C., Seebeck, T., Bettens, F., and Paepke, A. J. (1995). "MHC-Dependent Mate Preference in Humans." *Proceedings of the Royal Society B* 260: 245–249.

Wells, D. L., and Hepper, P. G. (2003). "Directional Tracking in the Domestic Dog, *Canis familiaris.*" *Applied Animal Behaviour Science* 84 (4): 297–305. https://doi.org/10.1016/j.applanim.2003.08.009.

Wieland, G. (1938). *"Über die Grösse des Riechfeldes beim Hunde."* Zeitschrift für Hundeforschung XII: 1–23.

Wilcox, R. M., and Johnston, R. E. (1995). "Scent Counter-Marks: Specialised Mechanisms of Perception and Response to Individual Odors in Golden Hamster (*Mesocricetus auratus*)." *Journal of Comparative Psychology* 109 (4): 349–356.

Yeshurun, Y., and Sobel, N. (2010). "An Odor Is Not Worth a Thousand Words: From Multidimensional Odors to Unidimensional Odor Objects." *Annual Review of Psychology* 61: 219–241.

Zell, Th. (1909). *Der Polizeihund als Gehilfe der Strafrechtsorgane.* Berlin: Verlag Guttentag.

Zuschneid, K. (1973). *Die Riechleistung des Hundes.* Dissertation, Freie Universität Berlin.

About the Authors

Ruud Haak is the author of more than 30 dog books in Dutch and German, and for over 40 years he has been the editor-in-chief of the biggest Dutch dog magazine, *Onze Hond* (*Our Dog*). He was born in 1947 in Amsterdam, the Netherlands. At the age of 13, he was training police dogs at his uncle's security dog training center, and when he was 15, he worked after school with his patrol dog (which he trained himself) at the Amsterdam harbor. He later started training his dogs in Schutzhund and IPO, and he successfully bred and showed German Shepherd Dogs and Saint Bernards.

Ruud worked as a social therapist in a government clinic for criminal psychopaths. From his studies in psychology, he became interested in dog behavior and training methods for nose work, especially the tracking dog and the search-and-rescue dog. More recently he has trained drug- and explosive-detector dogs for the Dutch police and the Royal Dutch Airforce. He is also a visiting lecturer at Dutch, German, and Austrian police-dog schools.

In the 1970s, Ruud and his wife, Dr. Resi Gerritsen, a psychologist and jurist, attended many courses and symposia with their German Shepherds for Schutzhund, tracking dog, and search-and-rescue dog training in Switzerland, Germany, and Austria. In 1979, they started the Dutch Rescue Dog Organization in

Ruud Haak with his German shepherd Yes
van Sulieseraad and Malinois Google van het
Eldenseveld.

the Netherlands. With that unit, they attended many operations responding to earthquakes, gas explosions, and lost persons
in wooded or wilderness areas. In 1990, Ruud and Resi moved
to Austria, where they were asked by the Austrian Red Cross to
select and train operational rescue and avalanche dogs. They lived
for three years at a height of 6,000 feet (1800 m) in the Alps and
worked with their dogs in search missions after avalanches.

With their Austrian colleagues, Ruud and Resi developed a
new method for training search-and-rescue dogs. Their methods showed the best results after a major earthquake in Armenia
(1988), an earthquake in Japan (1995), two major earthquakes in
Turkey (1999), and big earthquakes in Algeria and Iran (2003).
Ruud and Resi have also demonstrated the success of their unique

Resi Gerritsen with her Malinois Halusetha's All
Power and Malinois Google van het Eldenseveld.

training methods for tracking dogs as well as search-and-rescue
dogs at the Austrian, Czech, Hungarian, and World Champion-
ships, where both were several times the leading champions.

Resi and Ruud have held many symposia and master classes
all over the world on their unique training methods, which are
featured in their books:
- *K9 Complete Care: A Manual for Physically and Mentally Healthy Working Dogs*
- *K9 Drug Detection: A Manual for Training and Operations*
- *K9 Explosive and Mine Detection: A Manual for Training and Operations*
- *K9 Investigation Errors and How to Avoid Them*
- *K9 Personal Protection: A Manual for Training Reliable Protection Dogs*

- *K9 Professional Tracking: A Complete Manual for Theory and Training*
- *K9 Scent Training: A Manual for Training Your Identification, Tracking, and Detection Dog*
- *K9 Schutzhund: A Manual for IGP Training through Positive Reinforcement*
- *K9 Search and Rescue: A Manual for Training the Natural Way*
- *K9 Working Breeds: Characteristics and Capabilities*
- *The German Shepherd Dog: A Historical View of the Breed's Development, Prime, and Deterioration*
- *The Labrador Retriever: From Hunting Dog to One of the World's Most Versatile Working Dogs*
- *The Malinois: The History and Development of the Breed in Schutzhund, Detection and Police Work*

With Simon Prins they wrote *K9 Behavior Basics: A Manual for Proven Success in Operational Service Dog Training*; and with Dr. Adee Schoon, Ruud wrote *K9 Suspect Discrimination: Training and Practicing Scent Identification Line-Ups*. All of these books were published by Detselig Enterprises Ltd., Calgary, Canada (now Brush Education Inc.).

Ruud and Resi now live in the Netherlands. They are training directors and international judges for the International Rescue Dog Organisation (IRO) and the Fédération Cynologique Internationale (FCI). Ruud and Resi are still successfully training their dogs as detector dogs for search and rescue, drugs, explosives, and Schutzhund. You can contact the authors by email at resigerritsen @gmail.com.